MASTERING THE
HYPE CYCLE

Other Books in the Gartner, Inc./ Harvard Business Press Series

*Heads Up: How to Anticipate Business Surprises
and Seize Opportunities First*
by Kenneth G. McGee

The New CIO Leader: Setting the Agenda and Delivering Results
by Marianne Broadbent and Ellen S. Kitzis

*Multisourcing: Moving Beyond Outsourcing
to Achieve Growth and Agility*
by Linda Cohen and Allie Young

*IT and the East: How India and China Are Altering
the Future of Technology and Innovation*
by James M. Popkin and Partha Iyengar

IT Risk: Turning Business Threats into Competitive Advantage
by George Westerman and Richard Hunter

MASTERING THE HYPE CYCLE

How to Choose the Right Innovation at the Right Time

Jackie Fenn and

Mark Raskino

Harvard Business Press

Boston, Massachusetts

Copyright 2008 Gartner, Inc.
All rights reserved
Printed in the United States of America
12 11 10 09 08   5 4 3 2 1

Library of Congress Cataloging-in-Publication Data
Fenn, Jackie.
    Mastering the hype cycle: how to choose the right innovation at the right time / Jackie Fenn and Mark Raskino.
      p.   cm.
    ISBN 978-1-4221-2110-8
    1. Technological innovations—Management. 2. Organizational change. I. Raskino, Mark. II. Title.
    HD45.F42 2008
    658.4'06—dc22

                                                            2008027503

The paper used in this publication meets the requirements of the American National Standard for Permanence of Paper for Publications and Documents in Libraries and Archives Z39.48-1992.

To William Knight,

for just assuming I could do anything

I set my mind to.

Contents

Preface

Hello.

How do you do. Please state your problem.

I am feeling sad.

I am sorry to hear that you are sad.

My mother is driving me crazy.

Tell me more about your family.

She interferes in my life all the time.

Your life all the time?

She tells me who I should date.

You say she tells you who you should date?

The year was 1966. A secretary at the MIT computer science labs found a therapist she could talk to over her computer network. When she noticed her boss was watching one of her sessions, she asked if he would leave the room so that she could converse with the therapist in private. Her boss, Joseph Weizenbaum, was disturbed to learn that she was using the therapist—not because he was concerned about her mental health, but because it was a computer program he had written, and his secretary knew full well that it wasn't a real person.[1] Called Eliza, it was a simple pattern-matching program that often just replaced the pronoun *me* with *you* and played back the user's words in the style of a Rogerian psychotherapist. The experience led Weizenbaum, along with many others, to speculate on the role that artificial intelligence (AI) could play in people's lives and work.

Fifteen years later, we (Jackie and Mark) were delighted to rediscover Eliza during our studies at our respective U.K. universities. Like each new generation of students in the field of artificial intelligence, we spent endless hours interacting with it and similar programs and debating its larger significance. Did it pass the Turing test, whereby judges can't tell whether they are conversing with a human or a computer? Was it the start of computers that could think?

Weizenbaum wrote Eliza when AI was still a purely academic endeavor. By the early/mid-1980s, when we were both graduating, AI had begun its transition into the commercial realm, and companies were hungry for AI expertise. Much of the focus was on expert systems, which modeled a human's ability to solve problems such as diagnosis ("What is wrong with this patient?") and classification ("Is this person a high or a low risk to insure?"). Jackie joined Logica, one of the largest European software consulting organizations. Funded by government programs and leading-edge companies, she and her colleagues interviewed experts, extracted the "rules" they used to make decisions, and developed expert systems for such applications as product formulation and medical diagnosis. After a stint at Cable & Wireless, Mark joined British Airways (BA), which was then building a new experimental competency in expert systems, and worked in a small team of "knowledge engineers."

By the late 1980s, the initial rush of commercial excitement around artificial intelligence was waning. AI development environments cost too much, capturing expert knowledge proved more difficult than anticipated, and even systems deployed successfully often failed in a year or two because the companies using them lacked the skills or resources to keep the rules up to date. That period came to be known as the "AI winter," when the whole technology fell out of favor because it failed to live up to people's initial, overheated expectations.

Jackie and Mark moved on to other emerging technology projects with our respective companies. Jackie became involved with interactive television (delivering movies on demand and other interactive services), and Mark worked on early versions of customer relationship management and airport electronic self-service kiosks—all technologies that would take far longer to deliver their dues than anyone at the time anticipated.

In 1994, Jackie moved to Gartner as an IT industry analyst covering emerging technologies. Her role was to help clients—mostly technology planners within information technology departments of large companies and government organizations—understand the realities of new technologies. She saw the tremendous potential of technologies such as AI, video on demand, and the newly emerging World Wide Web, but had also experienced many of the challenges of putting immature technologies to work.

As she wrote research reports about specific technologies, Jackie realized there was a common pattern that most, if not all, of them shared. Again and again, she saw a rapid initial rush of enthusiasm for a technology's potential, followed by disillusionment in the face of real-world challenges, finally followed over time by a deeper understanding of what the technology could really achieve. She drew a graph showing the ups and downs of this recurring cycle, gave each stage a catchy name ("Peak of Inflated Expectations," "Trough of Disillusionment," and so on), and populated it with example technologies. In the two-page research report showing this graph, she added some advice for clients about how to make decisions at each stage, depending on how much risk they wanted to take. Her report appeared in January 1995, with the title "When to Leap on the Hype Cycle."

At British Airways, Mark saw Jackie's hype cycle chart, which became an important aid to thinking about new technologies at BA. In fact, he wrote the hype cycle into his job description as a relationship manager between IT and sales and marketing, to note that part of his job was to moderate overblown expectations and then bolster sagging confidence at different stages of a new technology's hype cycle.

At Gartner, Jackie didn't give much further thought to the note she'd written. She'd delivered it as a one-off "buyer beware" commentary for businesses adopting information technology. But the next year, clients began asking for an update. That seemed like a good idea, and so she picked some new technologies and the "Hype Cycle of Emerging Technologies" became an annual report. Soon other Gartner analysts covering other areas of technology adopted the graphic as a useful way to showcase a set of technologies within their technology domains; customer self-service technologies and Internet publishing were among the earliest examples.

As the number of published hype cycles proliferated, our Gartner analyst colleague Alex Linden proposed an annual "Hype Cycle Special Report," which would bring together all such analysis, cross-referenced and consistent. Since 2004, under Jackie's guidance, that report has appeared annually and is relied on by technology planners in hundreds of organizations. Many of those companies create their own versions of the hype cycle to analyze the status of their particular technology and innovation portfolios.

In parallel, Jackie has been refining a technology adoption process as a framework to feature the best practices from leading companies and government organizations. The STREET process (scope, track, rank, evaluate, evangelize, transfer) started life as a four-stage process created by Gartner analyst Martin Muoto in 1994. Jackie expanded the process on the basis of feedback from clients who were putting the ideas into practice, and is continually updating the ideas, activities, and approaches to support each stage of the process.

Mark moved from British Airways to Gartner in 2000 and has worked on various aspects of the hype cycle. He has published research showing how to use the cycle in conjunction with different organizational risk profiles, applied the cycle to management disciplines and emerging business and societal trends far removed from pure technology, and worked on measuring levels of people's expectations around new technologies.

As both authors have worked with the hype cycle over the years, we have been learning more about what causes the cycle, how it progresses, and the insights it can offer managers. Thanks to many additional contributions from our colleagues and clients, the body of experience around the hype cycle has grown to a level where we feel it is appropriate to share our perspectives and recommendations in book form.

Before we begin, we want to acknowledge that many of the underlying phenomena reflected in the hype cycle have been observed, adapted, applied to different purposes, rediscovered, and analyzed over many years by researchers, academics, and practitioners. In the 1920s and 1930s, economist Nikolai Kondratiev described fifty- to sixty-year-long waves of economic prosperity and depression, and Joseph Schumpeter noted how radical innovation drives recurring cycles of "creative destruction" that form the basis of entrepreneurship and capitalism.[2] Everett Rogers, a pioneer in researching and analyzing how ideas spread, showed clearly that innovation adoption does not happen as a straight line but follows a predictable S-shaped curve. He divides the population into five categories based on where on the curve they adopt an innovation: innovators, early adopters, early majority, late majority, and laggards.[3] Geoffrey Moore identified a "chasm" between early adoption and mainstream adoption that prevented many high-tech companies from expanding the market for a new technology beyond adventuresome early users.[4] Roy Amara and Paul Saffo at the Institute for the Future have spoken and written about the phenomenon of overestimating a new technology's short-term benefits and underestimating its long-term value, a concept that Saffo refers to as "macro-myopia."[5] Saffo has also pointed out that the cycle of expectation and disappointment is an essential part of the innovation process.[6] Howard Fosdick has described the distinct "publicity vector" that precedes a technology's usefulness.[7]

The hype cycle's particular contribution is in highlighting the challenge of adopting an innovation during the early stages of the innovation's life cycle. The hype cycle is also, we believe, the only model of its type that has moved beyond an abstract concept and been used in earnest as a working management decision tool, tracking thousands of innovations over more than a decade. It's a simple and highly visual way to represent the cycle of overenthusiasm, dashed expectations, and eventual maturity. But it's more than descriptive—it's also predictive, as we demonstrate in the book.

The hype cycle is helpful to anyone interested in the adoption of innovation—in particular, anyone who must make decisions about whether and when to adopt a new product, technology, process, practice, or idea. Much has been written about how to create innovation in the marketplace, but much less on the topic of how organizations should bring in innovations from the outside. In fact, most innovations originate outside your company—with very few exceptions, the number of innovations your company actually invents or creates is minuscule compared with the number that it finds in the market, learns about in the press, or adapts from other companies' ideas. While the hype cycle applies both to innovations you invent internally and to those you discover externally, it's adopting external innovation that is the subject of this book.

We focus in the book primarily on such decision making in a business context, where the scale of risk can be intimidating and the motivation to adopt an innovation must go beyond the satisfaction of a shiny new corporate toy. Although the hype cycle applies to most types of innovation, the book tilts strongly toward the world of technology, both because of our own extensive experience in this field and because technological innovation is now so pervasive in corporate life. Much of what is "new" these days has some critical technological component or link.

The book is presented in two parts. Part 1 introduces and explores the hype cycle: what it is, how it works, why it works that way, traps and opportunities it presents, and lessons to be learned. Part 2 presents the STREET innovation adoption process that can help managers and innovation leaders turn their understanding of the hype cycle into sound adoption decisions.

Part 1 will be the more interesting to a casual reader, but part 2 is crucial to those whose jobs require them to repeatedly make or participate in adoption decisions. The hype cycle is a product of human nature, not of innovation or technology. Thus, changing the adoption decisions we make requires more than simply understanding the hype cycle phenomenon, just as changing the hand we write with would take more than "understanding" that we are naturally right- or left-handed. Avoiding the dangerous pitfalls of the cycle requires both understanding and a disciplined approach to adoption decision making.

After so many years riding hype cycles ourselves and watching others ride them, we're pleased to bring what we and our colleagues have learned to a broader audience.

Acknowledgments

As the authors have learned through the course of a two-year writing project, creating a work of this type takes many people in a variety of supporting roles. We would like to thank the following individuals, without whom this book would not have been possible.

Professional writer Kent Lineback is a hidden treasure. He has helped many authors on business books you have either read or heard of. We were privileged to have his support and benefited greatly from his experience, writer's craft, and critical insight, particularly in composing some of the longer case stories.

Both authors write research reports for a living; nevertheless, we needed guidance on how to craft a book to the high standard that Harvard Business Press (HBP) expects for titles that carry its brand. Luckily, we had the luxury of two experts shepherding us along the path to book creation: Heather Levy in Gartner books and Jacque Murphy at HBP. We thank them for their help whenever we needed it and their trust when deadlines slipped a little.

This book is one of a series Gartner has published with HBP. That productive relationship is managed day to day by Heather and Jacque, but at Gartner, the buck stops with our erudite head of communications, Andrew Spender. Thanks to him for backing this title and making it part of a flourishing commercial relationship.

As with any project of this size, dedicating so much of the authors' time to the book meant that something else in their roles at Gartner had to give. Our managers defended the space and time we needed to get this book completed; they cleared our paths of obstacles and reassured others it was a worthwhile project. Thanks to Martin Reynolds, Daryl Plummer, and Jennifer Beck.

Over the years, a number of people have contributed key insights, new twists, angles, extensions, and variant uses of the hype cycle. In particular,

Alexander Linden in Germany is responsible for many significant enhancements and insights around the hype cycle. For contributing to the intellectual wellspring of the hype cycle and the STREET process, we also thank Nick Jones in the United Kingdom; Cassio Dreyfus in Brazil; Hubert Delany, David Smith, Martin Muoto, and Jim Sinur in the United States; and the many other current and former Gartner colleagues around the world who contribute new hype cycles every year, making it a living and evolving management tool.

Gartner analysts are always willing to help build each other's work by reviewing and critiquing drafts. Peer review is very important for a quality result. For reviewing this manuscript and being so generous with their time and insights, we thank Audrey Apfel, Ty Harmon, David Cearley, Carol Rozwell, Diane Morello, Anne Lapkin, and Barbara Gomolski, with special thanks to Mark McDonald and Kathy Harris, whose depth and detail of feedback went far above and beyond the call of duty. We also thank the four anonymous external reviewers selected by HBP. For particular observations and insights, we thank Alexander Drobik and Andy Kyte.

The hype cycle would be just an ivory tower observation if its practical use weren't constantly refined and debated in businesses and government organizations. For their unending support and inspirational ideas and feedback on the hype cycle and related research, we thank Dan Gossett, Brent Lowensohn, Jim Wasil, and the members of the Gartner Best Practices Council for Emerging Technology Management Executives. We also thank those who lent their good names and fascinating case stories: Mike Askew, Fred Balliet, Todd Brown, Erin Byrne, Frank Finocchio, Nick Gassman, Dan Gossett, Janice Jackson, Paul Jones, Martin Kagan, Sanjay Khunger, Roger Partington, Aaron Rajan, Fritz Schulz, Dan Simons, Jim Wasil, and Jeremy Wyman. Special thanks to Tom Wolf for his understanding.

Mark would like to thank Jackie for the opportunity and privilege to coauthor the book that arose from her original insight. Thanks also to Ken McGee for his mentorship and to Tim Ogden for encouragement.

Finally, to our families. For providing Jackie with emotional support and time to write—Tony. For helping keep things in perspective—Alex and Zoë. For always being there—Joan Knight and Sue Ramin. For emotional support, insight, and endless cups of tea to Mark—Pauline. For their irreverence and enthusiasm—Ben and Danny. For an education and a mission to use it—Audrey and Louis.

Part I

The Hype Cycle

One

Hype Cycle Winners and Losers

You always pass failure on the way to success.

—Mickey Rooney

"I RESIGNED ON THE SPOT."

So responded the marketing director of the independent British grocery chain Safeway in July 1999 when he learned that he would report henceforth to the COO, not the CEO, of his company. It wasn't pride that motivated Roger Partington to leave but the deeper meaning of the change. In demoting his role, Safeway was in effect abandoning the direction he had been hired to pursue six years earlier as Safeway's chief marketing officer.

Trained in marketing at Unilever, Partington had brought to Safeway something unusual in the grocery business: a focus on customer-facing strategy, brand management, and other basic aspects of traditional marketing that far surpassed the sales deals and discounts then considered "marketing" by most grocers. His job was to create a powerful brand for a group of stores that the Argyll Group had assembled by acquisition, including the U.K. subsidiary of the U.S. Safeway chain. (These stores, which by 2000 would become a $15 billion business, retained the Safeway name but had no connection with the U.S. company.)

The Safeway stores in the United Kingdom tended to be smaller than competitors' stores, a disadvantage Partington and his newly hired marketing team hoped to overcome by increasing the company's average transaction size. Key among the strategies for doing this was targeting families with young children because they were the market segment that spent most on groceries. Focusing on young families depended, however, on Safeway's ability to identify and address them specifically. "My challenge," said Partington, "was understanding who young family shoppers were. When you come into a store, there's no way of identifying who these people are. Nobody had succeeded before [in the grocery business] apart from mass-market communication or mass-market promotions."[1]

His solution was for Safeway to adopt a new management innovation that was causing a lot of hype in consumer-facing industries at that time. It was being called "one-to-one marketing," or database marketing, and was the forerunner of customer relationship management as we know it today. Advances in large-scale database technologies had made it economically possible by the late 1980s to store the full transaction histories of customers. The early successes of airline frequent-flier programs and credit card reward schemes in the United States had begun spilling over to Europe. New marketing theory was being formed by management academics and gurus who were bursting onto the scene. In 1993 Don Peppers and Martha Rogers's book *The One to One Future* became an international business best seller. Their ideas were seductive: look beyond market segments to the needs and loyalties of individuals. Focus on share of customer, not share of market. Consulting services and technology firms were quick to pick up the ideas and eager to help companies across various industry sectors that wanted a part of that future. A marketing revolution was in the air. There was an increasing sense among a generation of management high fliers that if your company didn't build up this new capability, it would appear blind and uncaring and become irrelevant to its customers. Many Safeway managers believed that customer data could be their secret weapon. The head of IT at Safeway announced, "Retailers must move from mass market to a marketplace of one. Anyone who doesn't go for mass personalization risks not being able to compete. Ignore the customer-specific path at your peril."[2]

In the United Kingdom, the clock was ticking. A company called Airmiles was already forging relationships with the retail sector to extend the redemption of mileage beyond free flights and into goods and services. The press started to hype the coming supermarket battle in public. "Loyalty has emerged as one of the main weapons in the food retailers' endless battle to outdo their rivals," declared the London *Times* in 1995.[3]

Partington knew that to build up a database profile of its customers, Safeway would need its own example of what the media was calling a "loyalty card." Safeway's card was called ABC. Shoppers would sign up for it, and if they swiped it each time they checked out, they could accumulate points toward discounts, gifts, or leisure activities. To shoppers it was a discount or rewards card, but to Safeway it was a way of paying for detailed information about what customers were buying, literally item by item. By analyzing purchases—of disposable diapers or baby food, for example—Safeway marketers could identify those high value family shoppers, study what they bought, and develop specific, targeted ways of motivating them to buy more.

Safeway certainly wasn't alone in offering a loyalty card. In fact, all major U.K. grocers in the early 1990s seemed to be in the grip of loyalty card fever. The big idea had broken out suddenly, everywhere at the same time. Every major chain, not just third-place Safeway, was testing such cards, including Sainsbury's, the market leader; number-two Tesco; and even number-four Asda, which was primarily a big box discounter.

But the concept was unproven in the U.K. retail grocery business. At Safeway, Partington and his team market tested the ABC card at a few stores in late 1994 and decided to wait until it had fully installed the data processing capacity to handle the flood of data the card would produce. According to Partington, Safeway's advantage lay not in the card itself, but in Safeway's technological ability to analyze the data. Though smaller than Tesco and Sainsbury's, Safeway was widely known as the most advanced, innovative, and aggressive of all chains in its data processing and analytic capabilities. In 1995, Safeway was probably best positioned technically to analyze and make good use of card data.

Tesco, however, seized the opportunity to launch its card first in 1995, several months ahead of Safeway. Sainsbury's launched nationwide eighteen months later, in 1996. Asda didn't launch nationally but continued extensive testing.

In the years after launch, Safeway's marketing strategy of focusing on high-spending young families began to yield the changes it had hoped for. Supported by card data, Safeway's efforts to attract this lucrative segment were producing an increase in average transaction size. For example, by analyzing changes in the goods a young woman was regularly buying, Safeway could identify that she was probably starting a family, and immediately make special offers with coupons. But, unfortunately, the financial benefits resulting from these changes weren't appearing fast enough.

Meanwhile, retail industry sentiment and investor impatience was turning against loyalty cards. "Skepticism about loyalty schemes is increasing," said one trade publication in 2000.[4] "They might have worked in the beginning, but recent research has shown that 'loyalty' cards are a misnomer—they simply don't make customers more loyal." Sainsbury's launched a reexamination of its card program. Asda, after years of trials, abandoned any plans to launch nationwide.

So, after four or five years, enthusiasm for loyalty cards in the United Kingdom began to wane. Their benefits seemed slow to arrive and hard to prove or measure directly, while their substantial costs were only too obvious.

That change in sentiment undoubtedly played a role in the deliberations of the Safeway board, whose members concluded that the market could only support a few major players and that Safeway needed to merge with another chain. To do that, the board felt, Safeway had to improve its short-term financials to make itself an attractive acquisition target. In a reversal of direction, the company abandoned long-term, customer-focused, database marketing strategies. It reorganized—which led to Partington's resignation—and hired an ex-Wal-Mart executive as CEO. (Partington went on to a more senior position with TXU, an energy company.)

Right away, the new CEO at Safeway installed a high/low strategy: lower prices dramatically on a few key items to attract customers while maintaining strong margins on all other products. One way Safeway chose to pay for this approach in 2000 was to abandon the ABC card, which the new CEO called a "backpack of stones" and a "flashy, worthless piece of plastic."[5] He promised to invest the annual £50 million operating cost of the card in lower prices. "People are bored by loyalty cards," he said. "When they go shopping, they open their wallet and have three or four cards, so it has stopped being a stimulant to visiting a store."[6] So much had sentiment for the cards changed that when Safeway announced the demise of the ABC card, the company's share price rose. In dropping the card, Safeway was abandoning a major innovation over which, at the trial stage, it had initially held a slender lead. Its board did not believe database marketing was the most effective way to attract customers or a competency that would make the company more attractive to a buyer.

Whether or not you lived in Great Britain in the 1990s, there's probably something vaguely familiar about this story. Some innovation comes along that captures people's fancy, and everybody, including the media, joins the parade with great fanfare and high expectations. Just as Safeway pinned much hope on its ABC card and the data it provided, this "latest thing" always promises to bring fundamental change and great success for those who adopt it—and great peril for those who don't. Then, when it fails to deliver the promised bounty right away, everyone starts bailing out, just like the Safeway board when it abandoned database marketing and its loyalty card. Cries of disappointment replace the earlier cries of hope and enthusiasm. The innovation that you "ignore at your peril" becomes "a backpack of stones."

We see this pattern all the time in business. The field of technology is rife with it. And it happens over and over and over—so much that you must wonder how capable companies, adopting highly touted innovations, so often fail to understand what's happening. Why do so many organizations seem to rush lemminglike to each new innovation, only to abandon it when it falls short of initial expectations?

This cycle of hope and disappointment is so common that we've given it a name, the *hype cycle*, because all the initial enthusiasm is built mainly on hope and hype. We've even charted it (see figure 1-1). The vertical axis

FIGURE 1-1

Beginning of the hype cycle

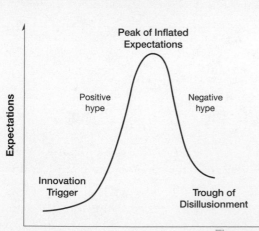

represents the expectations around an innovation, and the horizontal axis shows time. Each part of the curve has a name.

The Innovation Trigger. The hype cycle starts when a breakthrough, public demonstration, product launch, or some other event generates press and industry interest in some innovation. In the world of information technology, this is often referred to as the Technology Trigger, where an announcement about a technological development drives sudden interest. The innovation may have been under development for quite a period of time, but at this point it reaches a stage where word of its existence and excitement about its possibilities extend beyond its inventors or developers. More and more people hear of its potential, and a wave of buzz quickly builds as everyone passes on the news.

The Peak of Inflated Expectations. Companies that like to be ahead of the curve seek out the innovation and jump on it before their competitors. The suppliers of the innovation boast about their early prestigious customers, and other companies want to join in so they aren't left behind. A bandwagon effect kicks in, and the innovation is pushed to its limits as companies try it out in a range of settings. The stories in the press capture the excitement around the innovation and reinforce the need to become a part of it or be left behind.

The Trough of Disillusionment. As time passes, impatience for results begins to replace the original excitement about potential value. The same few stories of early success have been repeated over and over, but now a deeper look often shows those same companies still struggling to derive meaningful value. Problems with performance, or slower-than-expected adoption, or a failure to deliver financial returns in the time anticipated all lead to missed expectations. A number of less favorable stories start to emerge as most companies realize things aren't as easy as they first seemed. The media, always needing a new angle to keep readers interested, switches to featuring the challenges rather than the opportunities of the innovation.

If this were all there was to such things, if most innovations simply died in the trough, the curve would end there. And all those who deal with recurring hype, hope, and disappointment by ignoring them would be right. Perhaps Safeway and the other U.K. supermarkets would have been better off ignoring loyalty cards altogether. Cards were expensive to administer, and all that money could simply have gone to shoppers in the form of lower prices.

But, usually, there's more to the innovation than hype, hope, and disappointment. It *does* contain something of lasting value. It's just that the value can't be found and extracted before disillusionment sets in. The people or companies that give up, like Safeway, don't have the patience or the skill required to find the value. The truth is that innovations often need considerable experimentation and development, along with patience and tenacity, before they deliver anything worthwhile.

Such was the case with supermarket loyalty cards in the United Kingdom. There *was* something there for those with the patience and skill to find and exploit it. As we will see, a loyalty card would be heralded as a key to one retailer's meteoric success a few years later as it became a *Fortune* global 100 company and the United Kingdom's number-one retailer.

For such innovations—and many, if not most, innovations contain something of value—we extend the hype curve (see figure 1-2). We add two further stages because the trigger, peak, and trough are only part of the story.

The Slope of Enlightenment. Some early adopters overcome the initial hurdles, begin to experience benefits, see the light at the end of the

FIGURE 1-2

The hype cycle of innovation

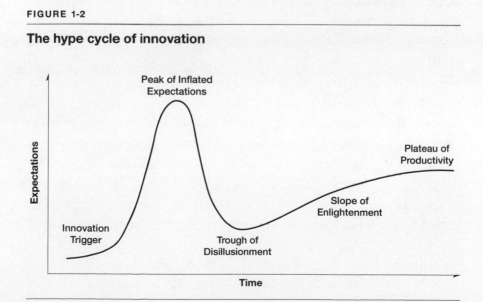

tunnel, and recommit efforts to move forward. Drawing on the experience of early adopters, understanding grows about where the innovation can be used to good effect. Over time, the innovation itself matures as suppliers improve products on the basis of early feedback. Methodologies for applying it successfully are codified, and best practices for its use are socialized.

The Plateau of Productivity. With the real-world benefits of the innovation demonstrated and accepted, growing numbers of organizations feel comfortable with the now greatly reduced levels of risk. A sharp uptick ("hockey stick") in adoption begins, and penetration accelerates rapidly as a result of productive and useful value.

Hype Is Everywhere

The hype cycle is not a new phenomenon, but one that repeats itself with each innovation that somehow captures people's imagination. The inventor of a new communications technology once predicted it would "bind man to his fellow-man in such bonds of amity as to put an end to war."[7] Government officials picked up the mantra, toasting the innovation that was "removing causes of misunderstanding, and promoting peace and harmony throughout the world."[8] These hopeful and familiar sentiments were expressed in the nineteenth century in a society smitten with the incredible potential of the telegraph. The same pattern occurred with canals and railroads in the 1700s and 1800s; the telephone in the late nineteenth and early twentieth centuries; automobiles and radio in the early decades of the twentieth century; the jet engine, rockets, and atomic energy in the 1950s and '60s; the Internet in the 1990s; and most recently biotechnology and nanotechnology. People have been swept up with the possibility and then disappointed with the initial reality of the next new thing for centuries.

While new technology is the catalyst for many of these wild rides through the hype cycle, the same effect occurs with higher-level concepts and abstract ideas such as management trends. Organizations have greeted innovations such as business process reengineering, knowledge management, activity-based costing, and Six Sigma with unquestioning enthusiasm and often heavy investment. And many of those organizations have gone on to the same kind of disillusionment they felt over the failure of some technical marvel to deliver on its initial promise.

In one example, we have tracked the hype cycle surrounding the management science concept of "business models." The term *business model* arose in the mid-1990s when the Internet offered new ways to structure and optimize commercial activities (see figure 1-3). With the dot-com crash, interest in the concept of new business models declined, until clear winners emerging from the crash showed that at least some of the new approaches were viable and triggered renewed activity.

Investors as well are only too aware of the hype effect as a new company or market gains in popularity. Though stock prices are influenced by many factors and are inherently unpredictable, a hot new company founded on a particular innovation can find its stock subjected to the forces of the hype cycle. Look, for example, at Amazon's stock price for the period 1998–2005, which included the Internet boom and bust (see figure 1-4).

This Amazon chart is not unique—the stock price charts for other companies founded on the innovation of the Web itself, like Yahoo!, followed exactly the same pattern over that period.

Hype cycles can also be found in macroeconomic phenomena, such as the recent "gold rush" of foreign companies investing in the hope of getting a share of China's rapid growth. Here the Chinese government statistic for foreign direct investment follows a hype cycle–like trajectory (see figure 1-5).

FIGURE 1-3

Number of articles using the term *business model* from 1990 to 2006

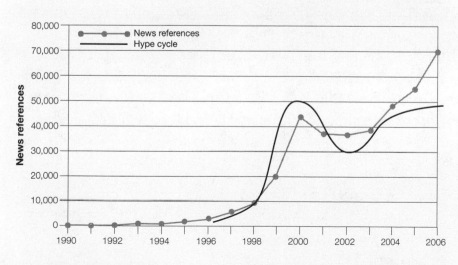

Source: Gartner research using Factiva.

FIGURE 1-4

Amazon stock price, 1998 to 2005

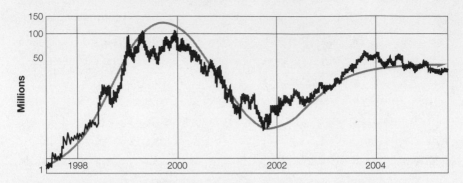

Source: Gartner and Yahoo! Inc. Reproduced with permission of Yahoo! Inc. ® 2008 by Yahoo! Inc.
YAHOO! and the YAHOO! logo are trademarks of Yahoo! Inc.

As we look across the range of areas where the hype cycle comes into effect, it's worth examining the axes along which we are measuring these effects. Whether it's a management trend, a new business process, or a new technology, when any innovation arises, it starts raw and gradually matures over time. The horizontal axis of the hype cycle is that inescapable independent variable of time. But what exactly is the variable on the vertical axis? It's more than just maturity. Historically, we have often labeled it "visibility." The premise is that the more visible an innovation is—in marketing, in conversation buzz, in news and media, in conferences and other places— the more "hyped" it is. But those are indirect effects that only tell part of the story—so in this book you will see the vertical axis labeled "expectations."

Across all types of innovation, the underlying variable that changes over time as the innovation progresses is really the market's assessment of its future expected value. As we will explain, this is impacted by the conjunction of the real engineering or business value progress the innovation makes and human perceptions of that progress—influenced by social phenomena. However, there is no standard unit of measure for "expectations."

In the case of financial markets, there are clear quantitative measures of expectation, as represented by stock prices and levels of investment that directly measure future expected value. In other areas, including business and technology innovations, the level of expectation has to be approxi-

FIGURE 1-5

Changing levels of foreign investment in China

Source: IBM Institute for Business Value study; Alan Beebe, "Winning in China's Mass Markets: New Business Models, New Operations for Profitable Growth," March 7, 2007. Reprint Courtesy of International Business Machines Corporation, copyright 2007 © International Business Machines Corporation.

mated indirectly. Fortunately, many proxy measures of expectation can be gathered so that a hype cycle can be detected or drawn up for an innovation or a set of innovations.

In the simplest case, the curve can be annotated with stories from the flow of industry news. This is at the very qualitative end of the spectrum. In the life of any new innovation, early stories tend to focus on the invention; later they focus on the applications and business results. Stories early on talk about the future possibilities; later they talk about the here-and-now practicalities. Stories early on gush with positive adverbs. Stories in the middle period often turn negative, cynical, and impatient in tone. The expert reader can see a hundred stories that reinforce the same basic sentiment, and then pick out the one that marks a real tipping point in changing attitudes and understanding. Such are the wonders of that marvelous pattern recognition engine: the human brain. Here's a real example laid out by Aaron Rajan—an IT strategist at Unilever—assessing the progress of radio frequency identification (RFID) technology (which allows a tagged item to be read by a scanner without contact or even direct line of sight) in the context of retail and consumer packaged goods (see figure 1-6).

As we saw in figure 1-3, which showed how the incidence of articles about the concept "business model" changed over time, the *number* of

FIGURE 1-6

Hype cycle for RFID based on press articles

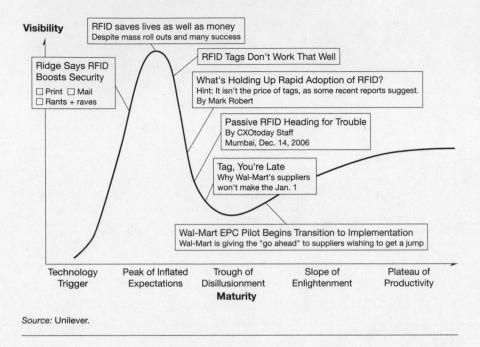

Source: Unilever.

newspaper and magazine article references to an innovation can be a very useful proxy measure of expectations. The more newsworthy an innovation is, the more expectations rise, and that becomes a reinforcing cycle. News counts are relatively quick and easy to measure using news database tools. On the basis of recent improvements in the field of *sentiment analysis*, which automatically detects the tone of a piece of text from the types of words used (positive or negative), we expect to see a growing availability of tools that will combine quantitative article counts with the type of previously subjective judgments contained in figure 1-6. But for now the hype cycle remains primarily a qualitative decision tool. As in so many areas of management practice, we still have to rely on the art of expert human judgment.

At the opposite end of the spectrum from business trends, technological revolutions, and financial markets (and with a decidedly fuzzy vertical axis), hype cycles also make their effects felt at a micro level on a local and personal scale. We've all felt the excitement of being involved with a challenging new project, only to be worn down into a Trough of Disillusionment once we realize the magnitude and difficulty of the task. Gradually, the long hours and late nights give way to a feeling of satisfaction as the project finally draws to a conclusion. This "internal" hype cycle can be felt by a team or a department involved in implementing an innovation. It can even be felt by individuals embarking on an ambitious undertaking, as we become impatient to see the gains from our investment. That exercise program, MBA, and novel are all harder work than we anticipated, and the rewards slower than we would have liked. And more than one observer has commented that the hype cycle seems to apply perfectly to their personal relationships.

It's Not Just Descriptive—It's Prescriptive Too

If the hype cycle is indeed inevitable—that is, we can assume it will occur with virtually every innovation—can it be used to forecast the future, at least to some extent? We believe it can, and for an example we'll turn to a colleague of ours at Gartner.

First, some background, for those who slept through the 1990s or have selectively forgotten how swept up they were themselves in the mania of the time. In 1997, an article by Peter Schwartz and Peter Leyden in *Wired* magazine described what they called "The Long Boom." The article's subtitle was, "We're facing 25 years of prosperity, freedom, and a better environment for the whole world. You got a problem with that?" which summed up the viewpoint that would dominate and fascinate conventional business thinking for the next three years.[9] The euphoria was based on developments in the world of information technology (IT). The industry had seen innovation before, some of it pretty big—the mainframe in the 1960s, the minicomputer in the1970s, and the PC in the 1980s. But what faced IT analysts in the late 1990s seemed like something genuinely new and different. The Internet, the Web specifically, was not only growing unbelievably quickly as a technology; it also seemed to be taking over business as an idea. Gartner analyst Andy Kyte recalls, "It seemed as if there was some hallucinogenic substance called 'e' being pumped though the air conditioning ducts into boardrooms everywhere."[10]

It went beyond things merely technological. It was the "new economy" and it had "new rules." Conventional business wisdom no longer applied.

Anyone who didn't share the enthusiasm clearly didn't "get it," to use the popular put-down of the era. The financial press, business journals, business thinkers, stock market analysts, venture capitalists, even the annual reports of blue chip companies, all caught the Internet bug. Stacks of new business books hit the shelves, all with one clear message: Get on the train or be left behind. It's a new world.

In a rather drab, gray office in Egham, a couple of miles from Heathrow airport on the edge of the urban sprawl in West London, one guy didn't "get it." Gartner analyst Alexander Drobik, with a long career in IT and telecommunications and a recent MBA, found it hard to believe that everything he had learned in work and business school had become junk. He had spent much time in the airline industry, where e-commerce had been mainstream for twenty-five years through reservation and global distribution systems. So the Internet didn't feel quite so revolutionary to him. He couldn't shake the feeling that something was wrong with the idea that this time around was truly different, with loss-making companies being valued more than profitable companies—even allowing for the normal start-up investment phase.

In the summer of 1999, Drobik found a way to articulate what was worrying him. He used a research tool, the hype cycle, that had been in use at Gartner since the mid-1990s, to look at the Internet and the "new economy." Figure 1-7 shows the chart he drew.

His analysis of previous hyped events—for example, the South Sea financial bubble of the eighteenth century—coupled with his deep understanding of Internet technologies and his assessment of the "capital pump" nature of the market (i.e., the frenzy for huge dot-com IPOs) all led to an inevitable conclusion. When he applied the hype cycle tool, he quickly convinced himself that the Internet and all things "e" weren't heading onward and upward forever; rather, the market was about to crash, and crash spectacularly. Drobik then had to convince his colleagues he was right. That wasn't simple. It took several months to argue his way through the research peer review processes that his company operated to ensure quality. But in the end he won the argument, on the basis of the insights and the strength of fit to the hype cycle tool.

On November 9, 1999, Drobik got his research note published to thousands of client companies around the world. Its opening words were:

FIGURE 1-7

Gartner e-business hype cycle, 1999

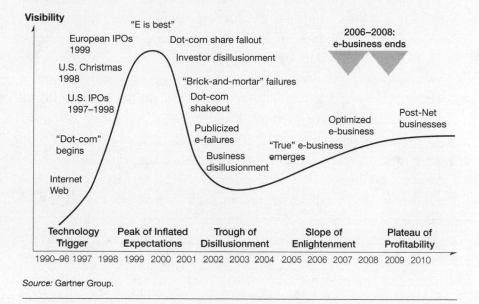

Source: Gartner Group.

"E-business is set to fall into a period of disillusionment by 2001, before successful organizations move through the 'hype cycle' and emerge fully transformed so that they can be referred to as just plain 'businesses' again."[11]

On March 10, 2000, the NASDAQ hit its final, record-closing high of 5,048.62 before crashing to half that value in 2001, along with all the technology companies that depended on the irrational exuberance of investors and executives.

Of course, what Drobik predicted wasn't the end of the Internet but the end of people's crazed expectations and the beginning of a period of disillusionment. If you look at the curve in figure 1-7, it's clear he was predicting not only the crash, but also that the Internet would emerge from the Trough of Disillusionment and find its rightful and extremely significant place in business and life. The Internet will turn out to be one of those innovations that actually exceed in the long run many of the original expectations. It's an example of situations in which the original expectations weren't entirely wrong—they were just premature.

So How Do You Deal with the Hype Cycle?

How should we as individuals and organizations deal with a recurring hype cycle and the overinflated expectations that occur with each new innovation? It's a crucial question, since every company adopts literally hundreds of innovations large and small every year. Should we all deal with the hype cycle by ignoring the hype, waiting for the innovation to mature as far as possible, and joining in only once it reaches the Plateau of Productivity? Safeway's example from our story of the U.K. loyalty card wars might be an argument for exactly such an approach, except that out of those wars emerged a spectacular winner, and that winner was Tesco.[12]

Few in the United Kingdom in the early 1990s would have predicted that outcome. Stuck in second place among supermarkets, and losing 1 to 2 percent of market share a year, Tesco struggled in the recession that gripped the United Kingdom, while archrival and market leader Sainsbury's continued to thrive.

Tesco had once thrived too. Its founder, Jack Cohen, imported American-style "pile it high and sell it cheap" supermarkets to the United Kingdom after World War II. Then he imported Green Shield stamps, a discount scheme that for over a decade enjoyed great shopper support. But when Tesco had to abandon the stamps in the 1970s, after shopper interest waned, the company seemed to be in the doldrums, with a merchandising strategy of merely copying Sainsbury's. So dramatic was its decline in the public mind that one school playground put-down among some British children was to call someone a "Tesco reject."

Tesco introduced its Clubcard loyalty card in February 1995, and by midyear its market share had nosed past Sainsbury's. By August of the next year, 8.5 million Tesco shoppers were using the card, which had rapidly become the "most popular, and the most recognized, loyalty programme in the UK."[13] Tesco was collecting data from two-thirds of the 600 million shopping baskets processed at its cash registers every year.

In spite of fundamental similarities, loyalty card programs could be different in subtly important ways. What set the Clubcard apart most significantly was that every quarter Tesco mailed vouchers and discount coupons to its cardholders. In other supermarkets, shoppers could obtain and redeem their points anytime they wanted at the checkout stand—simple, convenient, and very low cost.

But pursuing this variation of the basic idea was an act of some bravery by Tesco's then head of marketing, Terry Leahy (now Tesco's CEO). Every quarter Tesco sent millions of mail pieces to cardholders, in the process becoming one of the United Kingdom's major direct mailers. Since each piece had to be customized precisely to the recipient, each mailing was a major logistical challenge—and a security challenge as well because the pieces contained reward vouchers worth millions of pounds that could be spent like money for anything in a Tesco store. Each piece also contained discount coupons for specific goods aimed at the recipient according to his or her history of purchases.

Thus, the mailings were a vast but precisely targeted communication with Tesco's millions of customers. Since points accumulated over a three-month period, the vouchers were often worth several pounds. So they had some significance, as opposed to discounts taken frequently at checkout, which tended to be smaller and therefore felt less valuable. The mailings created what the company called "emotional loyalty." Research showed that Tesco shoppers came to think of their quarterly mailing as personal mail, akin to a bank statement, rather than junk mail. Though expensive, every quarterly mailing generated a sales uptick, much like those at Christmas and Easter, that paid for the mailing. Tesco claims it operated its mailing program from the very beginning for no net cost.

Shopper interest in the Clubcard may have been what lifted Tesco to first place among U.K. grocers, but it was arguably the chain's tenacity in exploring and exploiting the card data that delivered the deep payoff. According to an expert on U.K. loyalty card schemes, "the thing that set Tesco apart was the depth of its data analysis."[14]

Tesco used its card data in several important ways:

- *It found individual product opportunities.* For example, the data revealed that families buying diapers for the first time were good prospects to buy beer as well since, it turned out, the father no longer spent as much time at the pub.

- Through segmentation analysis, *it built richer and deeper understanding of its customers that revealed significant opportunities.* It confirmed that 20 percent of shoppers provided 80 percent of its total revenues and profits. But now Tesco knew by name and address exactly who those golden shoppers were.

- *Clubcard let Tesco track and respond efficiently to competition.* In particular, Tesco could fight the discounters much more effectively. Analysis showed not only which customers cared most about discounts (not all customers cared equally and some cared not at all) but also what specific products were most important to those specific bargain shoppers.

- And not least, *Clubcard data helped Tesco identify and introduce new businesses.* Tesco became the world's most successful online grocer by building on Clubcard data.[15] For example, Clubcard holders could view online what they had purchased in stores and select from that list what they wanted to buy online. Using Clubcard data to identify good prospects helped Tesco move into a variety of nonfood product lines. For example, with the Royal Bank of Scotland it created Tesco Personal Finance, which by end of 2005 produced £100 million in profit for the company.

Most important of all, Tesco didn't give up. It persisted, it learned, and as the insights built up, so did the value return on the investment. Tesco's board kept faith with the innovation and recognized its longer-term value to the company rather than reverting to simpler pricing tactics the way Safeway did.

From such an uncertain start at the beginning of the 1990s, Tesco emerged from the decade as the United Kingdom's leading retailer. It now ranks third in the world, behind only Wal-Mart and France's Carrefour, and in 2007 it entered the world's largest market, the United States, with its Fresh 'n Easy stores. Was all this because of the Clubcard? Of course not; business success at this scale never comes down to a single factor, but Clubcard heads the list of innovations CEO and now *Sir* Terry Leahy cites as the foundation of Tesco's success: "Our business has been built on innovations like Clubcard, Value lines, Finest products, Express stores, 24-hour shopping, and Tesco Dot Com."[16]

A recent British investment bank report said, "Contrary to popular belief, Tesco's most significant competitive advantage in the United Kingdom is not its scale. We believe Clubcard . . . is Tesco's most potent weapon in the ongoing battle for market share . . . it offers an ongoing engine of growth . . . indeed, it could also become an important force in Tesco's global expansion."[17]

Safeway, with its vaunted technical prowess, could and perhaps should have enjoyed all the benefits of the data provided by its loyalty card. But when the going got tough, in the Trough of Disillusionment, the Safeway board and the CEO abandoned the card. It's telling that the person who had headed Safeway's loyalty program and had left the company before it dropped the ABC card said, "Safeway didn't make a priority of the ABC card, and failed in using its technological expertise to gain a truly customer-focused approach."[18]

The challenge that Safeway failed to meet, apparently, was the one identified by Grant Harrison, a Tesco manager involved with its Clubcard. He realized card data would be worthless unless a company was willing to change the way it did business on the basis of what the data was saying. He said, "Do the stores want to run differently, do the retail directors, do the buyers? We all know that you can find 'interesting stuff' in the data. The challenge is how you get the business to engage and be prepared to change processes or decisions based on a new more detailed source of customer understanding."[19]

In hype cycle terms, Tesco was able to ride the loyalty card hype cycle to its most productive stage, while Safeway abandoned the innovation in the Trough of Disillusionment. Safeway's high/low strategy appeared to work for a couple of years, but the benefits didn't last. Canny Safeway shoppers soon learned to cherry-pick only the bargains. Strategic problems mounted and finally caught up with Safeway in the United Kingdom; it was bought for £3 billion in 2004 and absorbed into the Morrisons grocery chain, which had been a far smaller rival.[20]

Varying paths through the hype cycle sort winners from losers, whether at the level of whole businesses, such as Tesco and Safeway, or at the level of teams and individual managers. The hype cycle helps explain why people adopt, abandon, or ignore innovations inappropriately. Too many organizations are tempted to jump into an innovation prematurely, at the Peak of Inflated Expectations, while others wait too long and find themselves trying to catch up in an area where they wish they'd been more aggressive. Adopting innovation without understanding the hype cycle can lead to inappropriate adoption decisions and a waste of time, money, and opportunity.

The Hype Cycle Is the Key to Understanding Innovation Adoption

Given all this, what lesson about living with hype cycles might you take from the story of U.K. loyalty cards? First and foremost, it shows the importance of how you *adopt* innovation, and that differs markedly from what you find in other books about innovation, which are mainly about how you *originate* new ideas, usually for new products and services. Our focus in this book is elsewhere—on innovations you adopt from the outside. These innovations are often applied to internal capabilities and processes—like the database marketing insights Tesco obtained. The key difference is that the core ideas, techniques, and technologies come from outside your firm, and not from internal invention. The U.K. supermarkets did not originate the one-to-one marketing concept or the loyalty scheme; nor did they invent the relational databases and magnetic stripe cards technology that enabled them. They tried to adopt, adapt, and exploit these innovations, with varying success.

An external innovation becomes available to a group of businesses at roughly the same time; indeed, it's often actively sold to those businesses via carefully considered marketing strategies. There is a market discourse about the innovation, and a head of steam builds up around it. The choice is not simply whether to be first mover or fast follower. It's about how you time your adoption to leverage market hype about the innovation, how well you judge the shape of the unfolding curves of social sentiment toward that innovation and the engineering progress of its supporting technologies over time. It's about how you manage the dissonance between internal confidence and learning and the external, inevitable roller coaster of expectations. In the end, Tesco's management team rode the database marketing hype cycle better than Safeway. We don't claim that effectiveness at managing the adoption of a single innovation is what makes or breaks large companies. Multiple factors are always at work. But in this case, differences in navigating the hype cycle certainly helped Tesco on its way to spectacular success and contributed to Safeway's eventual demise. The stakes really can be that high.

The hype cycle also highlights the need for continual, ongoing awareness about your own decision processes when faced with never-ending waves of potential innovations. Over the coming decade, you, and the organizations you work for, will be adopting innovations faster than ever before. Our hyperconnected society exposes us more rapidly to more ideas and innovations than at any other time in history.

We've all heard how the pace of technology innovation adoption is accelerating as a result of underlying driving forces like Moore's Law.[21] You only have to look at the technologies you have built into your personal life over the last twenty years to see that—e-mail, iPod, DVD, laptop PC, and many more besides.

But another, less obvious change is at work that can be demonstrated by a quick visit to a place called Google Labs. To go there, you don't need special clearance and needn't pass a phalanx of security guards, because it's actually a section of the Google Web site, where you're greeted by this message: "Google Labs showcases a few of our favorite ideas that aren't quite ready for prime time. Your feedback can help us improve them. Please play with these prototypes and send your comments directly to the Googlers who developed them."

At one time, no company would dare send out half-baked product ideas like that just to see whether they worked. An innovative product or service would have to be comprehensively evaluated to calculate the cost of development, and its launch would produce an appropriate level of market adoption. But in the late 1990s, the Web fueled a much more experimental culture, one willing to create and consume millions of new Web sites and services. The cost of adding a new capability to a Web site is negligible compared with the cost of traditional product launches. The sheer number of ideas arising from this melting pot of innovation means that there are simply more and more innovations, at earlier stages of development, to evaluate. We have moved from discrete to continuous innovation—in fact, to a state of "perpetual beta."[22] Indeed, increasingly we are all asked to collaborate in evolving new innovations rather than having them handed to us—contributing Wikipedia entries, YouTube videos, or news blog reactions.

The skill of navigating waves of change—predicting their timing, judging their inflection points, and mitigating the moments of danger—is a skill that needs to become second nature. It is the goal of this book that you internalize the hype cycle. If you do so, you can develop different and better reactions as a manager to the key data points along the hype cycle and end up making better decisions that lead to far better results.

The concept of the hype cycle is simple, and we all recognize its truth intuitively. However, making decisions and taking action around it are difficult. They require both understanding and disciplined, systematic effort. The remainder of part 1 will be devoted to the understanding, and part 2 will focus on the systematic, disciplined effort.

Two

Behind the Hype Cycle

When people are free to do as they please,
they usually imitate each other.

—Eric Hoffer

T O UNDERSTAND WHY the hype cycle happens again and again with each new innovation, and why it keeps seducing even those of us who have been burned before, we must look more deeply at what drives the rise and fall of expectations that create the cycle.

In a theoretical, completely rational world ruled by logic, excitement about an innovation would track perfectly with the reality of what the innovation could do. As the performance of the innovation improved, and as people's understanding of how to derive value from it evolved, people would become increasingly confident about it, and their adoption of it would grow. But, as we saw in the opening stories of chapter 1, in the real world, wonderful, warm, passionate human beings repeatedly develop levels of excitement and disillusionment that don't match the current reality of what the innovation can do.

Why does this happen? Why do people's expectations rise far above the levels currently justified by the innovation, thereby causing the Peak of Inflated Expectations? And then why does it then take so long for the innovation to drive value, which leads to the Trough of Disillusionment?

In fact, the hype cycle arises from the interplay of two factors: human nature and the nature of innovation. Human nature drives people's heightened expectations, while the nature of innovation drives how quickly something new develops genuine value. The problem is, these two factors move at such different tempos that they're nearly always out of sync. An innovation rarely delivers on its promise when people are most excited about it. Expectations rise quickly and are easily frustrated, while innovations develop slowly, step by step.

These two factors can be described by two distinct curves. The first is a bell curve, which represents the initial enthusiasm and disappointment driven by positive and negative hype. The second is an S curve showing how an innovation's performance improves slowly at first, then picks up steadily, and finally yields diminishing returns.[1]

When we combine these two curves, we can see how the shape of the hype cycle arises from the offset timing of the two factors. The hype cycle is driven upward first by our collective emotional response and then, on the Slope of Enlightenment, by our logical response to an innovation's improving performance (see figure 2-1).[2]

In this chapter, we will take a deeper look at these two sides of innovation adoption: on one side, people's impatient excitement about the new and novel and, on the other side, the reality of an innovation's frustratingly slow actual development. By examining how these two sides contrast and interplay, we will see how the hype cycle plays such a key role in decisions about innovation adoption.

Expectations: Human Response to the New and Novel

The sudden, illogical acceleration of expectations around an innovation is a form of "irrational exuberance," to use the famous e-business-era phrase of then Federal Reserve Board chairman Alan Greenspan.[3] At least three aspects of human nature are at work here: our attraction to novelty, our social natures, and our tendencies to use shortcuts or "heuristics" in making

FIGURE 2-1

Components of the hype cycle

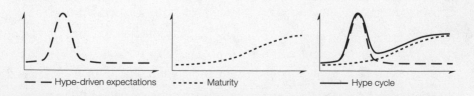

— — Hype-driven expectations   ...... Maturity   —— Hype cycle

decisions under uncertainty. All three stem from the ways we've evolved psychologically that keep us alive and relatively sane in a complex and sometimes hostile world. Unfortunately, all three can be causes of less than perfectly "rational" behavior with potentially negative consequences when we are deciding whether and when to adopt an innovation.

Novelty Preference and the Positive Role of Hype

We all love something new. From birth, we're all attracted to novelty. When babies are shown an object they've seen before, they spend less time looking at it than at a new object. This desire to spend more time looking at new objects and exploring new locations is called the *novelty preference*. Our senses are tailored toward novelty. We use peripheral vision to detect movement in our surroundings, and we instantly detect when a sound changes (the silence when the refrigerator switches off), even if we hadn't consciously noticed the sound before.

As adults, we continue to feel the attraction of the new and novel over the known and predictable. As long as we can set our own agenda and time frame for embracing the new (we don't like to be *told* to change), most of us show a marked preference for novelty. A new idea or opportunity piques our curiosity, and we feel compelled to explore it.

One of the most influential American psychologists of the twentieth century, Abraham Maslow, acknowledged this in late work that built on the hierarchy of fundamental human needs (such as food, shelter, and belonging) for which he is famous. "Above and beyond these negative determinants for acquiring knowledge (anxiety, fear), there are some reasonable grounds for postulating positive *per se* impulses to satisfy curiosity, to know, to explain, and to understand," he wrote in 1971, the year of his death.[4] He pointed to examples as varied as the way monkeys pull things apart and the drives of historical figures such as Galileo as sources of evidence.

More than the love of the new and novel is at work in the early stages of an innovation's life, however. As adults, all of us supercharge our innate novelty preference with *imagination*. We're able to take a possibility—an innovation of some kind, for example—and imagine an array of wonderful futures around that innovation. We're free to imagine the possibilities because, in large part, there is little else at this point in the life of the innovation to base our judgment and expectations on. The innovation is all possibility unencumbered by real experience.

Part of our love of novelty includes our desire to share it with others. Rather than simply viewing hype as a villain for inflating our early expectations about an innovation, we need to acknowledge that a certain amount of hype is necessary to expose us to novel ideas and inspire our imaginations to dream up new possibilities. The definition of the term *hype* ranges from "blatant and showy promotion," such as marketers often use in launching a new product, to "exaggerated or extravagant claims," which tend to occur as an industry's imagination catches hold and explores possible new directions, and finally on to outright fraud and trickery. If we exclude the latter from our consideration, we are left with a spectrum of behavior that involves overstating the case for an innovation to varying degrees in order to attract people's attention.

We need to communicate the value of an innovation to make people notice that something has changed and to open them up to new possibilities. Without a friend's recommendation, a vendor's press release, a professional guideline, a government regulation, or other similar source, we would never be exposed to important new ideas, or we would encounter them much later than we would have liked. And without ongoing discourse within a community that questions, prods, and develops the innovation, even the best ideas will fade into obscurity.

In the mid-twentieth century, a British biochemist called Joseph Needham began collecting and documenting discoveries and inventions from China through the ages. During this work Needham repeatedly encountered examples of ancient inventions that had been reinvented in modern times, with no realization of the earlier experience.[5] In one example, he came across the following law of physics penned in a work called the *Mo Ching* in the third century BC: "The cessation of motion is due to the opposing force . . . If there is no opposing force . . . the motion will never stop."[6]

Compare this to Newton's first law of motion, also called the law of inertia, written 2,100 years later: "An object at rest will remain at rest unless acted upon by an external and unbalanced force. An object in motion will remain in motion unless acted upon by an external and unbalanced force."

The words of the *Mo Ching* lay unacknowledged until Needham brought them to light, yet Newton's work found a foothold and flourished in the supportive intellectual and cultural framework of the eighteenth century. This led Needham and other academics to ask the question, Why were the critical insights and breakthroughs of the Chinese not recognized and developed earlier?

Reflecting on the *Mo Ching*–Newton comparison, John Lienhard at the University of Houston highlights the importance of sharing—some might say marketing—an idea in order for it to take hold: "The idea alone is necessary, but it's not sufficient. Invention isn't complete until we've shared it—until we've told one another, maybe even boasted a bit, about our latest wonderful new thing."[7] Against such a radically different cultural and philosophical backdrop from Newton's, the Chinese version of the law of inertia didn't get shared loudly enough or often enough to make an enduring mark on the world.

So we need communication and community discourse for an idea or innovation to flourish. But why doesn't that discourse remain reasonable and rational? Why does it so often cross the line into "blatant and showy promotion" and "exaggerated or extravagant claims," both by the originator of the innovation and by those who become enamored with the idea and spread it further? Why do we always feel compelled to boast a bit?

We can find some answers by looking a little closer at the first part of Newton's law of inertia: "An object at rest will remain at rest unless acted upon by an external and unbalanced force." Communication is the external and unbalanced force that sets an idea in motion, but to deliver on the "unbalanced" part, it often needs to overshoot reality—that is, it needs to slip into the realm of hype.

Marketers are practiced at this, and advertisements are fraught with superlatives that go beyond what we know can be reality. This doesn't necessarily reflect badly on the developers and marketers of innovations, as their belief in the value of their product and their enthusiasm to spread the word may be perfectly genuine. We even treat ourselves the same way when we "hype ourselves up" to motivate ourselves to change. Knowing that we will lose a quarter of an inch of belly fat may not be enough to launch us on an ambitious exercise program. Imagining that we can look like an athlete with a six-pack of abdominal muscle is more likely to motivate us, even if deep down we know that scenario is unlikely. Anyone trying to drive an innovation forward will at times need to overstate their case to others, to act as an unbalanced force on the status quo.

If a little marketing hype to ourselves and others is a necessary evil to get things moving, it's certainly not the only force in play in driving up the levels of excitement. One of the largest factors in the wild swings of the early stages of the hype cycle is the phenomenon known variously as social contagion or the bandwagon effect.

Social Contagion

Although we might not like to admit it, we humans are at our core extraordinarily sensitive to what others around us are doing and saying. We want to be seen as individuals, yet not be perceived as too different. Even those who refuse to conform to the norms of some larger group generally belong to a subgroup, if only to the subgroup of those who don't conform. Rare is the individual who forgoes social acceptance and genuinely seeks to be only him- or herself. Our choice of clothes, hobbies, spending patterns, and many other aspects of our lives are deeply influenced by the behavior and opinion of others—to a degree much greater than most of us would care to admit.

Perhaps you remember that old trick you might have played on your schoolmates at age six or seven. Two of you stood in the playground and stared up into the sky and pointed. "Look!" you cried out. "Up there! Can you see it?" Soon other kids joined in, straining at the sky, anxious to see whatever it might be. The small group became a slightly larger group and then, if you could keep it going long enough, a small crowd—a crowd of people all staring at precisely nothing.

As with many of our psychological predispositions, our tendency to be influenced by others probably originates from raw survival needs. Early humans who joined the crowd fleeing an unseen enemy probably lived to tell the tale. If they insisted on validating the appropriateness of their cave colleague's behavior through personal research, they probably found themselves wiped out of the gene pool by a herd of stampeding mammoths. But sometimes the crowd is mistaken, and instead of just wasting breath running away from a nonexistent enemy, the members of the crowd end up at best embarrassed and in many cases significantly out of pocket.

The role of social contagion in driving the adoption of positive and negative innovations is well documented. Once a critical mass of people show interest in an innovation—or stop to look at an empty sky—further adoption becomes self-propelling. In *The Tipping Point*, Malcolm Gladwell describes how interest in some new thing—whether a new product, teen suicide, crime cleanup, almost anything—grows slowly until it reaches a tipping point, after which it spreads rapidly, literally like an epidemic. Some researchers have even suggested ideas behave almost as if they were independent viral entities. Proponents of "memetics" have suggested units of cultural information are transmitted through populations like genes. Ideas have us rather than us having them.[8]

Once a bandwagon starts rolling, the press stories start to talk about what "everybody" is doing with the innovation. Senior managers are often at the receiving end of an executive waving an airline magazine that features the latest technology or management trend.[9] Or the executive is invited to a briefing by one of the company's management consulting or technology suppliers and is exposed to a great new idea. "What are we doing about this?" asks the executive, at which point the managers scurry off to get their own briefing and launch the next bold new initiative.

Over the last decade, the Internet has acted as an accelerator of such contagion, as news travels around the world almost instantaneously, growing exponentially via e-mails and blogs. For example, news of the outbreak of the SARS disease in Asia in 2002 affected international travel all over the world within a few days. Medical authorities as far apart as China and Canada, sharing critical information, designed containment procedures for it within weeks. Images direct from the front lines of war zones and terrorist incidents now move from mobile phone cameras to global TV networks in minutes. And when these things happen, mass online discussion and exchange of views breaks out very quickly. This force continues to grow stronger as wikis, video blogs, Twitter (mobile phone microblogging), and photo-sharing sites continue the evolution.

One of the most visible and dramatic areas in which you can see social contagion at work is the financial markets. History is rife with examples of stock bubbles and crashes because people followed the crowd rather than the reality, the "fundamentals," of what they were investing in. A number of extreme examples are documented in *Extraordinary Popular Delusions and the Madness of Crowds*, including the tulip mania that gripped Holland in the early decades of the 1600s, just after the flower had been introduced from Constantinople.[10] At one point, the price of tulip bulbs grew twentyfold in one month. Some people traded their land, livestock, and savings to buy one bulb.

In business, competitive threat acts as a powerful driver of contagion. When some new thing appears and we hear our competitor is adopting it, we pay special attention. You may recall in the book's opening story the effect on other U.K. supermarkets when Tesco was first to launch a national loyalty card. Of course, the sellers of an innovation take advantage of this by telling companies, "Your competitors are already doing it." That's guaranteed to get some interest.

Our attitude toward the early adopters that are leading the charge works as a further accelerator. One of the personality characteristics admired in many (but not all) cultures is the willingness to take risks. Teddy Roosevelt's words resonate with many of us: "Far better is it to dare mighty things, to win glorious triumphs, even though checked by failure . . . than to rank with those poor spirits who neither enjoy much nor suffer much, because they live in a gray twilight that knows not victory nor defeat." Even if most of us don't dare mighty things, we look up to those who do.

It is no coincidence, then, that the companies seen to be taking the most risk (i.e., the most innovative) are also among the ones most admired. Half of the world's top ten most innovative companies are among the top ten most admired companies in the world (see figure 2-2).

The nature of risk taking is such that spectacular success tends to be punctuated by equally spectacular failure. The companies that excel at innovation know this and plan their investments and innovation activities accordingly, using the kind of process we will explore in part 2. But for

FIGURE 2-2

World's most innovative companies, 2007, from *BusinessWeek*

Gray bars indicate inclusion in Fortune's "World's Most Admired Companies 2007," with their position in parentheses

1. Apple (5)
2. Google
3. Toyota Motor (2)
4. General Electric (1)
5. Microsoft (8)
6. Procter & Gamble (3)
7. 3M
8. Walt Disney Co.
9. IBM
10. Sony

World's Most Admired Companies

Source: "The World's 50 Most Innovative Companies," *BusinessWeek*, 2007, http://bwnt.businessweek.com/interactive_reports/most_innovative/index.asp; and "World's Most Admired Companies 2007," *Fortune*, http://money.cnn.com/magazines/fortune/globalmostadmired/2007/top50/index.html.

other companies watching the much-admired innovators, there is no way to tell which innovations will be the successes and which will be the failures. The contagion begins shortly after initial adoption by the innovators, not at the point where the real value is understood.

A more subtle but equally contagious influence is the impact of the *zeitgeist*, or the "spirit of the time." A common social framework of attitudes, outlook, values, and expectations works its effect subtly in ways that cut deeper than short-term fashion shifts. Innovations that fit within that framework are more likely to attract attention and generate excitement than those that take us in a fundamentally different direction. We're generally unaware of how much we are products of our times, and often our frameworks are evident only after they've changed. In one time and place, it is considered good to be loyal to your company, to eat high-quality meat protein, and to be a consumer whose purchases stimulate the economy. In another time and place, it's considered obvious that we should strive for personal independence, eat less red meat, and be frugal to protect the environment. We are more likely to adopt an innovation that fits the times, or leads them slightly, than one that doesn't.

Decision Heuristics

A vast body of research has demonstrated predictable tendencies in the way people make decisions when faced with alternatives whose outcomes are uncertain, such as whether to adopt a particular innovation or which one of multiple innovations will provide most value. Rather than attempt the (usually impossible) task of evaluating every alternative, people apply shortcuts, or heuristics, that get good-enough results most of the time. In the words of one of the early researchers in cognitive psychology, Herbert Simon, we "satisfice" (a marriage of *satisfy* and *suffice*) rather than optimize our decisions. If you need a new shirt, you may look at several before you buy one, but you won't evaluate every available shirt (although some people apparently want to try, much to the dismay of their shopping companions).

The heuristics we've developed usually serve us well in arriving at an acceptable decision in a reasonable amount of time, but they can also lead to flawed decision making without our realizing. For example, there's the availability heuristic: if something comes to mind easily—if it is more readily "available" to us—then we overestimate its probability.[11] For example, in the 1990s, people heard most about wildly successful dot-com IPOs, and so probably tended to overestimate the chances of success for the next dot-com IPO, while ignoring all the failures and nonsuccesses they never heard about but could have discovered if they'd looked.

That phrase *could have discovered* is telling. As you start to consider some innovation, you start to collect evidence for and against it. Or do you? Unfortunately, people tend *not* to look equally at both sides of a question. We all have a strong bias toward seeking out and collecting evidence that confirms our existing or preferred view. So if people are inclined toward adopting an innovation, they will seek out examples that show why it's a good idea. Even when explicitly instructed to look for "disconfirming" evidence, people still tend to look only for supporting examples.[12] Like the hype cycle itself, this is not a new phenomenon. As Francis Bacon wrote nearly four hundred years ago:

> The human understanding when it has once adopted an opinion (either as being the received opinion or as being agreeable to itself) draws all things else to support and agree with it. And though there be a greater number and weight of instances to be found on the other side, yet these it either neglects and despises, or else by some distinction sets aside and rejects, in order that by this great and pernicious predetermination the authority of its former conclusions may remain inviolate.[13]

These shortcuts in our decision making compound the effects of the novelty preference and social contagion in further escalating our expectations.

What Goes Up . . .

With excitement about an innovation driven to dizzy heights by these all-too-human tendencies, something has to give eventually. Either the innovation delivers on its promise or the Peak of Inflated Expectations has nothing to sustain itself and collapses under its own weight. It is the second scenario—collapse—that we see repeatedly.

Since virtually all innovations require time and experience to realize their real potential, it's almost inevitable that reports of early experiences will disappoint us. Once the excitement starts to wane even slightly, the same psychological and social factors that drove the excitement upward now begin to drive it right back down again. Novelty is not a long-lived characteristic, by definition, and so when the novelty wears off, we seek the next new thing. When negative sentiments start to arise, social contagion can spark a stampede *away* from an innovation as easily as it sparked the movement toward it. And our decision heuristics lead us to focus on the latest and most prevalent information—the stories of doom and disaster.

From this point on, expectations are no longer held aloft by hype and promise, but can only be raised out of the Trough of Disillusionment by real progress in the maturity of the innovation.

Reality: The Long, Slow Road to Value

Ask any teenager which company invented the digital audio player, and they answer without hesitation, "Apple." That must be frustrating for Diamond Multimedia, iriver, Creative Labs, and other companies that were pioneering and improving digital audio players for years before the iPod hit the shelves.

Apple developed the iPod in less than a year and launched it in October 2001, almost three years after the first digital player appeared. Known for its unique interface, ease of use, and clean design, the iPod went on to dominate the market, particularly after the launch in April 2003 of the online iTunes Store, where iPod users could purchase and download songs. As of mid-2005, the iPod's U.S. market share was 74 percent, and as of April 2007, Apple had sold over 100 million iPods.

Like most overnight successes, this one was long in the making. Early work on digital compression standards began in the 1980s, two decades before the iPod, and led to such early digital audio players as the Diamond Rio and Creative devices, as well as PC-based peer-to-peer file sharing via Napster.

Such a time frame is typical for technological and business innovations. For example, the peak of hype for customer relationship management was in the late 1990s, as Tesco was beating Safeway at the retail loyalty card game—yet the very first airline loyalty cards scheme, American Airlines "AAdvantage," appeared in 1981. In spite of popular stereotypes to the contrary, an innovation doesn't spring fully formed from the mind of the inventor and into the hands of the user. It needs a period of time to diffuse in markets, to become useful and usable. While some early adopters may gain early value from it, most users get dependable value only after a longer period of development.

Stages of Innovation Maturity

To reach a predictable level of value for most adopters, an innovation must pass through four characteristic stages of development along the S curve of maturity (see figure 2-3).

1. In the *embryonic stage*, it is still in the lab (or on the whiteboard) and has no commercial use yet. An example might be the early 1980s work on MPEG digital audio standards.

2. The *emerging stage* is characterized by early commercialization by suppliers, pilot projects by potential adopters, and deployments by industry leaders. For example, in November 1998, a two-and-a-half-ounce device the size of a small pager hit the shelves of Radio Shack and other electronics stores and became the first mass-market digital audio player with no moving parts to be launched in the United States. The Diamond Rio could hold about twenty songs and cost $199.

3. In the *adolescent stage*, the innovation develops more mature capabilities, process understanding deepens, and an associated infrastructure develops around the innovation. When Apple launched the iPod at the end of 2001, it offered one thousand songs for the $399 price tag. The infrastructure for delivering digital audio moved through a couple of false starts based around illegal file sharing before the launch of Apple's iTunes service on

FIGURE 2-3

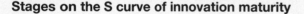

Stages on the S curve of innovation maturity

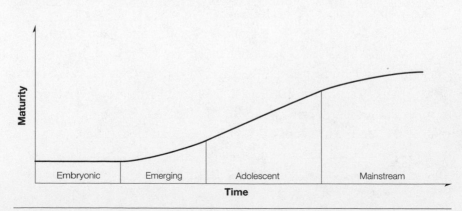

Windows machines (most of America's PCs) in October 2003, which set the standard for a more stable long-term infrastructure of legal downloading from online merchants.

4. In the *mainstream stage of maturity*, the innovation is considered proven, though its capabilities may continue to evolve. The innovation now has a relatively predictable value proposition and the risks are significantly lower compared with the embryonic or emerging stages. In the world of digital audio players, the launch of the iTunes Store ramped up popularity for iPods and established the beginning of the mainstream stage. Apple launched variations on the basic iPod with the iPod mini, followed by the iPod shuffle, along with major storage enhancements. By 2007, a $250 iPod could hold twenty thousand songs. With the price/performance ratio dropping, MP3 players began to be built into smart phones. When podcasting emerged as a simple way to capture and disseminate audio, mainstream companies became interested in the technology as a way to deliver corporate information.

The Time-to-Value Gap

Any nontrivial innovation—something beyond a minor modification or extension, such as a new scent of bubble bath—progresses through the stages above. Along the way, it matures from an uncertain value proposition with high risk of failure to a predictable value proposition with low risk, at which time it goes mainstream.

In regulated fields such as the medical and pharmaceutical industries, an innovation such as a new drug or procedure cannot be released until it has passed strict quality standards. There may be excitement around the potential of a new drug, but the public is protected from many of the early risks through a series of stringently controlled trials in which test patients are informed of the risks and give their consent.

In business and technology innovations (especially software innovations), the maturation process is exposed to the outside world in an unrestricted, unregulated way. Early adopters are the guinea pigs that get hit with the problems and risks of an immature innovation. In many cases, there is no "informed consent" in their decision to adopt. The innovation is on the market, so surely it will work—or so goes the hopeful thinking. The earlier people are exposed to an innovation, the longer it will take before they see the innovation reach maturity. As we noted in chapter 1, the broad use of the Web has compounded the tendency for innovations to go public early in their lives and led us into a world of "perpetual beta."

In many cases, an innovation literally cannot mature until a broad range of people and organizations put it to use under different conditions and test the limits of its performance and applicability. Such experimentation is a necessary part of the maturation process. The lone genius in a lab or garage is an inventor, not an innovator—the invention needs to be socialized, adopted, and adapted in order to deliver value. MP3 standards for digital audio, for example, evolved as musicians and other enthusiasts tested the capabilities through multiple iterations.

The time between people's exposure to an embryonic innovation and their ability to confidently predict its value as a mainstream innovation—the *time to value*—is inevitably longer than most people anticipate. We call this gap between initial excitement and ultimate value an innovation's *time-to-value gap*. The time-to-value gap applies both to the consensus of understanding and value in the broad marketplace for an innovation, and to the challenges felt by each organization that tries to drive the innovation into full and productive value.

Many types of challenges and risks create the time-to-value gap. We can categorize them into four main areas—four value gaps that need to be closed before an innovation can deliver on its promise to an organization or to the industry at large (see figure 2-4).

1. *Performance.* The innovation must work with consistent levels of accuracy, reliability, or other relevant performance metrics.

2. *Integration.* Even if the innovation basically works, it must be usable within cost and time requirements in a real, working environment, supported by a reliable supplier. For this to happen, adopters must develop a good understanding of how to incorporate the innovation into an existing environment, including process, technology, and organizational infrastructures, and often also a broader ecosystem of related innovations.

3. *Penetration.* A group or an organization may adopt an innovation, but for it to work successfully, individual users must accept and assimilate it into their everyday work. Not everyone embraces an innovation at the same time or to the same degree: the

FIGURE 2-4

The time-to-value gap

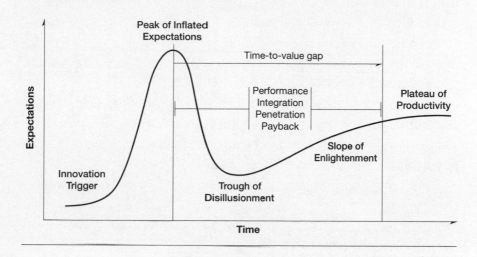

development of value may require that a critical mass of (or even all) users actually embrace the innovation.

4. *Payback.* The technology works, it scales and is reliable, everyone's using it, but there may still be problems with deriving projected business value because cost savings or other financial benefits aren't materializing as expected, or as quickly as expected.

Let's take a look at these four value gaps in more detail, to better understand what must happen to close the overall time-to-value gap.

Performance

With enough money and other resources, a small number of highly motivated adopters can put an innovation to good use in the early stages of maturity, but most potential users must wait until a useful level of performance is attained at much lower price points and resource requirements. What counts here is not just raw performance characteristics (for example, the speed of a computer chip or the fuel consumption of a car) but performance *within relevant constraints*, such as price, size, and power consumption. Some factors, such as reliability and serviceability, can only be improved by learning cycles from real-world experience with the innovation. Simple challenges such as devices overheating on an airport ramp in Kuwait, opening an access panel with gloved hands in a field in Finland, or securing against intellectual property loss in one of China's bright new cities are easily overlooked in the originating Swiss laboratory, California coding cubicle, or German engineering workshop.

To determine expected performance levels, you need to know what to expect from an innovation at each stage of maturity.

In the *embryonic stage*, there is a high risk that an innovation will not perform at all to the levels required. Little is known about the situations in which the innovation does and does not work, and what factors impact its performance.

At the *emerging stage*, the innovation has been shown to work effectively in some situations, and early adopters try to apply it in their environments. Much of the maturation that happens during this stage lies in understanding the limits of the innovation. In particular, laboratory demonstrations often fail to take into account the problems of deployment in a real-world setting. For example, early speech recognition technology showed impressive accuracy in converting people's words to text and commands—until the users took the technology into an office or factory setting and had to deal with background noise and everyday speech. Similarly, many companies jumped on RFID as a way to identify items without having a worker scan a bar code. But they soon discovered RFID couldn't read through metal or liquids, and that even where it did work, the read rates fell short of lab results.

During *adolescence* and *early maturity*, there is growing understanding of where and how required price/performance can be achieved reliably. Sometimes the performance levels limit the innovation to a niche status— for example, speech recognition is used to good effect in call centers and medical transcription, but it still is not a mainstream user interface.

User perception of performance or quality can also lead to the impression that an innovation is not yet mature enough, even if it does in fact have value. This is a particular challenge when the expected standard for a technology innovation is the performance level of real people. If a computer is supposed to understand speech or handwriting, we already have built-in expectations of what that involves on the basis of our experience with other humans. When the systems fall short of those standards, even if they are in fact useful, we're disappointed. Early experience with the

Apple Newton handwriting recognition is a good example. The popular press mocked the performance of the Newton's handwriting recognition (see figure 2-5). As a result, personal digital assistants (PDAs) floundered in the Trough of Disillusionment for several years, until the Palm Pilot launched in 1996 with a modified handwriting system called Graffiti.[14] That success pulled PDAs as a class of product into broader (though still not mass-market) adoption.

Integration

Any innovation must fit into existing, complex organizational environments of people, processes, and systems.

Some innovations can be deployed rapidly and easily either because they work out of the box or because they take advantage of mature interfaces that are relatively invisible to the user. A self-setting atomic clock is an innovation that adds value immediately but only requires plugging in to take advantage of the atomic radio signal that will make sure the clock always displays the correct time. Other examples might include flat-panel displays, a keyless door lock, or the latest search engine.

Other innovations—including most of those deployed in businesses—tend to be more complex and have a much bigger footprint across the organization. They can rarely be deployed off-the-shelf; they require customization and integration with existing infrastructure, processes, and

FIGURE 2-5

A 1993 *Doonesbury* cartoon mocks the Apple Newton's handwriting capability

ecosystems. RFID has proved to be a challenging technology to integrate, with its requirements for deploying two sets of technology—the chips and the readers—and modifying data systems and workflows.

Infrastructure challenges are a frequent cause of a long integration gap. By definition, infrastructure involves multiple elements—collections of systems, physical assets, or people. Designing and implementing the required changes in all these elements to introduce an innovation can be extremely complex. Earlier we saw the challenges of developing an infrastructure to deliver digital audio for the growing number of MP3 players. Electric cars for consumers will continue to face a challenge until a far broader range of locations offer recharging services.

Many innovations need to be modified in a minor—or sometimes major—way in order to work within the constraints of a particular organization. This process of *adapting* an innovation, rather than just adopting it, also arises from a desire for people to feel a sense of ownership of the innovation. Innovations that need to be adapted to a greater degree in order to fit into existing process, culture, or technological infrastructure are likely to result in a longer deployment, longer learning cycles and a slower path to maturity.

For some innovations that become popular in the consumer world before making their way into organizations, the integration gap arises from challenges in adapting the innovation to meet corporate needs for security, compliance, retention, and so on. Such has often been the case with personal productivity tools, where end users in corporations adopted for their own use instant messaging, desktop search, Web-based e-mail, and collaboration tools. These were of high value to individuals, but they often presented a nightmare for IT and legal departments. Should instant messages be "discoverable" corporate data? Is it acceptable, in terms of privacy and security, for e-mails and documents to be stored in free Web-based services? Organizations flail in the face of popular, free, easy-to use-consumer products that fail to meet the basic requirements for enterprise-class products.

Penetration

An innovation advances as it penetrates more deeply into its potential audience. There are two related but distinct facets of penetration: adoption and assimilation. Adoption refers to people using a technology, while assimilation refers to people using it in a way that allows them to derive its full value.

No matter how simple or ready an innovation is, or how obvious its benefits, it still needs time to spread among a set of users, assuming it spreads at all. Decades of research about how new ideas spread has pointed to an S curve of penetration, where initial take-up is slow, followed by a rush and then a tailing off (the same basic shape as an innovation's performance S curve).[15] The curve can apply both to adoption by companies in an industry and to adoption by users within a company that has officially brought in an innovation.

The rate of adoption becomes an issue when the time taken for employees to start using an innovation is slower than expected or desired. In some cases organizations can address this issue by mandating changes to the process or by rolling out software that forces the use of the innovation.

Assimilation challenges occur when the users of an innovation don't fully embrace the changes that arrive with the innovation, and so the value of the innovation falls short of what it could be.[16] A common example is the update to a new version of a word processor or spreadsheet—most users rapidly figure out how to perform their common tasks in the new environment, and never explore the new features. In these cases, expensive and time-consuming upgrades result in little overall value. As part of the assimilation process, any new innovation must overcome "Maslow's Hammer"—Abraham Maslow is commonly attributed with first saying that if the only tool you have is a hammer, you treat everything like a nail. It's true that new tools get used initially to solve the old problems, not for the new value they might bring. For example, the first TV shows were just like radio shows, with one person standing in front of a microphone, and the earliest corporate Web sites were just like printed brochures and printed annual reports.

Penetration is most often an issue when the people driving the adoption of an innovation (e.g., IT professionals or top management) are not the individuals who will be using it (e.g., customers or employees). Those who launched the innovation must wait for it to be adopted and assimilated among the target population.

The challenge of assimilation and adoption is compounded by the fact that people need to see personal value, not just organizational value, to adopt. For example, many early deployments of speech recognition in an office looked at replacing human dictation and transcription with direct text entry. Executives were told, "Try this technology. If it works, you won't need your secretary anymore." You can guess how well those trials went.

Payback

The challenge in the early stages of an innovation's development is to estimate its potential payback in the face of unknown risks and uncertain benefits. (Note that we use the term *payback* as a general indicator of value, rather than any specific measure of calculating financial return.) In fact, there are two ways to misjudge the payback: by getting the amounts wrong (costs, value of benefits) or by getting the timing wrong (how long before the benefits appear).

Overestimating the value or underestimating the costs can happen in a number of ways. First, the innovation must be applied to a problem that really matters. For example, it doesn't make sense to install a new help desk system in a company that isn't growing or has just implemented a self-service system, and therefore doesn't have many customers calling the help desk. When an innovation is adopted early, at the Peak of Inflated Expectations, the focus is often on the innovation itself, and many organizations approach adoption with the question "Where can we use this?" rather than "Should we use this?" When that happens, projects will be identified that can certainly derive some value from the innovation but not enough to justify the high price and unknown risks of early adoption.

Payback can be affected by any of the other three value gaps. Delays in achieving appropriate levels of performance and integration can lead to increased costs and delayed returns. Even after an innovation works technically as it should, payback can be reduced if the innovation is not adopted by enough users, or not assimilated deeply enough by users to produce actual business value.

Circumstances may change such that the payback calculations become invalid—you assume that costs are spread over a user base of a certain size, and then the company sells a major division. Or unanticipated costs may be associated with the ongoing use of the innovation, such as a required upgrade after only two years when the payback assumption was four years. If a project falls behind schedule, not only are the expected benefits delayed, but any anticipated savings from replacing a predecessor system or process will also be delayed.

The business model around an innovation is often a major risk factor that delays or diminishes payback. This was obviously a major challenge in the e-business era. Finding the way to make money flow from the innovation can take years. For example, in the 1990s, Alta Vista didn't manage to nail the search-term advertising mechanism that brought the fountain of wealth from Web search to Google through its use of AdWords in the 2000s.

Studies of companies adopting innovations have revealed an inevitable period of decreased performance before projected improvements kick in.[17] Companies often do plan for a time lag between the introduction of an innovation and the appearance of benefits, but all too often they fail to plan for an actual *reduction* in productivity while the innovation is implemented and assimilated. The drop in productivity is related to the obstacles that we discussed earlier: performance, integration, and penetration. Or to put it less formally, rolling out an innovation is inevitably subject to the rule: "Anything that can go wrong will go wrong." Payback calculations that fail to account for this performance drop are going to overestimate payback and lead to disappointment.

Certain types of innovations face challenges in ongoing usage. For example, in the 1980s a number of companies developed large expert systems that modeled company and industry rules. Initial performance was good, but over time the rules fell out of date. Because there were no budgets, people, or procedures to update the rules continually, many of these systems were rapidly abandoned by users, and the projects never achieved their anticipated payback.

Even the mechanisms and metrics to determine how to attribute the financial value of an innovation need time to develop. When the same innovation is offered to many companies, they usually start to share best practices in business case development. Just analyzing the cost components and finding the value metrics that work takes time. Successful spreadsheet template models need to migrate socially between executives in different companies and business situations, via conferences, job moves, and personal networking.

The Role of the Hype Cycle

The hype cycle reflects the full range of human response to an innovation—the rational and irrational, hope and reality, imagination and plodding thought, excitement and sober assessment, right brain and left brain. So it should, for all those elements are present, and have an impact, as we confront each new thing we bring into our work, organizations, and lives.

These responses combine to create the five stages of the hype cycle. The excitement set off by the Innovation Trigger rises because people like novelty, because we're social animals, and because we take shortcuts in our decisions, until it reaches the Peak of Inflated Expectations. Because the innovation's time to value occurs more slowly than expected, because of the inevitable performance, integration, penetration, and payback challenges, it sinks into the Trough of Disillusionment. Next, on the Slope of Enlightenment, there is a handoff from promise to actual value, when real experience takes the place of unfettered imagination as the primary driver of expectations. As the innovation's maturity develops and real adoption spreads, the innovation arrives at the Plateau of Productivity.

The great lesson of the hype cycle is that the early life of an innovation is fraught with moments of acute dissonance, dangerous groupthink, and self-doubt that can lead managers into misjudgment and error. The right decisions often feel counterintuitive at precisely the time of greatest opportunity, when delay can have serious hidden costs.

Knowledge of this danger is important but not enough. All of us know the secret of wealth on Wall Street—buy low and sell high—yet how many of us have made fortunes on the stock market? Why, then, would we confidently assume as professional managers that picking the right innovation at the right time is somehow easier? In the next chapter, we will help you better spot and understand some of the specific traps and challenges in the hype cycle.

Three

Hype Cycle Traps and Challenges

For a successful technology, reality must take precedence over public relations, for nature cannot be fooled.

—Richard Feynman, Rogers Commission Report on the *Challenger* Crash[1]

IN 2000, TIM B. JOINED ONE of the major Canadian banks to lead the bank's e-business strategy. His predecessor had left the bank in the wake of a costly and unsuccessful foray into Internet banking. Its online bank, like most others at the time, hadn't succeeded in enrolling enough customers quickly enough to pay off the costs of creating and launching the new service.

Tim joined the bank with significant experience in the world of innovation. He rapidly realized that Internet banking was neither product nor service but a channel—that is, one of several ways customers could access products and services they already used. Tim integrated the bank's online capabilities into the existing business and product lines. He succeeded in lowering costs by sharing services such as marketing and technology infrastructure across all channels, which had not been possible when the Internet bank was viewed as a separate product.

Then, in mid-2000, one of the bank's rivals started advertising what it claimed was the first mobile banking service in North America. Although the hard lessons from Internet banking were still fresh in their minds, the bank's managers felt compelled to respond to this move by one of their chief competitors. E-business leadership was a key strategy for the bank, and so mobile banking was not an area where they wanted to be seen lagging behind other banks.

With the retail banks, Tim and his group launched a mobile banking project, taking care to position it as a channel, not a separate product. It was a new way for bank customers to access a broad range of banking services. Unfortunately, only a handful of customers took advantage of this new approach.

There were at least three reasons for the poor response. First, less than 35 percent of Canadians used mobile phones at that time.[2] In addition, the mobile technology then available provided an online experience far inferior to the experience most customers were used to on their PCs. Finally, nobody in the banking industry knew what their customers wanted to do when they were mobile. Customers already had access to banking services via PCs and ATMs. The vast majority of Canadian online transactions were bill payment, and there was little benefit for customers in paying their bills as they waited in line for morning coffee.

Given the poor quality of the online experience, the bank was reluctant to promote mobile banking or invest more heavily. So it stopped funding the venture until mobile banking could find its role as part of a relationship banking strategy that provided different types of service for different types of customers. Mobile banking turned out to be an attractive channel for certain customers for certain services, but not for the broad customer base originally envisioned.

The bank fell into one of the most common hype cycle traps: a rush to adopt. A service based on immature new technology that severely limited user experience and provided uncertain benefits sounds like something an experienced innovation leader would have known to avoid. In hindsight, it's clear that the bank could have avoided the expense, misapplied resources, and customer disappointment with a more conservative adoption strategy. But the bank didn't want to risk damaging its reputation as an industry leader by being perceived as lagging in its market, so it felt it had to act on the competitive threat. "Fear fuels the hype and makes you more willing to take risks where you wouldn't normally," said Tim about management's feelings at the time.[3]

Even when they're aware of the hype cycle and how it affects their inclinations to adopt or avoid innovations, smart people and organizations still fall into certain traps. In this chapter, we will look at the factors that go into making a good adoption decision, and then see how the hype cycle repeatedly foils our best intentions.

Making a Good Adoption Decision

To make a good decision about when to adopt an innovation, you need to balance three variables: how potentially valuable the innovation is to you, how mature the innovation currently is (including consideration of the four value gaps), and how good your organization is at tolerating and managing risk.

Not all innovations are created equal in terms of their value to a specific organization. A pharmaceutical company may find high value in "smart" packaging that knows when it has been opened or tampered with, but have little interest in a new type of touch screen. For a retail bank with a network of ATMs, the priorities might be reversed.

The potential value of the innovation needs to be compared against the current maturity of the innovation. As we saw in chapter 2, most innovations of any degree of complexity are not static but mature over time. Consequently, early adoption usually brings with it higher costs and always a higher risk that the innovation may not deliver the expected value within the planned payback period. For an innovation that is potentially high value, this higher degree of risk may be warranted. For innovations of lower potential impact, it is often better to wait and let others learn the hard lessons. As the innovation enters the Plateau of Productivity, organizations know more about it and so can make informed decisions about when and where to apply it. Here the risk is much lower, so it may be worth adopting even if the payback is good but not spectacular.

In addition to value and maturity, the third factor in the adoption decision is the level of risk that an organization is comfortable with. Even if a high-risk innovation would be rewarded with a high level of benefit, not all organizations are able (or want) to manage that risk effectively. Like individuals—who range from early adopters to mainstream adopters to laggards[4]—organizations also tend to have a dominant *enterprise personality* profile in regard to the risks of adopting innovations.[5] *Type A* organizations are pioneers who consciously and aggressively adopt high-risk strategies to gain high-potential rewards and competitive advantage. To handle higher risk, type A organizations have developed the values, culture, processes, practices, and management skills needed to take risks intelligently and handle inevitable failures constructively. *Type B* organizations are willing to support moderate risk taking in the adoption of innovation and have the corporate skills and culture to support such initiatives. *Type C* organizations are cautious adopters of anything new. They are neither willing nor prepared to handle high levels of risk.

Categorizing all companies in this way is an obvious oversimplification. Every organization, whatever its style, contains pockets—departments, business units, divisions—that differ from the overall organization. Still, enterprise personality categories are useful because organizations do tend to have dominant traits, and everyone in an organization must understand those traits, even (especially) if his or her part of the organization takes a different course.

In general, type A organizations deliberately try to adopt more innovations early in the hype cycle because they are prepared to brave the risks associated with early adoption in return for the reward. Type Cs deliberately try to minimize risks by adopting late in the hype cycle, once the innovation hits the Plateau of Productivity. The type B majority try to hit the middle of the hype cycle in order to learn from the type As but not wait so long that they lag behind their competitors and become type Cs. Figure 3-1 shows when organizations typically start the adoption process for an innovation, although full-scale deployment usually comes later in the cycle.

FIGURE 3-1

Adoption activity for enterprise personalities A, B, and C

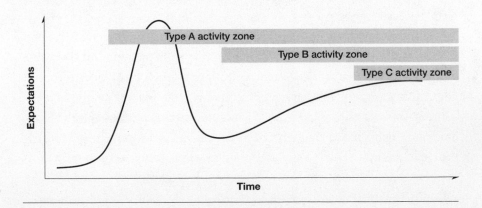

The trouble is, if an organization operates exclusively within its comfort zone on the hype cycle, it will miss opportunities. It will always tend to adopt everything early, or late, in line with its enterprise personality. Organizations should recognize their risk comfort zones *but be prepared to step outside them depending on the strategic importance of an innovation.*

The meaning of this guideline differs by type of organization. For type As, which want to adopt everything early, it means they should adopt early only innovations of genuine importance. Why waste corporate resources handling the risk of something that doesn't truly matter? Overall, type As will adopt a greater number of innovations earlier than type Bs and type Cs because they want the competitive advantage and are able to handle the higher risk, but they still should channel their energies into innovations that really matter. For type Cs, which want to adopt everything late, the guideline means being prepared to sometimes adopt early an innovation that is likely to make a strategic difference. For type Bs, which prefer to follow quickly but not too quickly, it means being an early adopter or even a first mover for an innovation of truly strategic importance. The overall lesson for all risk types is to be *selectively aggressive* and make sure an innovation adopted early is worth both the risk involved and the stress that risk places on the organization.

The goal of being selectively aggressive in adopting innovations is a simple one, but one deceptively difficult to achieve in practice. The constant barrage of positive and negative hype, the peaks and troughs of hype cycles for every innovation, pressure organizations to respond unwisely by adopting too early, giving up too soon, adopting too late, or hanging on too long. These are the four traps of the hype cycle.

Trap 1: Adopting Too Early

The most common trap associated with the hype cycle is the tendency to adopt an innovation too early, when the hype is peaking but the value of the innovation is not yet predictable. We've seen the power of social contagion, competitive threat, attraction to novelty, type A enterprise personality, and other pressures that lead organizations to dive in before understanding whether the value warrants the risk. The enthusiasm is often well intended: "One of the hardest things for us innovators to control is our desire to do something really cool for our customers," says Tim B. from the Canadian bank.

While the peak can bedazzle any organization into early adoptions that are inappropriate, the danger of early adoption is particularly acute for type B organizations. Unlike type Cs that know instinctively they need to wait, type Bs are trying not to get too far behind industry leaders. This means they're more likely to get sucked forward inadvertently into an adoption that is out of line with their risk profile (see figure 3-2).

The existence of this danger zone doesn't mean that type Bs and even Cs should never reach into more aggressive territory, but it means they should be aware when they do. They must make sure, first, that early adoption is justified by adequate potential value and, second, that they strengthen their corporate risk management skills. Adopting "too early" means adopting an innovation earlier in the hype cycle than can be justified by the innovation's strategic value in relation to the risk and stress it brings. Even a type A organization may adopt too early if it overestimates the value or the maturity of the innovation.

The greatest danger can come from the largest and most expensive innovations. These often involve a combination of business and technology innovation, like customer relationship management (CRM) programs and enterprise resource planning (ERP) systems in the 1990s or Web 2.0 initiatives today. Such innovations often suffer from a prolonged peak because they involve broad process and strategy changes and large system developments that may take years to implement. During this prolonged peak, many organizations will be exposed to the concepts and technolo-

FIGURE 3-2

Type B danger zone

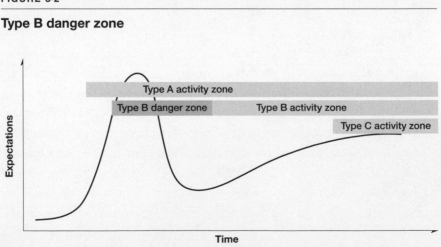

gies and will join the stream of adopters before news of challenges and failures hits the press. Type Bs and Cs can mistake the prolonged peak for the plateau and fail to realize the trough is yet to come.

Trap 2: Giving Up Too Soon

Companies that do decide to adopt at or around the peak are subject to another wave of pressure, but this time negative, as the hype cycle falls to the Trough of Disillusionment. When it becomes clear that the road to value is longer and harder than they anticipated, many organizations abandon their efforts. Even those companies that are actually on the right track in the long term—those that have selected wisely and are good at managing risk—may go into a quiet phase as they navigate their own internal struggles to derive the anticipated value. So the stories people hear most now are those of failure. The same forces and facets of human nature that caused a rapid rise to the peak cause a similar stampede, only this time in the opposite direction. The stories of failure grow, and along with them the internal pressure to abandon the innovation and to "stop throwing good money after bad." As U.K. Safeway found with its loyalty card scheme, it's all too easy to let go of an idea that has diminishing support. Many good adoption initiatives get terminated at this point, and organizations sometimes find themselves in endless rounds of hype chasing as the next promising innovation candidate raises its head.

In his motivational book *The Dip: A Little Book That Teaches You When to Quit (and When to Stick)*, Seth Godin talks about a phenomenon similar to the Trough of Disillusionment that affects individuals when they try to excel at anything. The dip is "the long slog between starting and mastery" that makes expert levels of performance so scarce. Godin uses snowboarding as an example. People take it up because it looks cool and exciting, but they soon quit when they hit the dip because of the difficult learning required. As he explains the choices: "The *brave* thing to do is to tough it out and end up on the other side—getting all the benefits that come from scarcity. The *mature* thing is not even to bother starting to snowboard because you're probably not going to make it through the Dip. And the *stupid* thing to do is to start, give it your best shot, waste a lot of time and money, and quit right in the middle of the Dip."[6]

Organizations face the same choices when an innovation hits the trough, and the same advice applies. It's a time when two doors open up: one is through the door marked "Exit" and the other is through the door marked

"Hard Work." Making the right choice involves deliberately reassessing your options, rather than following the knee-jerk reaction of the crowd to abandon. If you have indeed been swept up by the bandwagon and find yourself with an innovation that has little strategic value, or if you have discovered through early investigation that the innovation will probably not yield the value it first promised, then the Exit door may be the right one. In *The Dip*, Godin refers to this as *strategic quitting*, which is sometimes a necessary course of action if you are going to apply resources where they really matter. But you can make this determination only after you reexamine the situation rationally.

Determining that Hard Work is the correct door, and keeping a potential winner going through the trough, involves drawing on those same decision-making skills you applied in starting out—that is, assessing the potential value, the time and resources it will take to achieve it on the basis of the innovation's maturity, and your tolerance for the risks involved. You have more information to feed into this evaluation than when you started, as a result of the experience of your own and other organizations' investigations. Building in regular evaluation points for assessing each innovation's potential is an essential part of working through the trough, as the rethinking will be part of the planned activities rather than an unexpected crisis. A positive determination of the value will serve to reaffirm the organization's commitment. Most innovation ideas will eventually work out and deliver good returns if adopters are prepared to go through the multiple learning iterations and changes needed to get them right.

Sometimes moving forward requires most of the original project team members to be replaced. The pioneering spirit needed at the start of the project and the head-down tenacity needed to get through the trough usually aren't found in the same people. Caution is needed, however, as new players in the trough, given the negative pressures at that time, may be more inclined toward abandoning the innovation altogether rather than examining the realities of the current situation to make an updated determination of value.

Trap 3: Adopting Too Late

On a Thursday in late September 2004, researchers Dan Simons and Chris Chabris walked onstage at an award ceremony at Harvard University. As Nobel laureate Dudley Herschbach presented them with their award for contributions to the field of psychology, an audience of 1,200 cheered and threw paper airplanes, and a student in a gorilla suit bounded across the stage. This was no ordinary award ceremony—this was the "Ig Nobel" awards, organized by the *Annals of Improbable Research*, for scientific achievements that, in the words of the founder, "make you laugh, then make you think."

Simons and Chabris's achievement was to demonstrate how easily people miss things right in front of their eyes if they're not paying immediate attention. In their experiment, test subjects watched a video of two teams of students, one in white T-shirts and the second in black T-shirts, each passing a basketball among their own team members. Subjects were told to count the number of passes white team members made to each other. During the video, a gorilla (actually that same student in a gorilla suit) walked into the middle of the students, stopped, thumped its chest while the action continued around it, and then walked off. Guess how many subjects completely failed to notice that anything unusual had occurred while they were counting basketball passes? Perhaps a handful of the most absent-minded subjects? Try 50 percent. Half the people watching missed the gorilla entirely.[7]

Simons and Chabris's gorilla experiment dramatized a phenomenon called "inattentional blindness." According to Simons, "Approximately half of observers fail to notice an ongoing and highly salient but unexpected event while they are engaged in a primary monitoring task." In other words, you can miss even major events if you're not looking for them.

Inattentional blindness explains the third trap associated with the hype cycle—that of adopting an innovation too late and being blindsided by something you feel you should have noticed earlier. Many companies stepped up their focus on finding external innovations after the Internet years because they felt they'd missed a major wave of change that ultimately transformed their businesses. "We don't want to miss the next Internet" was the explanation often heard when companies formed a new innovation team.

So far we've talked about the hype cycle as if hype cycles occurred one at a time. A moment's thought will tell you that's not at all how the world works. People are actually inundated with recurring and simultaneous waves of hype about one innovation after another. In this environment, inattentional blindness manifests itself as an "attention filter" that most of us, individuals and businesses alike, apply as an essential coping strategy (see figure 3-3).

FIGURE 3-3

Attention filter as coping strategy

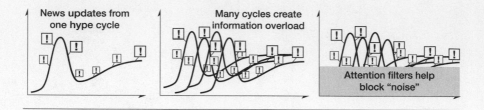

By blocking all but the loudest messages, we can find our attention limited to only two points on the hype cycle: the Peak of Inflated Expectations and the Plateau of Productivity. The hype is overwhelming at the peak, and by the plateau, competitors have probably already seized any competitive advantage to be had. During the early days of initial interest, and in the Trough of Disillusionment, the filter can create blind spots that cause us to miss urgent and important opportunities (see figure 3-4).

Again, this is a particular problem for type B organizations that might be sucked into behaving more like type Cs than they need to, or should do. Type Bs are most comfortable adopting once the innovation starts to climb the Slope of Enlightenment. Because the innovation is maturing and a growing body of knowledge and experience is available, they feel comfortable adopting the innovation. However, the upturn from the trough into the Slope of Enlightenment may not be very dramatic or visible, and so they're likely to miss it unless they're actively watching for it.

In one example, on February 14, 2006, after many years of planning, U.K. banks finally moved the whole nation away from magnetic stripe bank cards and paper signatures and over to chip cards and personal identification numbers. It was a move intended to cut paper, reduce fraud, and speed up the point of sale.

But a number of major retailers weren't ready. They'd had plenty of warning and lots of time, but they just didn't get it done. Their point-of-sale systems hadn't been converted to the new scheme. Inside the laggard retailers, there was apparently nothing to overcome inertia or to prevent managers from ignoring the signals of critical mass and serious intent among banks and other retailers. The result was that these last movers got punished, not just once but three times: in the media, by irritated cus-

FIGURE 3-4

Attention filter creates blind spots

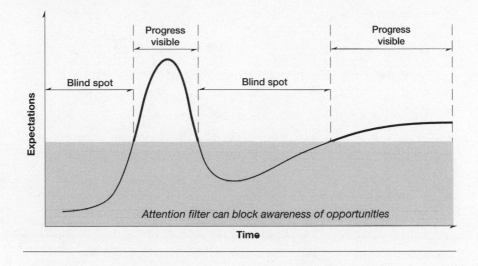

Attention filter can block awareness of opportunities

tomers at the checkout, and in the increased fraud they had to absorb for continuing to trade with old and less secure systems.[8]

Reliance on earlier decisions can also lead organizations to delay for too long. Even if managers do notice progress and increased activity in the trough (signaling the start of the Slope of Enlightenment), they may feel anchored in their earlier decision not to adopt. "We looked at this already" is a common response as an innovation nudges its way through the hype cycle.

To counter the blind spot and the persistent denial of an innovation's usefulness, an organization must build in review points for innovations not yet adopted, including those that have been investigated and shelved, as well as for those being actively evaluated. As an innovation moves further and further through the hype cycle, the biggest risks no longer come from *adopting* the innovation but from *failing to adopt* it and being left behind by competitors.

One other significant finding from Simons and Chabris's work on inattentional blindness is how unexpected these results are, even for those who follow the research. "For me, one of the most striking things about this phenomenon is that our intuitions are consistently wrong," says Simons. "People are convinced that if there is something that is important, or distinctive, or unusual, it is going to grab your attention. It is a really hard intuition to override, so much so that the researchers continued to have it years after we had done these studies."[9] As with so much of the hype cycle, just knowing about a phenomenon isn't enough to keep you from being tripped up by it, time after time.

Trap 4: Hanging On Too Long

During the late 1990s and early 2000s, thousands of companies bought customer relationship management (CRM) systems from leading vendors. Many have run into problems getting the applications to work. The software itself is quite complex, but so are the new business procedures, and the culture and organization changes that are needed to make it work. Often, highly visible parts of the innovation project, like the technology vendor or the management consultants, take the blame when things don't go well.

For example, during a public holiday period in 1998 a recruitment company tried to install a large CRM system for its three hundred telephone sales employees. But instead of speeding up sales, teething troubles with the system meant that the telephone representatives couldn't help customers, and the sales peoples' laptops were locked out of the customer database for a year. "The entire sales force—and everyone here—was very upset," said a senior manager at the firm. "Our business was hurt. At the time, no one understood how complex these systems can be."[10]

The manager's experience was very common. CRM went through a large and lengthy Trough of Disillusionment, and claims such as "over 60 percent of CRM projects end in failure" abounded. In fact, most of the projects didn't actually "end," but they did require very large follow-up investment sums to get the processes to work, amounts that sometimes exceeded the original investment.

You could say these companies set a great example in not falling victim to the second hype cycle trap: giving up too soon. Unlike Safeway, they ploughed through the trough and eventually got the systems working and, usually, derived some value from them, though perhaps not all they expected. If the decision to continue was a deliberate one, based on reexamining the likely value and payback of CRM in the light of what they had learned about the costs and resources required, then it would indeed be an example of avoiding the trap. However, in too many cases no such deliberation took place.

After the trough, the rise of the hype curve is gradual and may not be sufficient cause for people to reconsider their earlier decisions. We've seen how this can cause a problem when companies planning to adopt late don't notice the change and only realize too late they've been left behind.

Here in the "hanging on too long" trap, the problem concerns organizations that have adopted an innovation that was inappropriate for their strategies and plans or that, for reasons such as an excessively difficult implementation, is no longer a good choice. Such organizations may be struggling to make the innovation work, but there is no sharp turn along the Slope of Enlightenment that acts as an "external and unbalanced" force to drive them to reexamine their current course of action.

Even when an organization does realize that it is far off track from its original vision of the innovation, the decision to proceed is all too often made out of fear of stopping rather than the value of continuing. The message that needs to be delivered may well be something like this: "The $20 million investment we made in product X isn't working out too well, so now I recommend we start over and pay vendor Y $25 million to do the job instead." In the long run, the $25 million to do it right may be less expensive than plowing more money into the existing approach. But it would take a brave manager to deliver that message. A less risky approach for a project manager, though maybe not for the company, would be to blame the vendor for doing a bad job and claim to be doing all in one's power to make things right, even if that requires investing millions of dollars more in the same project.

Desire to avoid losing money invested so far is a major influence. Looking at *sunk costs*—what you've spent so far and cannot recover—can lead you away from the key question that should be asked throughout any project: "What is the best thing to do *starting right now?*" In your personal life, you may carry through a difficult but ultimately meaningless task for the personal satisfaction of finishing ("I'm going to complete this matchstick model of the Eiffel Tower if it's the last thing I do!"). But the human satisfaction of completion isn't enough in business. While it makes no sense to change course constantly for arbitrary reasons, it is important to assess periodically whether a major initiative still makes sense.

In making decisions, people "display a strong bias toward alternatives that perpetuate the status quo."[11] So typical management practices, where the default is to continue current projects, will perpetuate more "money pits." In fact, there was eventually a development that caused many organizations with floundering CRM projects to change path. A number of companies, with Salesforce.com leading the charge, moved to a services model of delivering CRM. Instead of a massive initial outlay, companies could pay a monthly per-user fee. This was a sufficiently different value proposition that led many companies to abandon their sunk costs. Part of the attraction was certainly the new business model based on operating expenses rather than capital investment, which changed the numbers behind the business case for CRM. But much of the attraction was the fact that here was an alternate path forward not available when the original decision was made. This new development allowed the original decision makers to save face even as they abandoned the millions of dollars already invested. Unfortunately, such an external justification for changing course is not always available.

A different version of the "hanging on too long" trap occurs when we extend the hype cycle to the end of its course. Usually, we end the hype cycle at the Plateau of Productivity, where the big surge of mainstream adoption occurs. But at times it is useful to consider two more stages that take the hype cycle through an innovation's full life cycle (see figure 3-5). Note that for convenience of terminology, we will continue to use the word *innovation* to describe the dying product, technology, management approach, or idea, even though at this point it is by definition no longer an innovation.

The Swamp of Diminishing Returns. After a period of productive use, the innovation is no longer appropriate for new applications, but

FIGURE 3-5

Extended hype cycle

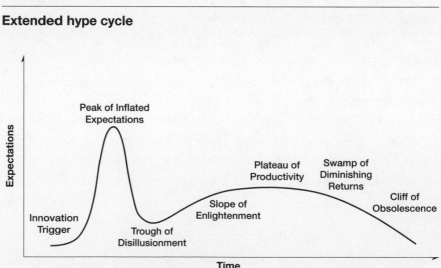

replacing it would take money, effort, and disruption. In the technology space, at this point one or two vendors often buy up the technology for its established client base and focus on maintenance revenues. Companies may wish to move away from the innovation but can't seem to make the business case to do so. This stage maps to a level of innovation maturity characterized as *legacy*.

The Cliff of Obsolescence. The Cliff of Obsolescence is not a dramatic precipice that innovations tip over to crash to their doom. It is a crumbling escarpment where erstwhile innovations begin the often long and drawn-out, and always irreversible, slide into oblivion. At this point, the innovation is rarely used, and equipment can only be obtained through the used or resale market. Skills are in short supply. The innovation can be classed as *obsolete*.

Some companies cling on, trying to extend the life of the innovation as the ground collapses around them. They persist in hanging on—to a piece of equipment, for example—in the belief that maintenance is cheaper than replacement. What they forget are the costs of missed opportunities. These are the opportunity costs of new innovations they're not able to adopt because of the obsolete innovation they're retaining—for example, a legacy computing infrastructure that consumes resources and limits the new capabilities they should be adopting to stay current. Although these end-of-life issues are not typically the primary focus of innovation adopters, addressing the retirement of old technologies or approaches may be an essential first step in moving forward with the new.

Other Adoption Challenges

The four traps represent pitfalls for adopters that result when media and market forces at work in the world around us combine with our natural tendencies and predispositions. Additional challenges arise from the nature of the innovation itself—in particular, those innovations that do not survive long enough to make it through the hype cycle and bring the anticipated value.

Falling Off the Hype Cycle

People often ask whether innovations can ever "fall off" the hype cycle before they reach the plateau. The answer is, they can.

Failure comes more often to innovations in a space where there are multiple ways to deliver the same capability or benefit. For example, broadband connectivity has made its way through the hype cycle over the last decade, but some of the techniques to deliver the capability (e.g., ISDN broadband) have fallen off the hype cycle along the way. That is, they've become obsolete before reaching the Plateau of Productivity. The actual capabilities—broadband, speech recognition, biometrics, videoconferencing, for example—do not fall off the cycle, whereas specific techniques, protocols, operating systems, products, and devices may be supplanted by alternatives.

Some innovations succeed but become embedded in other products and cease to exist as a distinct category or concept. For example, "push technology" rose rapidly onto the Peak of Inflated Expectations in 1997 through high-profile dot-com start-ups like PointCast and Marimba. Push technology allowed information providers to "push" news and information to users according to their prestated preferences and profiles, without waiting for users to request the material. Within a year, the technology sank into the trough, largely because home dial-up connections and corporate networks couldn't keep up with the traffic loads the technology generated. It was banned by many organizations. As vendors of push technologies sold out or shifted their focus, the key ideas were embedded in many other classes of technology. Marimba, for example, evolved to deliver software and security updates automatically over corporate networks. Today's highly popular Web feeds, such as RSS, offer similar functionality (although based on a different technology underpinning). The idea of pushing information to consumers is likely to be a staple in the emerging mobile commerce markets.

Signs that an innovation may be falling off the hype cycle into early obsolescence include a slowing adoption rate, even though the market is nowhere near saturated, with early adopters moving on to other approaches. The press and PR machines no longer cover the innovation, even in negative terms. Suppliers struggle, and investors are no longer interested in the market. When you spot these signals, it's usually time to cut your losses and see whether there is an alternate and more viable approach to achieving the same goal. The good news is that much of the learning around integration, usage, and payback issues will be transferable to the new approach.

Fads and the Hype Cycle

One other reason an innovation might not progress through the hype cycle is because it is a fad—a cycle that rises and falls, never to come back up. These innovations follow the path of the one-hit wonders of the music world or the latest must-have toy for the holiday season.

To borrow a phrase Gertrude Stein used about her hometown of Oakland, with a fad "there is no there there" The curve looks like the "hype" part of our curve, without the benefit of a maturity curve. There's nothing—no artifact, core idea, talent, or other value—to pull the fad out of the trough and on to eventual productivity. Hype without substance is destined to end up in the wasteland of obscurity, strewn alongside a collection of Pet Rocks.

Management trends without a technology component have the most similarity to fads, because they hang on an idea rather than a physical asset that acts as a "there." Research into management fads and fashions shows that a new idea typically replaces an existing trend with similar goals.[12] As disillusionment sets in with one approach, its decline leads organizations to embrace the next trend. Quality circles give way to Total Quality Management, which is replaced by Six Sigma. Business process reengineering leads to workflow, followed by knowledge management and business process management. Significantly, research shows that recent management fashions peak and decline more rapidly than in the past, but that they are becoming more difficult and require more substantial effort to implement.[13]

A major part of understanding the hype cycle, particularly when applying it to abstract trends such as management and marketing trends, is figuring out whether there is really something tangible (either a physical asset or an innate value) that will endure.

But I'm Not Like That . . .

The hype cycle has one more challenge for adopters, possibly the hardest one to avoid. When we examine the workings of the hype cycle, it's an analysis in which we usually exclude ourselves. We think we're somehow different. Others rush lemminglike up and down the hype cycle, but not us. Everybody else is foolish and irrational, but we're not. This perspective is so pervasive in our thinking that experimental psychologists have given it a name: the *fundamental attribution error*.[14] It means that we tend to explain our own behavior in terms of the situation or context we find ourselves in ("I was late because there was so much traffic"), but the behavior of others in terms of their personality or disposition ("He was late because he never leaves himself enough time"). Or "I adopted the innovation because I know it's the next big thing," but "They adopted the innovation because they're jumping on the bandwagon." We think that we wouldn't act the same as others who behave inappropriately, but in fact we do.

That's the danger. If we see the world as "them" (the lemmings) and "us" (the cool, rational ones), we'll never be able to see the situation (and ourselves in it) for what it is. Consequently, we won't be able to make decisions about it and ourselves that make sense, because we won't realize when we're caught up in the irrational aspects of the initial hype cycle ourselves. In fact, each of us is as capable of being as caught up as anyone else. We are most in danger when we forget that. Knowledge of the hype cycle can make us aware of its dangers but not impervious to them.

Such are the hype cycle traps and challenges for unwary innovation adopters. You may have noticed that the four traps represent a set of "damned if you do and damned if you don't" options. Distinguishing "too early" from "too late" or "too soon" from "too long" can only be a matter of judgment; for "too soon" and "too late" make sense not in relation to any objective time frame but only in relation to your organization's goals and risk profile.

By now you should be seeing some common threads in our recommendations on how to counter these traps and challenges. You need to understand what is most valuable to your organization, you need to be aware of the maturity of an innovation, and you need to understand but not be limited by your enterprise personality with respect to adoption risk—overall, you need to be selectively aggressive in your approach to adoption. You also need to build in regular evaluation points to reassess your decision on the basis of the experience you are gathering about benefits, costs, and risks. At the end of the next chapter, we'll formalize this advice into the key lessons that lead to the adoption process we follow in part 2.

But first, in case we have led you think the hype cycle is all danger and no fun, we move on to the *opportunities* that arise from an understanding of the hype cycle and how it works.

Four

Hype Cycle Opportunities and Lessons

The task is not so much to see what no one yet
has seen, but to think what nobody yet has thought
about that which everybody sees.

—Arthur Schopenhauer, 1788–1860

WHILE IT'S IMPORTANT TO UNDERSTAND the traps that can snare unwary adopters, it's equally important to examine the opportunities that arise from the inevitability of the hype cycle. Anytime you can predict major shifts in behavior—such as the major turning points on the hype cycle—you can take advantage by being ahead of the crowd. If avoiding the traps are the "Hype Cycle 101" lessons, then grasping these opportunities can be viewed as the graduate course in adopting the right innovation at the right time.

We see two types of opportunity arising from the hype cycle. The first set of opportunities comes from timing your adoption of each innovation with precision to optimize the amount of value you can derive. If you're going to invest your organization's time and money (and also some of its limited capacity for change) in an innovation, you want to make sure not only that it's the right one but that you jump in at the time that gives you the longest lifetime value at an acceptable level of risk.

The second type of opportunity lies in harnessing the energy of the hype cycle in the broader marketplace by taking advantage of the needs and actions of other players. Avoiding the traps that others fall into is one element of this. As the old hunting joke goes, you don't have to run faster than the bear that's chasing you; you just have to run faster than your friends. If you can be smarter than the crowd even some of the time in avoiding the money pits of adopting too early or giving up too soon, and the lost opportunity costs of adopting too late or hanging on too long, you'll come out ahead. But if on top of that you can anticipate the tendencies of suppliers, investors, competitors, and skilled individuals at each stage of the hype cycle, you'll be able to find the best deals, the best talent, the best publicity, and many other opportunities to advance your innovation adoption efforts.

In this chapter we'll take a detailed ride through each stage of the hype cycle and look at the major opportunities in timing your own adoption for maximum advantage and in building off the activities and attitudes of other players. To benefit from any of these hype cycle opportunities, you need to understand where an innovation is on its journey through the hype cycle. Figure 4-1 gives an overview of some of the key indicators that an adopter can glean from the intersecting market dynamics around an innovation, including the activities of suppliers, media, investors, and other adopters. As we move through the chapter and visit each stage, we'll fill out more detailed indicators and waypoints along the hype cycle. We'll finish with a summary of the key lessons that you will need to internalize and integrate into your innovation decision making in order to master the hype cycle.

The Innovation Trigger

All over the world, car driver's insurance is a very competitive business. Even in the more profitable markets, it is often highly standardized and a commodity competing mostly on price. In the worst markets, many insurers operate it at a loss, to create sales leads into other, higher-value financial products. Innovation opportunity is sorely needed but hard to find and often easily copied. At the tail end of the 1990s, two companies—Progressive Casualty Insurance Company in the United States and subsequently Norwich Union in the United Kingdom—recognized that an Innovation Trigger had been passed in the area of vehicle tracking and decided to use it as the basis of a radical new insurance offering.

FIGURE 4-1

Indicators of the hype cycle stages

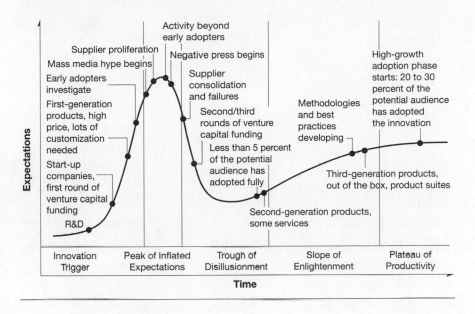

Vehicle tracking had been discussed for decades, all the way back to the 1970s, in traffic management think tanks. Satellite-based location triangulation technology was deployed by the military starting in the 1960s, and reliable mobile wireless data transmission became common in the early 1990s as digital cellular telephony took over from analog.

By the end of the 1990s, reliable, real-time location tracking finally became economical through the combination of low-cost GPS with widespread cellular telephony. Taking advantage of this combination, Progressive and Norwich Union decided the time was right to test behavior-tracked risk-pricing insurance models in their respective markets. Norwich Union has now fully commercialized a variant of Progressive's original model, which it calls "Pay As You Drive."[1] For the customer, it works a bit like pay-as-you-go cellular phones: you get a monthly itemized bill based on when and where you drove your car. Progressive found that less effective in the United States, so it evolved another version that it calls TripSense, where the driver periodically uploads data captured from a modern vehicle's standard onboard diagnostics computer, in order to receive a discount.[2] By acting early, both insurers now have massive head starts on competitors in their respective markets, in learning what does and doesn't work with this new type of insurance. Both have been smart enough to protect their ideas with patents—an unusual defense in that industry, opened to them by the technology components of the model. The innovation allows them to provide insurance with new pricing models that are difficult for competitors to match, in market segments that are often underserved (for example, very low mileage or unusually high risk drivers).

Opportunity: Getting the Jump on Competitors

Progressive and Norwich Union illustrate the two kinds of organizations that want to be ahead of competition—what you might consider an aggressive type A (Progressive) and a moderate type A (Norwich Union). One is a *first mover* and the other a *fast follower*. First movers seek to spot the initial trigger that launches an innovation up the slope toward the peak. The aim is to recognize the trigger, either just before or just after it fires, and make a move before everyone else notices that something has changed. Fast followers focus on watching the first movers as well as the hype cycle. They try to time adoption after the first movers but before the crowd. They let first movers scan for opportunities and trigger points, and try to take advantage of any early learning about what to do and not do. They want the advantages of moving early but also want to decrease risk by not being the first mover.

Between trigger and peak there is a relatively quiet period when first movers and fast followers can make stealth progress in early understanding and testing of an innovation. Acting early can also provide options for erecting obstacles for competition—for example, the patents taken by Progressive and Norwich Union provide local market control for both of them.

Opportunity: Optimizing Supplier Relationships

Early adopters have opportunities to develop favorable relationships with suppliers. At the very early stages of the hype cycle, relationships between adopters and suppliers or developers of an innovation can be very malleable. The supplier may not yet have packaged the innovation in a way it can sell and support according to its conventional terms of business. Indeed, the supplier may not be completely convinced of the market viability of the innovation, and may still be deciding how and whether to turn the innovation into a product. At this point, the supplier and the potential adopter can work together to the advantage of each. The supplier can find answers to some of its basic questions about how to proceed, and the potential adopter can get the earliest possible look at the innovation and even influence its development. In this situation, joint risk-and-reward arrangements are often drawn up that allow innovation teams on both sides to work together.

Suppliers will often put a great deal of effort into these first-customer initiatives and allow high-capability "backroom" technical staff to work directly with the customer. Later, such key people will be shielded from view so they're not overstressed, poached, or distracted from the task of technical progress on the innovation. They may only work with one or two early adopters. So, for an adopter, the opportunity at the "bleeding edge" can be to gain insight into the very core of the innovation as it is being created.

If an early adopter is willing to go public about its use of the innovation and so act as a reference for a supplier, it may be able to negotiate a significant price break, or even obtain free products and services, particularly if it commits to a certain level of purchases if the initial evaluations are successful.

Spotting the Trigger

It is not always straightforward to spot the little kink in the curve that indicates the trajectory of the innovation is changing. A trigger is anything that sets off a period of rapid development and growing interest, and it is different for each innovation. It may be a product launch, a major improvement in price/performance, adoption by a respected company, or simply a rush of media interest that socializes and legitimizes the concept. The challenge is that innovations can have an extremely long research and development preamble before they reach a meaningful trigger point, including several false starts with minor peaks and troughs.[3] Premature buzz around a research breakthrough may lure companies into the trap of adopting too early, when the innovation is not really developed enough even for a type A organization. To stay in touch with evolving capabilities, type As watch start-ups, go to venture capitalist (VC) meetings, and tour industrial and academic labs to try to assess when trigger points are being reached.

The gap between trigger and peak is often quite short. For an innovation that takes ten years from trigger to plateau, the rise from trigger to peak might only take one to two years, and it's only in the first half of that rise that visibility remains low. First movers and fast followers need to act quickly and decisively.

The most common indicator that an innovation is past the trigger is that it becomes available for purchase. Other indicators that an innovation is past the trigger but has not yet reached the peak include the following:

- Only a handful of suppliers are selling the innovation (often only one or two).

- The suppliers are funded by seed rounds of venture capital.

- The innovation requires significant customization to work in an operational environment. The customization is performed primarily by the supplier.

- The price tag is high relative to the cost of production and to the cost of related but more established products.

- Suppliers are not yet able to provide references.

The Peak of Inflated Expectations

Although the Peak of Inflated Expectations features as the biggest hype cycle trap in driving unwary adopters into adopting too early, it also offers opportunity for those who remain realistic. The peak is a necessary phase of early exploration and learning, of pushing an innovation to its limits. Those who can look beyond the superficial promises can translate the early experiences of others to their own benefit.

Opportunity: Finding Your Angle

At this period of the hype cycle, when the early adopters have already staked their claim to being there first, new opportunities arise if you can find the unique angle that makes your adoption of the innovation notable. A number of "firsts" can be enjoyed even at the peak, such as the first to adopt the innovation in your industry, in your geographic region, or for the particular purpose that you have in mind. If you do find yourself jumping in when the bandwagon is in full swing, you should take care to learn from the early adopters and use the innovation in a better, smarter, or cheaper way.

For example, in the late 1990s, the major Netherlands bank ING Group founded a new enterprise called ING Direct. This business was a wholly electronic online consumer bank focused solely on savings accounts, not full-service banking. Because of very low overhead costs, ING Direct could offer a sustained higher-than-average interest rate to savers. Using this model, the new bank was able to enter international markets country by country, cherry-picking savings business. Being without conventional encumbrances such as brick-and-mortar bank branches, it could "build" a new country operation very quickly. By 2007 its operations had successfully penetrated a number of countries, including Australia, the United States, the United Kingdom, France, and Germany.

Another opportunity is to evaluate the dynamics of longer-term trends more realistically than others may be doing at the frenzy of the peak. Hype at the peak is about not only the innovation itself but also its potential for blasting apart established industry models. Predictions of such large-scale industry shifts are often justified, but as with all trends, they will take far longer to traverse the hype cycle than most people realize. Acknowledging the realistic timing of the trends allows you to formulate practical applications for the innovation in the short term while preparing strategies for the longer-term shift.

Opportunity: Acquiring Talent

When first introducing an innovation, an organization often finds that it lacks staff with the necessary background, skills, or aptitude. Then the question arises of where to obtain the right people. Organizations that adopt very early, before the peak, usually have no option but to evolve the skills internally. But those adopting at the peak or later can go to the open market for the right people. If an adopter times its search and selection well, key moments in the hype cycle can be used to its advantage in the search for scarce talent.

The first point of opportunity occurs around the Peak of Inflated Expectations. Seasoned, midcareer professionals who have lived through a few cycles will know intuitively that "what goes up must come down." If they've been lucky enough to be involved with a cutting-edge innovation at a type A company, they might consider leveraging the excitement at the peak to sell their knowledge and skills at a premium in the job market. The time from peak to trough will be long enough for them to settle in with a new employer, and if they feel that employer takes the innovation seriously enough to press through the trough with it, they may choose to make the leap. So an adopter planning to be a fast follower can hire crucial skills around the peak. Of course, the price will be high, but poaching rare skills at this stage might have the added benefit of slowing down a competitor.

Beyond the peak are two other moments of opportunity to pluck experienced people from their existing roles in other organizations. During the trough, a professional who has pursued the innovation within one firm can feel battered and undervalued as the great innovation they've been associated with is no longer a boardroom favorite. This is a good time to woo highly experienced talent with the promise of a more dynamic and committed work environment. Finally, at the transition from slope to plateau, external consulting firms have sometimes reaped the most they can from the innovation and are looking for the next one. Consultants with considerable relevant experience may be enticed to work with organizations that are adopting a little later. In addition, some consultants like to stay aligned with a specific innovation rather than move into a new area, and so want to make the move from advising to implementing in a real-world environment.

Opportunity: Maximizing the Publicity Value

Sometimes a decision to adopt an innovation early is driven as much by the desire to be *seen* to be innovative as by the expectation of more quantifiable business objectives. There is a particular opportunity at the peak to use the publicity value to your advantage when the reporters come looking for case studies. It's the nature of the hype cycle and the peak that success stories will be told over and over. Sometimes a lead executive might be asked to do twenty or more press interviews and a dozen trade conference speeches in a year, which is all free marketing for a willing company. For example, in 2007 Starwood Hotels was mentioned at least fourteen times in major news and business publications, including the *New York Times* and the *Wall Street Journal*, for experimenting with Microsoft's Surface touch screen coffee-table computer. The same year, Starwood got over forty mentions for its experimental presence in the 3-D online virtual world Second Life.

Well crafted and well placed, a story of initial success can enhance customers' view of the adopter's brand as cutting edge, make the adopter appealing to potential employees, create options for the adopter for contract concessions with vendors, accelerate development of the innovation itself, and help the adopter guide the innovation in directions it wants.

Spotting the Peak

As the peak crests, the innovation seems to be featured on the front cover of every business and industry magazine. Suppliers in the marketplace align themselves with the hype, and the marketplace roils with overlapping, competing, and complementary offerings. Suppliers adopt the latest buzzwords into their marketing arsenals to make themselves more attractive. When investors see an emerging hot spot in the market, they want "one of those" in their portfolio, which encourages the proliferation of companies with similar offerings.

Hype bubbles in the consumer world may last from a few months to a year or so, but in the commercial world, the peak of hype usually lasts at least a year because of the slower pace of corporate decision making and investment. Major peaks, such as the dot-com era or 'green' technology, may last for two or three years.

Indicators that an innovation is at the peak include the following:

- The trade and business press run frequent stories about the innovation and how early adopters are using it.

- A popular name catches on in place of the original more academic or specialist engineering terminology; for example, the wireless networking technology called 802.11b became "WiFi."

- Analysts, bloggers, and the press speculate about the future impact and transformational power of the innovation.

- A surge of suppliers (often thirty or more) offer variations on the innovation.

- Suppliers with products in related markets align their positioning and their marketing with the theme of the innovation.

- Suppliers can provide one or two references of early adopters.

- Investors aggressively hunt down a representative supplier for their portfolio. Some early-stage VCs may sell at this point.

- Toward the end of the peak, one or two early leading suppliers are bought by established companies in expensive, high-profile acquisitions.

The Trough of Disillusionment

The trough is the most common home to the hype cycle trap of giving up on a potentially valuable innovation too soon, and sometimes also to the flip-side trap of hanging on too long. As we have seen, avoiding both traps involves reassessing the current course of action in an objective manner at regular checkpoints in the adoption process. If appropriately managed, these review points also provide opportunity by allowing you to bank your experience so far if you decide not to continue, or to take advantage of the slump in the broader marketplace if you do decide to continue.

Opportunity: Banking Your Experience

If, after due deliberation, the decision is to discontinue investment, you should take the time to turn your abandoned investments into value for a later date. Adopters that drop worthwhile innovations often find that the innovation returns later as something they're compelled to adopt, except now they're playing catch-up. If you can capture key facts and learnings about your experiences with the innovation and maintain a knowledge base of this information, others who need to revisit the decision can build on the earlier work instead of starting over. Later in the innovation's maturity cycle, the specific lessons you have learned about what did and did not work in your environment can be combined with the growing body of knowledge in the broader marketplace about how to apply and deploy the innovation. Even though elements of the innovation will have changed (in particular, the performance levels, costs, and suppliers), your understanding of how and where it applies in your specific context will still be relevant. You will be in a strong position to move rapidly with the innovation at the relevant time, compared with other organizations that are learning from scratch. However, to achieve this, you will need a deliberate, and most likely centralized, activity to maintain this type of corporate knowledge over a period of time. We will discuss approaches to this in part 2.

Opportunity: Planning Your Purchases

Whether you purchase an innovation at the peak or the trough can make a major difference in how fast you achieve payback. In 2000 there was a fashion for a new idea called *e-procurement*, which is the use of the Web to manage an organization's purchases of goods and services more effectively and at lower cost. Gartner research fellow Andy Kyte was the European lead analyst on the topic at the time, taking inquiry calls from senior clients and giving them strategic advice. One of the most common calls at the peak of e-procurement interest was, "Which software should I buy? Ariba or Commerce One?" They were the two leading packaged products of the day. For most clients, Kyte's advice was to wait for a couple of years, as payback based on the costs in 2000 was likely to take three to five years, not the eighteen months that was being claimed.

Kyte's advice turned out to be wise. As e-procurement settled into the trough, which coincided with the trough for e-business in general, Kyte estimated that the price per user dropped to one-eighth the price at the peak—a drop of nearly 90 percent. Both Ariba and Commerce One struggled to survive but rebounded (Commerce One was bought in 2006). Now e-procurement functionality is a mainstream, high-value tool for effective purchasing departments.

Spotting the Trough

Usually there is no actual drop in the overall adoption numbers as an innovation slides into the trough. Instead, the anticipated rapid growth in adoption is simply delayed. What suppliers and investors anticipated as a "hockey stick" uptake remains a depressingly slow growth path.[4] As a result, supplier consolidation and failure occur because there is too little adoption growth to sustain so many similar products.

Indicators that an innovation is, or will soon be, in the trough include the following:

- The tenor of press articles turns negative, featuring the challenges and failures around the innovation. For example, following a major wave of Six Sigma adoption in the early 2000s, *BusinessWeek* ran a story in June 2007 with the title "Six Sigma Stifles Innovation at 3M."

- There is general cynicism about the transformational potential of the innovation.

- Supplier consolidation starts, including buyouts by larger companies and investors.

- Second- and third-round funding by investors is required to sustain suppliers.

- The same few case studies and references for successful adopters are used by suppliers.

Length of the Trough

Before we move on to the opportunities and indicators of the Slope of Enlightenment, it is worth spending some time to understand how long an innovation is likely to spend in the trough. The length of the trough is one of the most variable parts of the hype cycle. With the average length of the trough ranging from two to four years, a rapidly moving innovation may suffer a temporary setback of six to nine months, while others may fester in the trough for a decade.

As we saw in chapter 2, the trough is caused by the four value gaps—performance, integration, penetration, and payback—that can delay the anticipated benefit from the innovation. If these value gaps are minimal, then an innovation moves on a *fast track* through the hype cycle. If they are severe, the innovation acts as though it is progressing along a *long fuse* before it leaves the trough and progresses through the rest of the hype cycle into mainstream adoption.

Fast-track innovations go through the whole hype cycle within two to four years because the innovation itself matures rapidly. In these cases, real performance begins to drive expectations before excitement wanes (see figure 4-2). The innovation largely bypasses the usual Trough of Disillusionment, with the result that many companies are caught unawares by the sudden maturity and applicability of such innovations.

Fast-track technologies still typically have a slight trough. Even the juggernaut of the Web browser suffered a temporary downtick in expectations. As Web sites became more ambitious in their use of graphics and other more complex designs, people started to complain about the "World Wide Wait" until bandwidth caught up with people's response-time expectations.

Long-fuse innovations take a particularly long time to deliver on their potential and so spend longer than average in the Trough of Disillusion-

FIGURE 4-2

Fast-track hype cycle

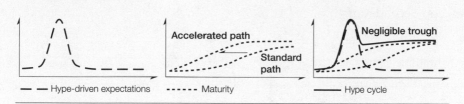

ment (see figure 4-3). As a result, they can require one or two decades to reach the point at which adoption takes off. An extreme example is the videophone, which was featured at the 1964 World's Fair but took forty years to achieve significant levels of use, driven eventually by webcams and mobile phones.

The forces at work on fast-track and long-fuse innovations can come from any of the value gaps. Tracking the indicators for long-fuse and fast-track hype cycles provides companies with an edge in precision timing their adoption for the upswing from the Trough of Disillusionment.

PERFORMANCE

Fast-track innovations work "out of the box," such as a new computer algorithm that offers immediate performance improvement—for example, Google's use of the "link analysis" algorithm to improve search results. Long-fuse innovations frequently require advances in basic science and engineering and take decades to reach maturity, regardless of how much excitement they generate. Often, with long-fuse innovations, there is a science fiction–style fascination that is far ahead of its real capabilities—for example, robots or nanotechnology. Such innovations are teasers because

FIGURE 4-3

Long-fuse hype cycle

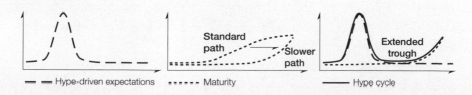

they never seem able technically to deliver on the dream people construct around them.

INTEGRATION

A fast-track innovation is simple to install and use, such as instant messaging, or it uses an existing infrastructure, such as a Web browser that simply drops into an Internet-connected PC. A long-fuse innovation may rely on a new infrastructure (ecosystem) that needs time to evolve. For example, smart cards need readers, and fuel cells require a distribution network. The need for professional skills can also delay adoption by requiring training and education that may take years.

PENETRATION

Everett Rogers identifies five attributes of innovations that foster a fast-track adoption: high relative advantage (compared with the current solution), high compatibility with the current environment, the ability to see others using the innovation and to try it out easily, and low complexity.[5] The cell phone is an example of an innovation that met all these requirements—it offered the advantage of mobility but was compatible with the existing phone system, you could see others using one and could try out a friend's, and people could immediately learn how to use it. On the other hand, long-fuse innovations require significant behavioral change (such as PCs for primary care physicians) or involve a delay in the visible benefit (such as employee contributions to a pension plan). Similarly, in "chicken and egg" situations, individuals won't adopt until the infrastructure is in place, and providers won't roll out infrastructure until people adopt. Many smart card implementations around the world failed for this reason.

PAYBACK

A fast-track innovation fits in an area where benefits are easy to quantify and it delivers immediate value for all parties—for example, a self-service check-in kiosk at an airport that shortens lines for travelers and reduces staffing costs for the airlines. Long-fuse innovations require changes in business processes or the creation of a new business model around the innovation that may take years to develop.

Some long-fuse technologies can be particularly challenging to navigate as they seem to be perpetually emerging and swing periodically between public enthusiasm and disillusionment. These phoenixlike innovations experience multiple mini peaks and troughs before the push that finally launches them up the Slope of Enlightenment.

For example, in the early 1990s there was a great deal of excitement in the telecommunications and media industries about the possibilities of "interactive television." Millions of dollars were invested based on the expectation that TV viewers would soon be using their remotes to flip through a wide range of digital services such as banking, holiday booking, and pizza ordering. However, before the telecom and cable companies could overcome the technical hurdles (for example, slow speeds and weak integration with the data "backchannel"), the Web stole their thunder in delivering a broad range of interactive capabilities. There is nevertheless still a role for interactive television as a "lean back" digital channel with the user sitting back in a comfy armchair, not huddled over a computer on a desk. With the arrival of each new TV delivery improvement of the last decade, such as digital cable and digital broadcast, hopes have flared again for interactive television. When the Web and TV fully converge in a home media hub, interactive television may rise up the Slope of Enlightenment. Meanwhile, it will see more false dawns as it bumps along an elongated trough.

The Slope of Enlightenment

If you decided for good reason not to take on a potentially useful innovation early, you still have opportunities as the innovation is revitalized after the trough. By the slope, many of the big lessons have been learned, and the reputation of the innovation is rising again. What's learned is incorporated into second- and third-generation products, and methodologies and tools are created to ease the development process. For some innovations there is a new capability or a performance improvement that changes the value proposition and makes the innovation more broadly useful. The marketing around these maturing products or the new capability acts as a minitrigger to launch the innovation out of the trough.

Opportunity: Leading the Mainstream Wave

Just as the rise to the peak provides opportunity for type A organizations, the beginning of the Slope of Enlightenment offers an opportunity for less aggressive adopters to move ahead of competitors. Products become easier to use, require less support, and are faster to produce value.

For example, radio frequency identification (RFID) has been moving through a long-term hype cycle. It rose rapidly to a peak after Wal-Mart decreed in early 2003 that its top one hundred suppliers would have to use the tracking technology by January 2005. A huge amount of learning has taken place since then as the technology has been tested in retail supply chains. However, the whole concept of RFID went into a Trough of Disillusionment as its challenges were uncovered—for example, the performance gap we noted earlier regarding the RFID signal's inability to travel through metals and liquids. By 2007, RFID was crawling up the Slope of Enlightenment, with major leading retailers beginning to stock clothing items that are RFID tagged. You can see how one manager at Unilever kept track of this hype cycle in figure 1-6 (chapter 1). Yet the vast majority of retailers have yet to take up the technology. Those who act quickly enough will still be able to adopt before most of their competitors while benefiting from the lessons learned by early adopters.

Spotting the Slope

Unlike the dramatic swings of the peak and the trough, the transition from the trough to the Slope of Enlightenment is more subtle, and therefore more difficult to spot. As we saw in the trap of adopting too late, news that an innovation has passed a threshold of interest may fall victim to our individual "noise filters" that we erect for our sanity in a world of information overload.

To get ahead of the mainstream wave in a relatively low-risk way, organizations need to be able to spot when a potentially relevant innovation is starting up the slope. This involves tracking and revisiting innovations on a regular basis to see whether the innovation has reached a threshold that makes it interesting to your organization. For example, during 2006–2008 many organizations have been tracking the price of RFID tags to see when they reach a low enough price point to make them viable for use with lower-cost goods.

On occasion the start of the slope is anything but subtle. A surge of supplier activity, new product versions, or marketing will launch an innovation out of the trough and up the Slope of Enlightenment in a particularly dramatic way (see figure 4-4). When this happens, it can look like

FIGURE 4-4

Double-peak hype cycle

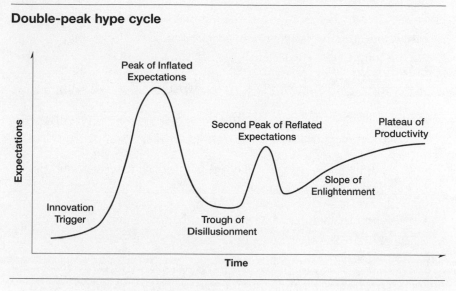

another Peak of Inflated Expectations. But because it is driven by genuine progress and understanding, the rise and fall will be far less dramatic than the initial peak.

Sometimes, if this second peak occurs long enough after the first or among a different adopter community, people may have forgotten or not know about the first peak. They may mistake the second minipeak for the first and miss the fact that this is actually the beginning of the path to a period of rapid adoption. Those who recognize the coming activity and value can move ahead more aggressively. For any innovation of potential interest, it's important to understand its history.

At the beginning of the slope, serious penetration among the target audience (beyond trials and prototypes) may be less than 5 percent and usually no more than 10 percent. However, in innovations with a particularly long time to value and a high level of hype, many more companies are pulled into some level of adoption before the trough hits—possibly as much as half the potential market. This has been the case with a number of large-scale enterprise applications and initiatives, such as customer relationship management. Management and organizational innovations are particularly prone to this as the expected benefits, or lack of them, may take several years to realize.

The journey up the slope may last from one to three years before the innovation reaches the beginning of the Plateau of Productivity. Indications that the innovation is moving up the slope include the following:

- Suppliers of the innovation offer second- or third-generation products that work with little or no consulting from the supplier.

- For technology innovations, suppliers offer product suites that incorporate the innovation into a broader range of tools.

- Consulting and industry organizations publish methodologies for how to adopt the innovation.

- Press articles focus on the maturing capabilities and market dynamics of the suppliers.

- New success stories and references start to proliferate.

- Reliable figures regarding costs, value, and time to value become available.

The Plateau of Productivity

Even as an innovation enters the Plateau of Productivity and the start of rapid mainstream adoption, there is still opportunity for competitive advantage. At the turning point from the slope to the plateau, often only 20 to 30 percent of the target market has adopted—the majority has yet to move. An organization that adopts here will still be ahead of many competitors. Adopters can leverage low costs and risks yet still find unexplored opportunities.

Opportunity: Leveraging Lower Costs and Risks

The plateau offers opportunity for less aggressive adopters, and also for aggressive adopters considering lower-value innovations. In both cases, waiting later in the cycle allows you to take advantage of lower costs and lower risks. There comes a point when most of the problems and unknowns have been ironed out of the innovation by earlier adopters, and the cost and functionality of products have stabilized. The trick is to leave adoption as late as possible but still early enough that the useful lifetime of the innovation allows time for the required payback.

Opportunity: Expanding a Niche

Some innovations reach maturity but fail to attain their full potential. Such *lowlanders* function as intended and enjoy a certain level of adoption. They move beyond the trough but end up in niche applications rather than mainstream use, and so their plateau is lower than average (see figure 4-5). Some find a home in specific types of applications—for example, after the major hype around artificial intelligence in the 1980s, expert systems have come to be used for insurance underwriting and data mining for customer segmentation. Artificial intelligence as a whole is still lingering in the trough, but expert systems and a number of other useful techniques have been spun off as lowlander technologies with the potential for much broader use.

Because they have not picked up the growing attention associated with a rising slope, these lowlander innovations are often little known and not well covered in the press. Organizations with a strong innovation-tracking culture can find these relatively mature but underapplied techniques and approaches and deploy them strategically within their business.

Opportunity: Imagining the Implications

Even though the direct value of an innovation is relatively well established by the plateau, the indirect consequences are not as well explored.

FIGURE 4-5

Lowlander hype cycle

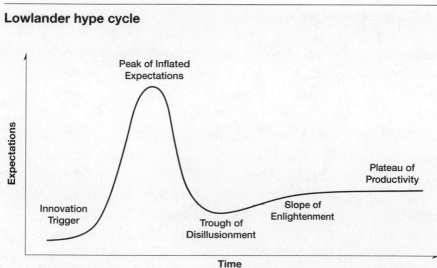

At this point in the hype cycle, there are many examples of successful applications, but far fewer examples of companies who have taken the next step and answered the question "Now that I have this innovation, how can I build on it?" This is not the wild speculation of the peak, but a more calculated exploration of the longer-term implications for your organization. For example, many companies have supported some of their staff working from home some of the time using a PC and a networking connection ever since the 1980s. In the 1990s it became a more usual flexible work practice as PCs became more common and the Web arrived. But a few companies have taken the same basic technology and idea to a whole other level. The airline JetBlue, which first flew in the year 2000, decided it still needed customer call centers—not everything could be done over the Web. But it created "virtual" call centers in which *all* the agents worked from home all the time (apart from occasions such as training and personal reviews with their supervisors). According to the founder and then-CEO David Neeleman, this allowed the company to save 20 percent per flight booked over a conventional call center—for example, from savings on office space.[6]

There is a particularly strong opportunity in those cases where the long-term impact of an innovation looks set to surpass the original expectations. While neither the telegram nor the Internet have brought world peace, they have had a deep and enduring impact on business and society in ways that, for the Internet, are still unfolding. For a few such innovations, the eventual impact is higher than the original inventors or marketers anticipated. Who would have foreseen that a "horseless carriage" would lead to the suburbs and shopping malls that so dramatically reshaped patterns of twentieth-century life, work, and commerce? Forecaster Roy Amara has pointed out that people tend to overestimate the effect of a technology in the short term and underestimate the effect in the long term.[7]

Such *high-flier* innovations end up with a plateau that levels off at a higher altitude than the peak (see figure 4-6). High fliers usually involve major technological developments that work within a broader supporting ecosystem, such as cars in a time of mass production and cheap oil, or PCs and the Web in an era of cheap worldwide electronic communication. The broad potential impact of these innovations means that there is a prolonged period of opportunity, often occurring in waves, for those able to sift through and make sense of the catalog of experimentation, successes,

FIGURE 4-6

High-flier hype cycle

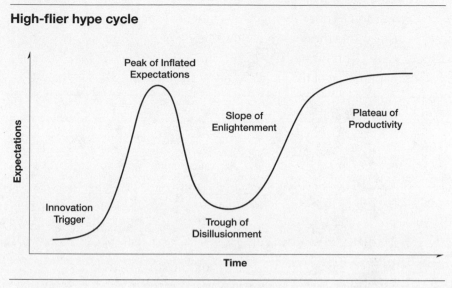

failures, and business transformation that surrounds the innovation on its long path to the plateau.

Spotting the Plateau

By the time they reach the plateau, innovations are increasingly delivered as out-of-the-box solutions, and the need for service support decreases. As an innovation matures, particularly if it is a major, high-profile innovation, an ecosystem of related products and services often evolves around it. As an innovation achieves full maturity and supports thousands of enterprises and millions of users, the hype around it typically disappears and is replaced by a solid body of knowledge about the best ways to apply and deploy it.

Indicators that an innovation has reached the plateau include the following:

- Trade journals and Web sites start to focus on best-practices articles about how to deploy the innovation.

- Clear leaders emerge from the many suppliers that have joined the market during the slope.

- Investment activities focus on acquisitions and IPOs.

- Many examples of successful deployments can be found in multiple industries.

- The terminology around the innovation becomes part of everyday speech, such as Googling, texting, and blogging.

Hype Cycle Lessons

The hype cycle offers a simple and clear message to those who want to avoid the traps and enjoy the opportunities: don't invest in an innovation just because it is being hyped, and don't ignore a technology just because it is not living up to early overexpectations. Aim to be selectively aggressive, and move early with innovations that are potentially beneficial to your business. For innovations that are of lower impact, let others learn the hard lessons, and adopt the innovation once it is more mature.

But as we have seen in the last two chapters, the reality of being selectively aggressive is not as simple as the idea. Organizations need to be continually alert to the hype cycle traps and constantly vigilant for the opportunities. From our years of experience studying the hype cycle and watching its effects in organizations of all types in all industries, we believe that consistently good adoption decisions require the following lessons to be applied to each adoption decision.

Lesson 1: Decide what's valuable to you and how much risk you'll take to get it. Understand where it is most important to innovate and how much risk you are willing to take on to achieve your innovation goals. This helps avoid the trap of adopting too early and supports opportunities to identify relevant value propositions for your organization.

Lesson 2: Seek out relevant innovations and track their progress along the hype cycle. Instead of waiting for each new wave of hype to alert you to a new idea or technology, be proactive about seeking out innovations that may make a difference in the areas you have identified as important. This protects against the trap of adopting too late. Continuing to track relevant innovations over time drives opportunities in managing resources and relationships to get the most value from other players, including suppliers and talent.

Lesson 3: Consider alternative candidates. Instead of automatically running with the current favorite, assess how an innovation shapes up against your organizational needs and against other potential candidates for the same resources. Prioritizing a set of candidate innovations is the best way to tread the fine line between the traps of adopting too early and too late, and also protects against repeatedly giving up too soon.

Lesson 4: Build in regular evaluation and decision points. Manage the risk of early adoption by building in explicit decision points about whether to continue. Factor in the impact of external pressures—in particular, the drive to abandon at the trough—in arriving at a sound decision. To avoid the trap of bringing in an innovation too early compared with the readiness of the organization, make sure to institute an appropriate level of risk management and encourage a tolerance for experimentation and interim failure that is appropriate for the maturity (or lack thereof) of the innovation. Also consider whether the innovation will endure to create payback—is it a fad, or might it be made obsolete by an alternate approach?

Lesson 5: Inspire, educate, and involve other people. Few innovations affect only the person making the adoption decision. Moving forward with an innovation requires the cooperation and support of many parties, so it is critical not only that you internalize these lessons, but that you also help others understand and apply them. Within your own organization, you need to create enthusiasm where it's missing and dampen unrealistic expectations where necessary. Helping others understand the hype cycle and encouraging a realistic and objective assessment of opportunities are essential elements of successful adoption.

All of which leaves us still with the challenge we identified as the biggest obstacle to good adoption decisions: people's inability to accept the powerful contextual influence of forces such as the hype cycle. To counter the belief that you are immune to the effects that you see so clearly in others, you need to do more than intellectually acknowledge the lessons. You need a way of forcing yourself to address them, time after time, each time an innovation comes your way. The best way we know to do that is through a systematic, disciplined framework that ensures that you incorporate the lessons of the hype cycle into every adoption decision that you make. You need to follow explicit steps and activities to counter the traps and drive toward the opportunities. Even if a formal process is incompatible with the level of effort your organization puts into innovation, you still need a way to remind yourself to periodically assess your innovation options in the light of your needs and the influences and opportunities in the outside world.

In part 2 we will present a process that meets the requirements for explicitly addressing the lessons we have learned in part 1. We'll use this process to dive into the adoption practices and approaches of organizations that have mastered the hype cycle and consistently use innovation to drive their organizations to excellence.

The STREET Process

Five

What It Takes to
Master the Hype Cycle

*If you can't describe what you are doing as a
process, you don't know what you're doing.*

—W. Edwards Deming

L
ET'S START OUR JOURNEY into the world of process with a
trip to Pennsylvania Dutch country. Here we find the Old Order
Amish, a centuries-old Christian community widely known for its apparent rejection of all things modern. At first glance, the Amish would seem a
poor model for our innovation-hungry modern-day corporate cultures,
but a closer inspection yields some important insights for our own adoption process.[1]

Living in settlements concentrated in Pennsylvania, Indiana, and Ohio,
Old Order Amish still use horses to pull carriages and farm equipment.
They eschew automobiles, radio, television, the Internet, telephones in
their homes, even electricity. They dress plainly. The strictest members use
hooks and loops in their clothing rather than buttons. To most observers,
they seem like people trying to stop time.

However, a closer look at how they live and work reveals something
more complicated. What appears to be rejection of anything modern turns
out to be in actuality a sophisticated interaction with the world of innovation. For example, they do use disposable diapers, modern gas barbeque
grills, and communal phones. It's common in Amish areas to see small

outbuildings set by themselves in fields. These phone shanties contain a telephone and often an answering machine that are shared by several families in the surrounding homes. Many Amish homes boast propane- or kerosene-powered refrigerators. Some Amish who run businesses do use electricity, but electricity drawn from batteries charged by their own diesel generators. Many employ cell phones in their work but drop the phone off each evening to be charged by an "English" (non-Amish) neighbor.

What drives all this behavior so strange to outsiders is a set of beliefs taken from their reading of the Bible. They believe the Bible commands them to remain separate from the world and to avoid anything that smacks of individuality, status, pride, or arrogance—anything, in short, that might cause one person to stand out from others. Striving for composure and humility, the Amish put family and community ties uppermost.

Nothing in their beliefs explicitly forbids the use of electricity, automobiles, or any other technology. Their actions are driven instead by concern for the effects of modern conveniences. They recognize that every innovation, every new technology, can change the people who use it and their lives. Since they aspire to live certain kinds of lives and be certain kinds of people, they choose or reject an innovation on the basis of whether it will help or hinder them in these aspirations.

For example, they reject a phone in the home because they believe it bridges too easily their separation from the world. It violates the privacy and sanctity of the family. It disturbs proper interaction with others—community—by replacing face-to-face communications with more impersonal voice-only interaction. Radio, television, the Internet, and even electricity from the public power grid foster the intrusion of the outside world.

Yet they recognize that many innovations are far from unmitigated evils. Farming by hand and horse makes their work less economical, which threatens their ability to live the lives they want. So certain power equipment may be used in certain ways on a farm—if, for example, it's horse drawn and not used to extend a person's independence and diminish his or her need for community effort. The benefits of the telephone are real—in their businesses or to summon help in an emergency—and so the shanties. In each case, they seek those aspects of an innovation that support the lives they want, and avoid those aspects that weaken or detract from such lives.

What's pertinent here for our purposes is the way the Amish go about deciding what to adopt and what not.[2] Typically, some of the more adventuresome members will try something new—a cell phone, for example. Others join them. Over the next few weeks and months, or longer, members will discuss the pros and cons. Eventually, the Amish bishops (elected from among the membership by Amish ministers, themselves elected by fellow members) will take up the question at one of the periodic meetings where they discuss church matters. There the bishops will decide whether and how the innovation may be used.

Not all Amish groups come to the same conclusion about the role that a technology should play in their lives. Disagreements about which innovations should be embraced, and which avoided, have led to multiple splits in the community. In *Plain Secrets: An Outsider Among the Amish*, Joe Mackall describes a visit to The Home Depot with Samuel, his Swartzentruber Amish neighbor. The Swartzentrubers are even more conservative than Old Order Amish. As Mackall notes:

> The Swartzentrubers do not need to look at refrigerators, stoves (unless there's a woodburner around), freezers or air-conditioning units. All the fancy front doors are unnecessary. There's no need for the aisles of tile, linoleum, or carpet . . . If Samuel were not a Swartzentruber but were instead a member of the Andy Weaver Amish, he'd be able to have linoleum or varnished floors, couches and cushioned chairs, and an indoor toilet, tub and shower. But no. If he and his family were members of the Old Order, he could have everything permitted by the Andy Weaver Amish plus window blinds, continuous hot water, and central heating. But no. And if he were to join an even higher church than the Old Order and become New Order, he'd have everything in this paragraph plus bottled gas appliances, a gas freezer and natural gas lighting.[3]

All these Amish groups live by the desire to remain separate from the world, but have arrived at different decisions about how to maintain that objective.

Most of us live in a complex world, in which we are constantly exposed to innovations and the implicit assumption that innovation is always good. The Amish challenge that assumption, and in doing so remind us that nothing actually compels us to adopt every new technology and embrace every new idea. Even though we may be well advised to evaluate innovation opportunities, by removing the assumption of inevitable adoption, the Amish approach to innovation highlights two points that should inform any adoption decision.

First is the importance of recognizing that *no innovation justifies its own use*. Every innovation must be considered in light of some broader purpose it enables or fosters. For the Amish, it is their religious beliefs. For the rest of us, it is the purpose and goals of our own lives or the goals and strategies of the organizations where we work. Considering this broader purpose makes it clear that the "right" innovation is not the same for every individual or every company. The horse and buggy are symbols of Amish tradition, but a closer look at a New Order Amish buggy will reveal rubber tires, whereas the wheels on a Swartzentruber buggy are simple wood with a steel band.[4] Rather than blindly following the decisions of others (including, in some particularly controversial cases, the decisions of the U.S. legal system), each Amish group comes to its own determination of whether an innovation is appropriate within its community.

Second is the recognition that *adoption decisions should be made by a careful and deliberate process*—a set of systematic steps taken with consistency and discipline. The Amish process is consistent: initial use by members, followed by ongoing discussion of pros and cons by members, with ultimate settlement by bishops. Nothing is decided without careful investigation and consideration that can take months, and even years, to conclude. The outcome, though it may appear odd to an outsider, always makes sense within the context of the Amish community and its own goals.

The Value of an Adoption Process

When companies adopt innovation well, the whole process looks effortless. We take for granted Wal-Mart's unparalleled operational efficiency, Vanguard's low cost structure, Nike's design excellence and customer choice. In fact, all their capabilities have been driven by many individual decisions to adopt or avoid specific innovation opportunities on the basis of a keen understanding of the purpose each innovation will serve. Leading innovators suffer the same hype cycle pressures as the rest of the world, but they've learned to excel in managing to their advantage the cycles around significant innovations. They leverage the enthusiasm when justified but provide well-researched alternate perspectives when sanity needs to be restored. None of this happens magically or serendipitously. It is the result of conscious organization, method, and discipline.

This deliberate, considered approach to adoption has been called a *mindful* approach, where "mindful decision making involves discriminating choices that best fit a firm's unique circumstances, rather than familiar and known behaviors based on what others are doing."[5] The key to being a mindful organization is recognizing that each organization needs to evaluate an innovation in its own unique context (including corporate goals, resources, capacity for change, and so on), rather than relying primarily on the external context of the innovation's hype cycle.[6] As we saw in part 1, people are consistently unable to recognize the pressures of context on their own and others' decisions. Organizations need a systematic process that forces decision makers to focus deliberately and continually on the organization's internal context. Otherwise, it is all too easy to slip back into hype-driven adoption based on the lure of the bandwagon.

An adoption process also provides organizational resilience beyond the success or failure of any single innovation. In chapter 3 we followed a Canadian bank's experience with mobile banking, where a competitive threat led the bank to adopt wireless data services while the underlying technology was still unproven and high risk. Although the initial rollout was not a success, the bank's foray into mobile banking was not disastrous. The mobile banking initiative was one of several innovation projects funded each year through an infrastructure tax and other funds contributed by the various banking divisions. In this environment the risk could be minimized (though not totally eliminated) by closely monitoring each stage of the project and shutting off resources if necessary, as the bank did once it realized the low levels of usage. Even a major failure may be tolerated if balanced by other, more successful undertakings in a portfolio of innovation projects. In fact, the leaders of a type A organization that aims to compete through innovation typically consider *a lack of* project failures a warning indicator that the organization is not being aggressive enough. So, even though the bank fell into the trap of adopting too early in the face of competitive pressure and growing hype around a new capability, it had a process to minimize the damage and balance the risks.

Effective innovation adoption is a competency that every company needs to develop and sustain. Mindful adoption can help in situations where the hype cycle drives organizations to move too early or too late, give up too soon, or hang on too long. The right process helps early adopters and laggards alike embrace the opportunities of the hype cycle and avoid the traps, as it helps them rationalize both the decision to adopt and the decision *not* to adopt.

In fact, the decision not to adopt a relevant innovation needs to be as deliberate and mindful as the decision to adopt, for two reasons. First, an organization needs to determine how not adopting will impact its competitive position or its customers' perceptions, particularly if competitors are moving ahead with adoption. Second, even if management decides not to adopt an innovation, its employees may be blissfully unaware of its decision. Individual employees, for example, may be downloading corporate data onto mobile devices, installing free software onto their desktops, or chatting with their peers on a social network. Unless the company has evaluated such innovations and determined an appropriate policy regarding their use or nonuse (and a suitable way to ensure compliance), any corporate decision may be overridden by employee action. An adoption process helps organizations become competent at determining the impact of adoption or nonadoption no matter what, whether they are habitually early or late adopters.

Every company already uses a multitude of processes. There are project management processes, change management processes, audit procedures, quality assurance processes, health and safety procedures, new product development processes, research processes, and on and on. Do organizations really need yet another? Can't some existing processes be tweaked to handle innovation adoption? We think not. While some other processes may contain elements relevant to adoption (e.g., project managing an innovation evaluation project), we have found none that adequately cover all the activities required for selecting appropriate innovations.

Introducing the STREET Process

After a decade of studying the hype cycle and how companies succeed and fail at innovation adoption, we have evolved a set of activities and tools based on best practices across a variety of companies, industries, and situations. We have encapsulated these activities in a process we call the *STREET* process. STREET addresses key challenges in selecting the right innovation at the right time and then in laying the groundwork for broad use of the innovation within the organization. STREET ends at the point where an innovation becomes a part of the mainstream project development or management processes. Very deliberately, STREET does not cover the later stages of full deployment and rollout of an innovation. These stages draw on established business techniques of project, program, and change management that we will not repeat here. However, the challenge of reaching the threshold of the deployment stage of adoption is neglected in many organizations and much of the business literature. STREET therefore focuses on the path up to the "transfer" step—where the innovation adoption decision has been made, socialized, and embraced.

The stages of the STREET process are scope, track, rank, evaluate, evangelize, and transfer.[7] We'll describe each stage briefly here, including how they address the lessons from part 1 (highlighted in each stage), and then cover each in detail in the following chapters.

> *Scope.* The scope stage is where you *decide what's valuable to you and how much risk you'll take to get it.* In this stage you specify why you need to innovate—that is, what organizational purposes must be served—in order to provide focus and context for innovation investments and to counter hype-driven temptations that lure you into following the crowd and adopting too soon. The scope stage leads you to understand your corporate mission, objectives, strategies, needs, and values, as well as business opportunities and aspirations, and to determine how aggressive your organization wants to be with respect to innovation adoption.

> *Track.* Here you *seek out relevant innovations* from a broad range of sources and *track their progress along the hype cycle* to notice advances in their maturity. You are aiming to find candidates that broadly match your organization's scope of needed innovation and fall within its risk comfort zone. As you identify such opportunities, you capture them in a way that can be communicated to others in the organization and that lends itself to further decision making. The track stage drives you to be proactive about finding worthwhile innovations.

> *Rank.* In this stage, you *consider alternative candidates* by ranking potential innovations and selecting those worthy of immediate attention. The aim is to identify those innovation ideas that look most likely to

bring significant benefit to your organization within a time frame that fits your risk profile. This involves asking probing questions about the potential of each innovation and, where possible, comparing multiple innovations against each other. A virtue of ranking multiple innovations at the same time is that it helps you avoid the danger of assessing an innovation simply on its own merits (which at the Peak of Inflated Expectations can be hard to determine) rather than in relation to other options for investing the same limited resources. Ranking is a key but often overlooked step in adopting the right innovation.

Evaluate. In the evaluate stage, you investigate each of the top-ranked innovation candidates where a lack of knowledge or understanding still prevents you from deciding whether to move forward. Activities here include laboratory and paper investigations, as well as prototyping and piloting, to understand each innovation's value and eliminate its value gaps. Here you *build in regular evaluation and decision points* by creating a staged evaluation program that incorporates many points of view. You also project the likely path an innovation will take through the hype cycle—in particular, its speed of progress—to determine the right time to adopt. The result of the evaluation stage is a decision to take one of four courses: (1) move forward with adoption and progress to the evangelize and transfer stages; (2) revisit the evaluation in revised form—for example, with a different product or an alternative process; (3) return the candidate to the track phase until it matures further; or (4) drop the innovation from further consideration.

Evangelize. For each innovation you decide to pursue, you need to *inspire, educate, and involve other people* to obtain the cooperation and support of all those who will influence the successful adoption of the innovation by its ultimate users. Marketing, educating, networking, and inspiring others take place throughout the adoption process, but their importance is most apparent here after the evaluation phase. You must overcome organizational resistance by inspiring key decision makers to appreciate the innovation's business impact. You must also exploit or counter the emotional effects of the hype cycle—for example, by urging realistic expectations at the peak and focusing on future benefits during the trough.

Transfer. Here you need to continue to *inspire, educate, and involve other people* to transfer responsibility to those who will implement or use the innovation. This requires more than transferring knowledge (for example, teaching people how to use a new device). It's about sparking the enthusiasm and sense of ownership required for the innovation to take hold. For successful transfer, the players ultimately responsible for driving or using the innovation must be involved in earlier stages of the STREET process—in particular, the evaluation activities.

Flow of the STREET Process

It's tempting to see the STREET process as a simple sequence of steps. Do first one, then the next, and then the next. But in practice, STREET involves continuous activities and multidirectional feeds among the various stages. Figure 5-1 shows the principal flows and interactions within the STREET process.

Understanding the scope and context for innovation is an essential prerequisite for any adoption activity. The scope activities drive knowledge of what types of innovation to track. Track is typically the most active and resource intensive of the first three stages. It's a continuous activity, although many organizations conduct a periodic, usually annual, trend or technology scan. In contrast, an organization's scope—its mission, strategies,

FIGURE 5-1

The STREET process for innovation adoption

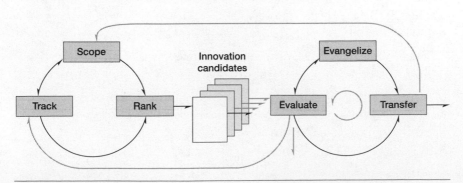

plans, and so forth—is likely to be relatively stable over the course of a year or longer, with changes triggered by major new business initiatives, external forces such as regulations or competitive actions, or an annual strategic planning exercise.

On occasion, a particularly disruptive innovation that falls outside the current scope (for example, a new business model) will come to light during the track stage. Because a company's scope should itself be subject to innovation over time, this type of innovation—a "game changer"—also needs to be accommodated by the process. A game changer is shown in figure 5-1 as an arrow from the track to the scope stage. If the game changer is determined to have merit after appropriate evaluation and consideration, typically by the most senior executives in the organization, it may cause a permanent change or expansion in the organization's scope. Since any senior executive evaluation of a change to the scope should itself follow the STREET process (to avoid being swayed by the latest management fad), the full path of the game changer is shown in figure 5-1 by the arrow from the transfer back to the scope stage.

The innovation candidates identified by the track stage feed into the rank stage, where the organization's scope is used to assess and prioritize the potential of each candidate. Obviously, a candidate's potential depends on its value to the organization, and that can be determined only in relation to the organization's needs and goals, its scope. Ranking can occur for each innovation candidate one by one or by periodically comparing a set of candidates with each other. Assuming that the right kind of information is collected during tracking, rank is an essential but typically brief activity. At the end of the rank stage, one candidate or a set of prioritized candidates will have been judged worthy of further action.

The right side of figure 5-1 shows the flow of the final three stages—evaluate, evangelize, and transfer—that applies to each innovation candidate that is selected during the rank stage.

The four arrows extending from the evaluate stage show the four possible decision outcomes: proceed to evangelize and transfer, reevaluate, return to track, or drop. In general, the activity flow is from evaluate to evangelize to transfer, but we have shown a direct link between evaluate and transfer to highlight that these two stages often do (or should) overlap considerably. As noted above, evangelize and transfer activities actually need to begin earlier in the process, at the latest toward the end of the evaluate activities.

Who Performs the STREET Process

Defining a process is one thing, but making sure it's followed is another. If the whole value of the process is to make sure certain key activities are consistently done, then it's important that somebody assume or be assigned responsibility for doing them.

As we work through the STREET process in the following chapters, we'll refer to this somebody as an *innovation leader*. An innovation leader is a person who identifies a relevant innovation and drives it into the organization. This person may or may not make the formal, final adoption decision, but he or she is the one who shepherds the process leading to that decision. In short, the innovation leader takes the innovation through the STREET process.

Depending on the scope and scale of the innovation, an innovation leader might be:

- A member of a distinct team—such as a strategic planning, product R&D, or emerging technology group—responsible for innovation adoption

- An executive responsible for overall business improvement, or a business, department, team, or project manager responsible for improving his area of responsibility

- The kind of person who hates to see a good idea go to waste and decides to champion an innovation whether or not it falls within his or her formal responsibility

These three types of innovation leader represent the three main ways that innovations are driven into organizations: (1) through a centralized team with responsibility for innovation; (2) as part of the decentralized activities of business units and departments; and (3) by bottom-up, often informal, experimentation by individuals. All three approaches can benefit from explicit attention to each stage of the STREET process.

Centralized Innovation Adoption

Visitors to the third floor of Fidelity's Summer Street offices, next to Boston's South Station, are greeted by wide-open spaces and sleek curves. An orb the size of a crystal ball glows on the backlit reception desk, its colors changing in sync with the movements of the stock market. In the center of the space, an oval pod hosts a demonstration theater with a band of screens showcasing research projects and prototypes. Outside the pod, a frieze stretches along one wall, depicting a timeline of Fidelity's sixty-year history, including its many industry firsts. Two full-height screens slide freely back and forth along the wall; positioning a screen over one of the specially marked historical events triggers a short video presentation about the event.

This is the Fidelity Center for Applied Technology (FCAT), founded in 1999.[8] The center acts as a focal point for finding and evaluating technology innovations that will improve Fidelity's business performance. Although Fidelity's various business units are diverse—ranging from its well-known financial services all the way to a luxury hotel property and a multibillion-dollar lumber company—many of the projects developed at FCAT provide value across the organization. Activities include usability testing and investigations into emerging technologies such as biometric identification.

Removing risky or speculative projects from the immediate responsibilities and budgets of operating managers allows companies like Fidelity to investigate opportunities for which there is not yet a proven business case but which may provide significant benefits once they are better understood. Pulling the activities into a dedicated center also allows organizations to bring in a broader set of skills and perspectives than would otherwise be feasible; for example, Fidelity employs behavioral economists and engineering psychologists to assess how various innovations are likely to affect the usability and impact of its Web site.

The value of addressing innovation centrally is not limited to the commercial world. Paul Jones serves as chief technology officer of England's National Health Service (NHS) "Connecting for Health" organization.[9] The NHS itself is a government-funded health-care system that employs around 1.3 million staff members and expends around $200 billion annually—so a lot is at stake.[10] Many technology-enabled initiatives are initiated and run in the various regions and divisions of that huge organization, but some issues and innovation opportunities are best judged and shaped from the center. For example, one problem shared by many Western countries is an aging population. Providing health care for the elderly will rapidly become a major social issue in these countries as current health-care facilities prove inadequate. One promising possibility Jones and his team have been looking into is home-based health care that takes advantage of the powerful home entertainment systems, linked via broadband connections and home networking, that are found in growing numbers of homes. It is hoped such technology will be adapted and used in ways that allow people to look after themselves at home via remote medical monitoring, advice, and counseling.

The potential of this approach seems great, but no one knows yet what the outcomes will be. Investments in technology and programs for home health care could be a nationwide success and a political victory, or they could be a money trap that causes major political embarrassment. This approach could liberate people from having to spend time in the hospital, or it could lead them to feel they're getting second-class service. It could be a way of bridging generational differences by relieving taxpayers of some of the burden of supporting those in retirement, or it could accentuate the "digital divide" between those with the necessary equipment at home and those without. The opportunities, questions, and potential problems are endless and need to be sorted out systematically.

For the National Health Service, it makes great sense to have someone like Jones and his team investigate and assess those opportunities, questions, and potential problems. Situations like this call out for a centralized approach.

Many large organizations, particularly those with risk-embracing type A cultures, have centralized innovation teams that act as focal points for leading-edge ideas and technologies.[11] Very large companies with independent subsidiaries or business units may create a small corporate innovation team for coordination and leverage and also place innovation teams within the individual units. Less aggressive organizations that want a centralized function without the cost of a full-time team often establish a task force or committee to perform the role, with members assigned part-time who retain their regular full-time roles. Alternatively, such organizations assign responsibility for innovation adoption to a key individual, such as a chief strategy officer or chief technology officer. These part-time approaches are often augmented by contributions from designated individuals and experts across the company.

A centralized approach to adoption provides a number of benefits. First and foremost, it acts as a focal point for innovation adoption and the innovation review process. An individual or a group with full-time responsibility for innovation adoption not only helps the organization identify and understand specific innovation opportunities, but that person or group also develops competency in managing and improving the innovation adoption process for all parts of the organization. The person or team becomes skilled in spotting opportunities, managing risk, conveying the value to others, and performing the other key activities of the STREET process. A central team is better positioned to:

- Avoid the hype cycle traps by keeping an eye on multiple opportunities simultaneously and prioritizing the options.

- Identify and drive the game-changing opportunities that would otherwise fall between the cracks of traditional organization structures and management responsibilities.

- Educate the broader organization with a consistent view of the innovation.

- Coordinate innovation activities among disparate corporate groups and departments.

- Identify and remove structural obstacles that impede innovation adoption throughout the organization, such as a lack of seed funding for pilot projects.

- Help the organization transfer learnings, build on successes, and avoid duplicate efforts.

One objection to a central group—in particular, one at corporate rather than business unit level—is that it sometimes becomes too theoretical, too much an "ivory tower," and loses touch with the needs of running the business day-to-day. When a centralized innovation adoption group is disbanded, this is the most frequent reason given. However, a group that swings too far in the other direction and focuses primarily on short-term activities will not add value beyond the type of innovation adoption already done within business units; it is likely to miss the larger, more strategic innovation possibilities. While the primary purpose of an innovation group is to identify and promote strategic, high-impact innovations, in practice it needs to balance both strategic and tactical opportunities. The use of a portfolio approach in the rank stage of the STREET process can ensure that innovation efforts are deliberately matched to both current needs and future aspirations and help a central team stay relevant to the business.

A centralized innovation group should not and need not be large. Certainly, it must avoid the accusation of merely being more overhead and bureaucracy. A typical group size is three to five people, with the largest around thirty. Some of the most successful groups we've seen comprise not more than a handful of staff in organizations with employee counts in the tens of thousands.

Decentralized Innovation Adoption

Whether or not an organization uses a centralized innovation team, operating managers around the company must themselves innovate to some degree. If a company is to thrive, its managers in all areas and at all levels must constantly improve the way they run the business.

In practice, individual managers vary greatly in their enthusiasm and abilities around innovation. Some operational managers have goals and incentives tied to consistency, and so they value smooth operational efficiency above all else. Innovation involves change and risk, which can be seen as a threat to operational consistency (even though the right innovation might actually *improve* consistency). Other managers thrive on the challenge of continuous improvement and constantly scan for innovations that will help their departments perform better. We see this frequently in high-technology companies; because the managers understand technology, which is the source of so many innovations, they know where to look and how to assess what they find.

The key strength of decentralized innovation is that individual managers know what matters in their areas of the business; that is, they have a strong understanding of their scope, so innovations they adopt are more likely to lead to real business improvement. Also, the attitude of line managers plays a pivotal role in the successful adoption of an innovation by employees within their area. If a manager is the driving force behind an innovation, his or her enthusiasm will ease the challenges of usage and assimilation.

However, innovation adoption is only one of many demands on a manager's time and skills. Operating managers are particularly prone to hype cycle traps when they're inundated with ideas from suppliers and employees and can't find time to track or rank the candidate opportunities. To give adoption decisions the attention they need, managers must look carefully at how they and their departments track and prioritize relevant innovations and how they determine whether an innovation is ready to be deployed. They may need to institute a version of the STREET process within their departments or work in partnership with a central innovation team that has the necessary time, skills, and resources.

Individual Innovation Adoption

Innovation adoption happens constantly at an individual level, as we modify our work spaces, processes, habits, practices, and technology environments to suit our own desires for collaboration, comfort, productivity, and whatever else we personally value. In the corporate world, these individual innovations can have an impact far beyond the person who originates them, even if that person is not in a position of authority. In these cases, if you look closely, you'll find some version of the STREET process in play.

Consider a hypothetical individual, a programmer, let's say, in the information technology department. She is in tune with the goals of the organization and her roles within it, and is constantly looking for ways to improve her own and her group's contributions (scope).

She runs a blog in her spare time where she shares ideas and pointers with others. She voraciously pores over other like-minded blogs (track). She often comes across tips—for example, for a new desktop search engine or a new debugging tool. She doesn't have time to try out everything, but those that look most interesting or that other bloggers recommend (rank) she tries out to see how well they work for her (evaluate). She uses some of the best ones in her own personal work environment, which is far ahead of the standard configuration provided by her company. She's often asked for advice by her colleagues and enjoys sharing her knowledge and helping them figure out what might make sense for them to use (evangelize). Quite a few of her colleagues act on her advice and adopt the innovations she has tested. Once in a while, she recommends to her manager a tool that she thinks the organization should adopt more broadly (transfer).

Individuals like this, who naturally follow the STREET process as part of their work DNA, are a valuable source of innovation in companies. They may not always be appreciated, particularly if their people or political skills fall short of their technological skills. Maverick early adopte rs can be irritating if they constantly berate the company for failing to keep up with the latest tools or methods. But, if handled well, their energy and expertise can be harnessed as a key resource in the innovation adoption process.

Some companies actively encourage individual innovation. Google is famous for encouraging its engineers to explore their own innovative ideas, which can include homegrown ideas as well as adopted and adapted external innovations. Each engineer is permitted to spend 20 percent of his or her time on personal research projects. Some of the best ideas end up in public view on the Google Labs Web pages. From there, the ones that survive public scrutiny move on to become actual products.

But Google's culture is unusual, and we've found that an organic, bottom-up approach to innovation alone usually falls short of what an organization needs. While every organization should encourage and leverage this approach to innovation adoption, no organization should depend on it solely. Centralized or departmental perspectives have a role to play. Even Google, to make its highly decentralized approach to innovation work, has its vice president of search products and user experience, Marissa Mayer, listen to the ideas that arise from employees' innovation time and determine which warrant further corporate attention.[12] Organizations need a combination of individual, departmental, and centralized innovation adoption processes, all taking advantage of STREET activities to guide their adoption decisions.

In sum, the STREET process can be used by a central group responsible for the top-down mapping of corporate needs and goals, by managers responsible for specific processes or functions, and by any individual employee seeking to encourage bottom-up organic innovation adoption. Like most management methods, the STREET process works best when adapted to the specific culture and context of each organization that adopts it. What's critical is that every organization needs a process, a series of thoughtful systematic steps taken with discipline, if it wants to master the hype cycle.

In succeeding chapters, we will cover each stage of the STREET process in depth. We will look at techniques, models, and practices that we have seen used to good effect in real organizations. Many of the examples will be from centralized innovation and emerging technology groups, because these groups have formulated and articulated their approaches in a way that makes them repeatable within their organizations and sharable with others outside. Some of these ideas will be directly transferable to your organization, and some will need to be adapted to your particular environment, but we hope that these chapters provide value for all innovation leaders.

Six

Scope: Establishing the Context for Innovation

My success, part of it certainly, is that
I have focused in on a few things.

—Bill Gates[1]

NO ORGANIZATION CAN INVESTIGATE, let alone adopt, every innovation that comes along. So how do managers in an organization decide which innovations are worth pursuing? We have seen how this is the source of most danger in the hype cycle—that an organization will make adoption decisions based primarily on the hype and hope that often surround something new.

Imagine someone who's never seen San Francisco and now finds himself about to spend a weekend there. He's eager to see something of that famous and beautiful city. What's the best use of his time? He might ask the hotel doorman or fellow guests he meets on the elevator. He could simply walk out the front door of his hotel and see what he finds, in which case he'll see what happens to be nearby, what's attracting the biggest crowd, what makes the most noise, what flashes the biggest neon sign, or whatever attracts his attention at that moment. Only by pure luck, however, will these approaches produce a satisfying weekend.

Most people would probably advise this fellow to buy a guide book and review all the sightseeing possibilities beforehand. That's a better approach, because he does need to know his options. But there's an even earlier, more crucial step. He should first ask himself, "What interests and fascinates me most? Is it natural wonders like the sea and seashore and mountains? Man-made wonders? Great universities? Parks? Sports?" San Francisco has great sites in all those categories, but no one can see them all in a weekend. Choices are required. Starting with his own objectives and interests and *then* reviewing the options is far more likely to produce a satisfying time.

Dealing with the hype cycle is no different. Just like the San Francisco tourist, your company faces far more innovation opportunities than it has time and resources to explore. A random walk isn't likely to uncover the best opportunities. Simply responding to the hype and excitement around something new is exactly like going to a big new city and being guided only by noise, signs, crowds, and the opinions of passersby. It's better to look at all the options for adoption at once and then choose among them. But it's best by far to start with personal interests—or for organizations, with the goals and needs of the organization.

That's precisely where we start the STREET process. The purpose of the scope step is to articulate an organization's objectives, aspirations, and compelling problems. The challenge, just as it was for our visitor in San Francisco, is dealing with the huge number of possible innovations a company could adopt. The trick is to find the ones most appropriate and valuable *to your company* in light of its unique context. In this chapter, we'll describe how to go about identifying such things.

The scope stage constructs the filter that will be used to determine what types of innovation should be gathered during the track stage, and also acts as a basis for more fine-grained filtering during rank and evaluate. This filter involves two main elements: the business value context, determined by the nature of an organization's business needs, and the risk context, determined by the amount of risk an organization is comfortable exposing itself to.

Business Value Context: Focusing Methods for Innovation Adoption

If you're like most people, the natural places to start innovating are the problems and processes that surround you every day. They are uppermost in your mind either because somebody's complaining about them, because you have to report on them to your boss, or because your annual bonus depends on them. If you are responsible for a business process such as manufacturing or call center operations, or a business function such as competitive intelligence or human resources, the chances are you have a combination of ongoing challenges you would like to solve and metrics that you want to improve. These act as a natural focus to filter and prioritize the potential innovations you encounter.

However, once you look outside clearly defined process or functional responsibilities, the means to focus are not so clear. There are hundreds of innovations that would improve the company. How can you uncover what is most important to your organization's business value?

Your business value context for innovation can come from a number of different avenues, ranging from a pervasive sense of corporate core brand values, through current business objectives, on to speculative forecasts of how your industry might change—or how your company might drive that change. We will examine the role that each of these three avenues—corporate core, current business objectives and initiatives, and speculation and aspirations—play in focusing innovation activities. Note that we will use the term *business value* broadly to include the value context of government and not-for profit organizations as well as for-profit companies.

Focusing Method 1: Corporate Core

Why do Disney theme parks dominate the top slots for amusement park attendance year after year?[2] They don't have the wildest roller coasters, the highest Ferris wheels, or even the tastiest food, yet over 100 million visitors pay nearly $300 for a family of four to spend a few hours in the Magic Kingdom or another Disney park. What's the big deal?

Long billed as "the happiest place on earth," Disneyland and the other Disney theme parks that followed owe their popularity to the total Disney experience rather than any single "must see" attraction. As the company overview claims, "Since its founding in 1923, The Walt Disney Company has remained faithful in its commitment to producing unparalleled entertainment experiences based on its rich legacy of quality creative content and exceptional storytelling."[3]

To deliver the experience, cast members (as the company calls its employees) wish their guests (as they refer to their customers) a "magical day" and go out of their way to help. If you're organizing a family reunion, you don't make a group booking; you organize a magical gathering. Potential obstacles to happiest-place status, such as standing in line in 90-degree heat, are dealt with through innovations such as the Fastpass kiosks, which issue tickets to come back later to an expedited line, and biometric access for annual pass holders.

Disney's core value proposition permeates everything it does: "Wherever the Guest experience takes place—in our parks, on the high seas, on a guided tour of exotic locales, through our vacation ownership program—we remain dedicated to the promise that our Cast members turn the ordinary into the extraordinary. Making dreams come true every day is central to our global growth strategy."[4] Like any strong personality, it rubs some people the wrong way, and there are those who recoil from the squeaky-clean image. But love it or loathe it, people know what to expect from Disney experiences and can embrace or avoid them accordingly.

In terms of innovation, the clarity of Disney's core customer value proposition acts as a guiding beacon for where to focus the most attention on new ideas and where it's worth moving ahead of the crowd. Disney is an aggressive adopter of technology innovation, but instead of the sleek, high-tech feel of, say, an Apple Store, Disney delivers the technology in a way that blends into the overall experience. Take a look at how Disney decided to notify strolling guests about special events and line lengths at popular rides. A text message to a parent's BlackBerry or mobile phone would have done the job, but instead Walt Disney World developed an electronic plush toy companion, "Pal Mickey," for kids to buy.[5] Using a wireless link to a central notification system, Pal Mickey relays real-time, location-specific information to its owner, turning the youngest kids into information hubs for the whole family.

You may be inspired to higher excellence by this Disney example, or you might be intimidated by it. As with GE, 3M, Amazon, and some other "supermodel" case studies that come up frequently, you may feel that they are in a different league and thus irrelevant to your own company's situation. In fact, all organizations have a corporate core: something that defines their personality and culture, even if it's not quite as strongly developed and disseminated as that of companies like Disney.[6] The corporate core is an enduring expression of what is important to the organization, and therefore where it's important to innovate.

The corporate core may be expressed in multiple ways—for example, as a mission statement, vision, core value definition, or corporate profile. Look at the following examples taken from each company's Web site:

- For nearly a century, The Neiman Marcus Group has stayed focused on serving the unique needs of the luxury market. Today, that commitment is stronger than ever. We have stayed true to the principles of our founders—to be recognized as the premier luxury retailer dedicated to providing our customers with distinctive merchandise and superior service.[7]

- As the first airline to introduce low fares, Ryanair has revolutionised European air travel and the revolution is set to continue. We now offer choice, competition and much lower fares on all routes where we compete with some of Europe's biggest and strongest airlines and in all cases we beat the socks off them.[8]

- Lexus has revolutionized the luxury motoring experience through its passionate commitment to the finest products and the most satisfying automobile ownership experience. We vow to value the customer as an important individual; to do things right the first time; and to always exceed expectations.[9]

While such statements are sometimes aspirational pages written by corporate PR staff to paraphrase the CEO or founder, others are more formally enshrined. For example, that Lexus quote sits alongside a founding credo called "the Lexus covenant," set out when it was launched by its parent, Toyota.[10] When a mission statement accurately captures the corporate core, it can be extremely useful in helping employees at all levels in the organization focus their innovation efforts. Employees at Neiman Marcus can rally around "distinctive merchandise and superior service" as a catalyst for using their initiative to innovate in small and large ways.

On the other hand, some mission statements are so generic as to be worthless for the purpose of focusing innovation. Is there a company that the following extract from a real mission statement could *not* be applied to? "We will provide value and distinctive products to our customers, a superior return for investors, and challenging and rewarding work for our people in an environment that respects and values their contributions." "Distinctive merchandise" may be a meaningful attribute for a high-end retailer like Neiman Marcus, but are "distinctive products" really at the core of an airline, which issued this mission statement? And are distinctive products inherently compatible with "providing value" as a core attribute?

Innovation leaders seeking to anchor innovations to corporate missions and values must review them critically first. Ask yourself whether the statements really have integrity. Were they born from a serious attempt to capture the essential spirit of the corporation, or are they standard playbook sentences from a management consulting exercise?

In fact, many companies lack a well-formulated mission statement or other explicit expression of the corporate core. If that is the situation, how can you still recognize and apply your corporate core as a means of focusing innovation? Even in cases where the corporate core is poorly articulated, it still exists, implicit in the company culture as a powerful driving force for the company. You just have to work a little harder to tease it out. Fortunately, there are a number of ways to approach this challenge.

The management literature discusses many ways to examine and articulate what is at the heart of an organization's values and value proposition. We won't enumerate them all—and even if we did, new ones would soon appear. Looking at your core value in a new way often triggers new strategies and goals that drive your company forward, so this is an area that itself is ripe for frequent innovation. Every few years, a noted academic, consultant, or best-selling business author provides a new way of examining and evolving the corporate core.

We will, however, mention four noteworthy ways that innovation leaders can think about corporate core as a focus for innovation. Three are classic management strategy approaches to determining how a company brings value to the market: value disciplines, core competence, and value curves. The fourth, persistent business needs, provides an additional level of detail by focusing on specific business activities that are essential to delivering the corporate core.

VALUE DISCIPLINES

One of the most useful ways we have found for innovation leaders to think about focusing innovation is the idea of *value disciplines*, identified by Michael Treacy and Fred Wiersema.[11] They contend that there are three different approaches or values an organization can use to differentiate itself in the marketplace. *Product leaders* push the boundaries of product performance, such as Nike and Apple. *Operationally excellent* companies provide lowest total cost through a combination of price, product reliability, and service convenience. Examples include Ryanair and Costco. *Customer-*

intimate companies deliver best total solutions by tailoring products and services to satisfy unique customer needs, such as Neiman Marcus and GE Healthcare (which offers hospitals a full range of training and management programs for high-end GE medical devices). Gartner analyst David Flint observed a gap in this and found it useful to add a fourth value discipline to the three identified by Treacy and Wiersema: *brand mastery*. Brand masters excel in their ability to control customers' perception of the company and its products and services, such as The Coca-Cola Company and Rolex. Brand mastery can be viewed as a type of product leadership, but it differs enough in terms of focus and innovation activities that we believe it warrants a separate category.

Treacy and Wiersema's research suggests that leaders pick one, and only one, value discipline to excel in. In today's competitive environment, enterprises cannot succeed by trying to be all things to all people. Each value discipline results in a different corporate core. Therefore, a market leader wins by focusing on one value dimension and molding its entire organization to excel in that dimension.

The value discipline selected by a company as its primary focus helps determine the processes most essential to its growth and the most promising places to focus innovation. This doesn't mean other value disciplines are ignored. There is a minimum threshold of performance in each area that must be met through ongoing innovation. Operationally excellent companies like the airline Ryanair still aim to deliver acceptable customer experience— as Ryanair claims, "We provide all of the essential customer services, but clearly we do not provide all of the back up services ('expensive frills') that . . . high fares carriers promise, but then with our lower prices and better punctuality, 99.9% of all our passengers won't need them."[12] It does mean that innovations not central to an organization's value discipline are best adopted later in the hype cycle, when they are lower cost and lower risk.

Contrast Ryanair's relentless focus on operational efficiency to drive low fares and on-time arrivals with the core value of an airline that offers a much more customer-intimate proposition—Singapore Airlines: "Rediscover the romance of flying once again. Step into a place where exclusivity is made more personal, where space can liberate your senses and the level of comfort will soothe your mind and body."[13] Singapore Airlines' value discipline is clearly reflected in its emphasis on personal service, and it will focus innovation in that arena. Taking its cue from the hotel industry, the airline greets first-class passengers as they arrive in their car, provides porter service for their luggage, and checks them in while they relax in a special lounge.

Given the different value disciplines of the two airlines, Ryanair will typically be highly aggressive about seeking out innovations that reduce the cost of its operations and actively resistant to those that improve customer experience by adding cost. Singapore Airlines will proactively seek out new and better ways to provide a sense of romance and exclusivity, even if they result in higher fares, because it seeks customers who will pay a premium.

What we like most about value disciplines is that even if an organization's executives haven't explicitly stated (or thought about) their value discipline, we find that most management and professional employees, once introduced to the approach, can discuss and agree on what their company's value discipline is. We also like value disciplines for another reason. They make clear that creating an innovative product is not the only route to success, contrary to the impression given by the disproportionate attention to product innovation in business literature. Innovating a company's services, operational processes, business model, marketing and sales, customer experience, managerial philosophies, supplier relationships, partnerships, and even its strategy—all are potential routes to market growth.

CORE COMPETENCE

C. K. Prahalad and Gary Hamel introduced the concept of core competencies around 1990.[14] A core competence is defined as providing the capability to develop new products and services, making a significant contribution to the customer value proposition, and being difficult for others to emulate. Thus, it is the key source of a company's competitive advantage. Companies that have developed deep expertise in technical, process, or scientific domains often identify these capabilities as the core asset that fuels their innovation programs. One of the examples Prahalad and Hamel suggested was Honda, whose core competence of combustion engine design enabled it to develop a variety of quality products, from lawn mowers and snowblowers to trucks and automobiles, all based around the company's core competence. Disney also qualifies as a company with a strong ability to build out from its core competence, as the Disney magic ripples out from movies into theme parks, hotels, retail stores, and even a real Disney town (Celebration, Florida).

As with value disciplines, much of the work on core competencies relates to how they can be applied to create new strategies for market growth. Where core competencies have been identified for this purpose, they can also act as a powerful focal point for other types of innovation by highlighting areas where improvements will make a significant impact on the business. However, unlike with value disciplines, there is no pre-identified short list of core competencies to select from, because a core competence is relatively unique to the company that possesses it. This makes identifying your company's core competence a more difficult undertaking if the corporate strategists haven't already figured it out. In fact, value disciplines could be viewed as simply a list of generic core competencies.

VALUE CURVES

Whereas value disciplines and core competencies involve introspection about what a company does best, other approaches to defining strategic positioning focus on external market opportunities. One such approach is *value curve analysis*, introduced by W. Chan Kim and Renée Mauborgne and expanded on in their book *Blue Ocean Strategy*, which aims to identify where a company can innovate to break away from the pack.[15] In value curve analysis, a company charts the key value propositions for its product or service and for those of its competitors. Such value propositions for an airline might include cost, passenger comfort, and frequency of flights (see figure 6-1).

To break the mold, a company uses the value curves of existing players to identify value propositions where it could differentiate itself. Southwest Airlines' focus on low cost at the expense of meals, lounges, seating choices, and other value elements, with the addition of friendly service and fast turnaround, gives it a value curve radically different from others' in the industry. Similarly, Westin changed the value curve of a hotel room by revamping its entire chain with the highest-quality beds, luxury bedding, plush towels, and other valued amenities. Once identified and established, the differentiating value propositions become an enduring way to focus innovation where it matters.

PERSISTENT BUSINESS NEEDS

However your company expresses its corporate core—explicitly or subtly, through mission statements on its Web site or a proclamation after the

FIGURE 6-1

Value curve for Southwest Airlines

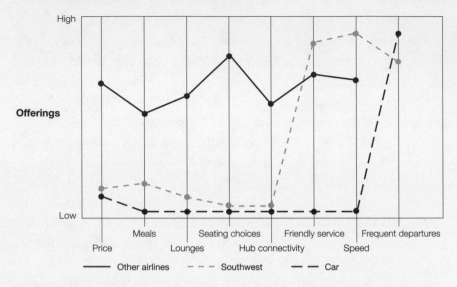

executive retreat with the latest management guru—translating the value propositions into specific targets for innovation typically requires an additional step. You need to ask the question, What specific attribute of the business do you actually want to change and in what direction do you need to move it?

To make the corporate core more tangible, we have found it useful to think in terms of *persistent business needs*, a term coined by Gartner analyst Mark McDonald, which we define as the activities that a company is always striving to improve. A persistent business need is expressed as an action—a verb—and an intent to change in a beneficial direction or to maintain acceptable performance levels. Examples might be "*shorten* product development cycle" for a product company, "*leverage* assets to new channels" for a media company, or "*comply* with regulations" for any company in a regulated industry.

Some of these needs are universal across all companies. Growing revenue is a universal need in every for-profit business and is typically quantified as an explicit annual goal for the company. Even if growth is not a company's highest priority, an innovation that can contribute to revenue growth would probably still be welcomed and adopted. In the same way, cutting costs is a universal need as well for all organizations, including not-for-profits and government departments. Even if cost cutting isn't the highest priority at the moment, an innovation that can significantly reduce costs is likely to be adopted nonetheless. But cost and growth aren't the only universal needs. In many business sectors, safety is equally a key concern and a top priority. In aviation, rail, nuclear, mining, utilities, chemicals, and other sectors, the potential costs, brand damage, and social consequences of accidents can be so high that any innovation that significantly improves safety will be a priority. For example, BP now declares its priorities as safety, people, and performance, in that order.[16] This refocusing followed incidents that affected its reputation for years, such as the forced closure of the Prudhoe Bay, Alaska, oil field in August 2006 because of pipeline corrosion and leakage.[17]

In addition to persistent business needs that are common across every enterprise, there are needs that vary in priority among organizations. Some will be determined by industry. A pharmaceutical company making batches of drugs will aim to speed the time to release a batch and minimize deviations in the process. Hospitality, travel, and retail industries have a persistent business need to reduce customer wait time, although the innovative solution may be different in each case—from Disney's Fastpass, to the airlines' use of kiosks for check-in, to Tesco's use of thermal heat sensing to detect how many people are standing in line at a cash register.[18]

An organization's corporate core underpins its persistent business needs. If we use the value disciplines to analyze the core, then related persistent business needs might include decreasing the time to new product introductions (product leadership), decreasing order-to-fulfillment time (operational excellence), increasing the number of touch points per month per customer (customer intimacy), or defending the brand against mischief, abuse, and fraud (brand mastery).

Whereas all organizations address many of these needs to a certain extent, the ones that fall within an organization's corporate core require proactive, aggressive innovation. For example, all organizations need to dedicate some effort to protecting their brands. But for brand masters like Disney, trawling through massive amounts of information to identify and stop unauthorized activity that could harm their brands is a persistent business need that demands significant amounts of resource and can therefore benefit greatly from innovation. All companies want to improve their customer service quality and response times, but customer-intimate companies make large investments in constantly refining and innovating channels and value-added services that lead to improved customer satisfaction.

Like value disciplines, persistent business needs work well as a focusing mechanism because most people inside an organization or department can agree on what their persistent business needs are.

Focusing Method 2: Current Business Objectives and Initiatives

One of the most direct ways to align innovation is through that staple of management focus: corporate goals and strategies that represent the organization's business objectives for the current fiscal year or other planning period. Goals and strategies, emanating from senior management formal communications, reflect marketplace pressures or opportunities, such as the need to grow market share, improve margin, or brace for recession. This might be stated in specific terms: the desire to stay in or move into the top three in revenues in the industry, the wish to beat out a specific competitor for market share, or the requirement to conform to new regulation. Strategies and goals often relate to new product or market opportunities, as in the following statement from GE: "The most exciting global opportunities for GE are in the developing world . . . Nearly 60% of our growth will come from developing countries in the next decade versus 20% for the past 10 years."[19] GE's focus on developing countries is likely to shape not just new products and services, but also other innovations to support the communications and marketing requirements of operating in dramatically different geographic and cultural contexts.

Without new goals, the weight and inertia of most large organizations cause them to focus their energies on maintaining smooth business operations. It's only by forcing a disruption through new strategies and goals that collective thinking will turn toward finding and accepting innovations in the way an organization runs. Business leaders set stretch targets or discontinuous goals to force deeper change and innovation across a company. For example, a new CEO's challenge goal to cut the cost of after-sales service by 50 percent over three years will force a search for innovations that change the way the company does business. Or a goal to increase revenue organically by 75 percent in five years can jolt managers into an innovative state of mind. This leadership approach has been referred to as a BHAG (Big Hairy Audacious Goal) by James Collins and Jerry Porras.[20]

Another type of business objective can be triggered by a specific event or business challenge that the company rallies around, creating a natural innovation target. A good example is a big physical move, such as new offices or a new manufacturing plant, which can be a catalyst for innovation in many aspects of equipment and operations. Think of the number of opportunities opened up when Boeing announced moving its headquarters from Seattle to Chicago in 2001.[21] Should the new campus be wireless? Can it be greener? Can new knowledge work methods be enabled? Each of these goals may require innovating technology and processes.

A crisis can force rapid innovation, as shown by JetBlue's experiences with a Valentine's Day snowstorm in 2007. The storm left JetBlue passengers at JFK airport in New York trapped for up to ten hours on planes, reportedly with no food.[22] Over one thousand flights were canceled over six days as the airline's operations descended into near chaos, and JetBlue's stock price took a hit. The CEO's appearance on the David Letterman show a week later was introduced with the quip, "We'll make him wait for a change."[23] The event was a public relations disaster, particularly for a company that claimed to be a customer service champion.

JetBlue needed to show a rapid and meaningful response. It offered immediate and generous (compared with other airlines' responses to similar incidents on other occasions) refunds and financial compensation to affected passengers, and looked at its internal processes in responding to crisis situations, such as dispatching managers and other employees from the head office seven miles from its hub at JFK airport, to help with luggage and other ground operations. But the centerpiece of its response was the introduction of a new "Customer Bill of Rights" guaranteeing refunds and vouchers for delays and missed connections under JetBlue's control.[24] The concept of a Customer Bill of Rights had been broadly adopted in the health-care industry; now JetBlue adopted this management innovation into the airline industry. Legislation mandating similar measures for U.S. airlines followed in some states soon after, but JetBlue was able to regain its credibility by innovating so rapidly in response to the furor caused by the events of February 14.

A more diffuse crisis, such as an economic downturn, can focus innovation as well, such as happened with many airlines after the Gulf wars in the 1990s and the early 2000s, and in particular after the terrorist attacks of 9/11. The number of passengers flying international routes fell off drastically, and the airlines found themselves with an urgent need to slash costs. The resulting cost-cutting initiatives accelerated adoption of self-service automations such as airport check-in kiosks and Web-based direct selling.

Sometimes a company must innovate to conform to new legislation or industry mandates; for example, Securities and Exchange Commission (SEC) regulations designed to enforce the Sarbanes-Oxley Act of 2002 required U.S.-listed public companies to become more transparent in their financial reporting.[25] The result of such regulatory change is frequently a permanent revision of internal operating procedures or even the creation of a new executive-level role, such as the growing prevalence of chief compliance officers after Sarbanes-Oxley. The smartest companies turn these types of issues into opportunities by exploring potentially desirable consequences of the required change. If a company must develop higher levels of reporting transparency, perhaps that will help it attract investment on more favorable terms or keep its customers more engaged with the company's activities. Likewise, if a company must introduce RFID tags into its supply chain because Wal-Mart or the Department of Defense mandates it (as both did in 2005), perhaps it can use the same technology for other innovations—for example, to make it harder to counterfeit its products. A forced innovation becomes an opportunity.

Sometimes organizations launch initiatives and create new objectives in response to external trends or societal pressures. Broad trends such as a growing concern for environmental impact and global warming become formulated as corporate goals; for example, in 2007 Marks & Spencer (M&S) CEO Stuart Rose announced "Plan A," which included the following goals: "By 2012 Marks and Spencer aims to be carbon neutral in its operations and send no material to landfill."[26]

This leverages the environmental trend, particularly in waste and climate change. Notice there is no specific innovation path outlined—just a goal. Rose does not know which possible future suppliers, halfway around the world, with some new vegetable-based packaging or energy-saving refrigeration process, might help. But he has set a clear focus that will help M&S managers seek and find them, wherever and whatever they are. Innovation fits naturally into this type of wide-ranging endeavor because there is less pressure to calculate direct payback. Rose has since stated,

"While we've estimated Plan A could cost around £200 million over five years, we haven't actually done a hard cost-benefit analysis."[27] What's more, this type of broader goal has a tendency to transcend tactical business conditions and cycles. After difficult trading conditions and weakened results over the 2007 holiday season, Rose goes on to say, "We could have heeded critics who said, 'Times are tough, best ditch the fluffy stuff.' But we didn't." This type of commitment has become more common as the business philosophy of corporate social responsibility (CSR) has grown considerably in recent years.

Focusing Method 3: Speculation and Aspirations

In addition to using their organization's corporate core and current business objectives as a catalyst to focus innovation adoption, innovation leaders can tap into longer-term planning initiatives that target speculative future opportunities and scenarios. These scenarios act as a focal point for innovation either by creating an aspiration, even if the company has no idea yet how to achieve it, or by highlighting the range of possible futures that the company should prepare for. These speculations and aspirations are not usually tied to a specific financial goal and, unlike the current business objectives, there is no sense of failure if they are not achieved. But by defining these future states and keeping them in circulation within the company, the organization is more likely to spot a relevant innovation that can drive toward a desired scenario.

One fruitful source of speculation is to identify opportunities to break through the current constraints of your organization or industry and then deliberately look for innovations that will achieve such a breakthrough.

Some organizations achieve these kinds of breakthroughs by taking a management team off-site, giving them a hypothetical start-up package of capital, and asking them to design a new business model that will destroy the existing industry. Because most people use their current situation as the starting point, on the first iteration a team will tend to state everything that must happen and all the conditions required, according to their experience. Most of these assumptions will be the constraints, taken as given and immutable, that surround that organization and industry. For example, a banking team might start with the assumption that branch location matters. A mobile telecom team might start talking about the mast infrastructure. A downstream oil company might start talking about gas stations.

The next step is to force the team to invert each assumption systematically. Assume, for example, that the new model for a bank can't have branches. Assume this cell phone company won't be allowed to put up additional masts. Assume that the gas company isn't allowed gas stations. This exercise may not lead immediately and directly to a breakthrough, but it does begin the definition of the invisible boundaries. These then become targets for finding innovations that change or remove them.

Using creative workshop exploration, management teams sometimes identify scenarios and ideas that would be extremely desirable but can't be achieved economically or technologically today. These are always good targets for innovation. For example, in 2007 UPS started to offer a service called "UPS Delivery Intercept," which allows customers to request a redirection or return of a parcel in midshipment, after it has entered the UPS transportation system. This was a customer need that the UPS new products group had known about and talked about for years, but the logistics systems of the firm just weren't ready for it until they crossed a threshold of capability in the mid-2000s. As Todd Brown at UPS says, "Once we got to the point where we had critical mass in our PFT (package flow technology), we realized that by stitching together systems that in the past hadn't talked, they could come together to provide a new service."[28]

Scenario planning, such as the approach used by Global Business Network, forces the creation of multiple alternative futures rather than a single future environment.[29] The value of this approach is that companies have to explicitly acknowledge and plan for potential futures that may *not* be the ones they most desire. The alternative scenarios are created by looking at the most important yet hardest-to-predict factors that could influence the future. For example, a key uncertainty in the hospitality industry might be whether the level of international terrorist attacks during the next decade influences people's willingness to travel. This key uncertainty creates two scenarios, each of which is plausible: one involving growth in international travel and tourism and one with a higher emphasis on local entertainment and vacation activities. There is nothing the industry can do to change or influence the alternate paths, but by understanding and exploring the two different futures, a company can look at what strategies, and what innovations, would make sense in the different scenarios. In particular, innovations that add value in both scenarios are the most desirable. Scenario planners often work with two or more key uncertainties to create a higher number of (but not so many as to be unmanageable) alternate scenarios.

One of the challenges of working with speculative activities such as constraint busting and scenario planning is to keep them alive and in people's minds after the scenario planning or visioning activity is over. Scenario planners often define "indicators" to track for, which show how each of the possible scenarios is becoming more or less likely according to how current events are unfolding. But innovation leaders still have to remember to check the indicators periodically. In most cases, the value of these speculative activities is to generate a burst of creative thinking that may turn into a more tangible initiative.

Risk Context: Enterprise Personality Profile

Using one or more of the focusing methods we have discussed, an innovation leader should be able to discriminate those places where innovation adoption is likely to generate high value. But that still leaves a hidden gap you need to take account of before setting out on the innovation trail: the question of the attitude of the company toward innovation risk in general.

In chapter 3 we described a simple way that organizations can categorize their enterprise personality as type A, B, or C. Is the organization often an aggressive early adopter? That's type A. Does it generally prefer not to go first but not to wait too long, in case competitors get too far ahead? Type B. Or does it tend to wait until an innovation is clearly planted on the Plateau of Productivity before adopting? Type C. Surveys of Gartner clients over the years have led us to understand that in the world of information technology, about 15 percent of all enterprises are type A, about 55 percent are type B, and the remaining 30 percent are type C. However, these proportions might vary for other categories of adoptive innovation that do not carry a strong technology component. Within each type, there is a spectrum of behavior—for example, we have heard moderately aggressive type B companies describe themselves as type B+, and fast followers claim to be type A−.

We also see that no organization is through and through one type, or one type for all times and in all seasons. A common scenario is that a company creates leading-edge products and services, but its manufacturing, supply chain, internal technology, and employee management practices are highly traditional and slow to evolve. An aggressive financial services company may have one or two lines of business that are notoriously conventional in their thinking. Or, companies may be temporarily shocked into more aggressive behavior based on current circumstances. In a study of the game show *Deal or No Deal*, in which contestants have to decide whether to take risks that could result in a very high payoff, researchers found that contestants who had just suffered extremely unfavorable outcomes or enjoyed extremely favorable ones were more likely to take big risks than contestants with a more balanced experience.[30] Organizations operating out of crisis or abundance are likewise more open to transformational innovation. To understand your context for innovation, you need to recognize the dominant tendency along with the organizational and situational variations on that tendency.

But how do you diagnose this? We have some useful behavior trait indicators that can help you make the determination. The characteristics of type A and type C are set out in table 6-1, with type B defined as being in between the two.

Type As are generally found among larger organizations, where there is more likely to be some level of slack in available resources. They also tend to be populated by individuals with advanced expertise, education, and management skill, who are well linked by interpersonal networks inside and outside their organizations.[31]

TABLE 6-1

Traits for enterprise personality profiles

Factor	Type A trait	Type C trait
Information use	We analyze all information on emerging trends to foresee possible changes.	We analyze our own achievements and mistakes to consider the necessity of change.
Risk tolerance	Taking the risk of implementing changes is a requirement for our executives.	Our executives' main virtue is stability of execution.
Attitude to change	We welcome more changes because we can deal with them better than our competitors.	Numerous and rapid changes overwhelm our capability to address them.
Strategic intent	Our strategy is to initiate change and impose it on our competitors.	Our strategy objective is not to disrupt our well-optimized business.
Complexity	Our structures and processes can be rearranged rapidly.	Our structures and processes are rigid and hard to explain.

One thing is common: when companies act against type and move outside their comfort zone, the lack of appropriate skills and mind-set will increase the chance of failure. However, we've seen that a key lesson of the hype cycle is that every organization at times must act contrary to its own risk personality. On some occasions, for example, it's in the best interests of a type B or C firm to adopt earlier than usual. And there are times a type A organization should wait. On such occasions, those organizations are taking special risks that cut against the grain of their corporate personalities. They must do it, but they also must know when they're doing it so they're prepared to deal with the special problems that arise when acting out of character and with the additional resources required to cope with that situation. That's why recognizing your organization's risk profile is a key part of the context for innovation adoption.

Finding and Capturing the Scope

Now you know what your company's business value context should look like—its corporatate core, current business objectives and initiatives, and relevant speculation and aspirations—and you understand how to define your risk context in terms of one of the three enterprise personality types. But if your company doesn't have its mission statement, annual goals, key business initiatives, or enterprise personality type nailed to the wall of every conference room, you'll need to figure out how to track down and document indicators of these focusing methods. Three of the best ways are to draw on company metrics, your own networking abilities, and external sources.

The Role of Metrics

It is often possible to identify at least some elements of your business value context by looking at the business metrics that are measured and rewarded within the organization. A focused organization determines what is important and figures out ways to measure progress along relevant dimensions throughout the organization. In many cases, this involves appointing a specific individual to be responsible for a corporate goal or a persistent business need. It involves forcing strategies and goals to become the goals of everyone in the organization by cascading down relevant and measurable targets through organization structures into performance appraisals and bonuses. In an ideal world, with every employee appropriately motivated, innovation naturally becomes focused on meaningful change to achieve corporate goals and objectives.

Unfortunately, many metrics lose sight of the core value they are aiming to improve. For example, most organizations claim to value quality over quantity, but measuring a person's productivity (calls per hour, lines of code) is always easier than measuring the quality of his or her work. Another challenge is that some persistent business needs are easier to measure (order fulfillment time) than others (avoiding brand damage).

Over the last decade, the Balanced Scorecard approach to objectives and metrics has become popular in many larger corporations. This allows companies to blend multiple factors and helps compensate for the biases of outcome and unintended consequences that simpler measures tend to introduce. More recently, Robert Kaplan and David Norton have attempted to improve further on their metrics-driven approach by adding strategy maps to plug the gap caused by the traditional blind spot of intangible assets such as corporate knowledge or processes.[32] These techniques can be very powerful when properly implemented, and if you are in a company that is following them with genuine intent, they can be very helpful as a focusing technique. Your scope for innovation adoption should be guided toward positive improvements in Balanced Scorecard measured outcomes. However, we also recognize that half-hearted attempts at deploying these techniques can linger in some companies in the shape of superficial metrics reports that are not actually driving business decisions, so you should take equal care not to tie your innovation activities to irrelevant or abandoned outcomes.

Where metrics exist and are relevant, looking at the impact that an innovation is likely to have on those metrics is a clear way to assess its potential value. And figuring out which metrics are most important, because they contribute directly to corporate goals or persistent business needs, will tell you where to be most proactive and aggressive with innovation. If the right objectives and persistent business needs are managed and measured in the right way, then an innovation that drives even incremental gains can significantly improve competitive position.

Internal Networks

What if corporate goals and strategies aren't explicit? Welcome to the other half of the business world, where—somehow—businesses are progressing nicely or perhaps even thriving without the collections of well-communicated management artifacts that business school theory suggests should be in place. Perhaps it's because of quirky governance structures, private and secretive ownership, partly protected markets, charismatic but confounding founders. In most organizations, explicit drivers and clear metrics represent only a fraction of the corporate context for innovation. As we will see repeatedly as we continue to traverse the STREET framework, in this situation, and others, the ability to build strong personal networks within your organization will be essential to innovation leadership. It is unlikely that a complete and succinct description of the corporate context and the risk context for innovation are anywhere to be found within your corporation, so you will need to do some work pulling together the views of different people in disparate parts of the organization to create a mosaic picture for yourself. Some of the sources described earlier, such as strategic planning documents and statements of mission, core values, and corporate goals, are a great starting point when they're available. But they don't tell the whole story, particularly for the risk context. It's therefore critical for innovation leaders to set up relationships with the teams and individuals who have an understanding of what matters, and what will matter, to the company. These contacts may include your manager and your manager's manager, other senior executives, the strategic planning group, the information technology architecture team, competitive intelligence analysts, the chief financial officer, and other influential roles within the company. In smaller companies it may be true that only the CEO knows, especially if he or she was the founder of the firm. In that case, the upside at least is that you know there is only one place to do your research.

Public Sources

Another way to find out more about the strategies and tactics of your company is, believe it or not, to look on the Web. That's not as facetious as it may sound, and it's particularly relevant to large public companies. Since the Sarbanes-Oxley Act of 2002, the suggestion that real-time disclosure of material information is a commendable business tactic has become a much more conventional view. What this new business culture means in practice for managers and employees in midsize and large companies is that they shouldn't expect to hear things internally first, because markets are legally required to be the primary communications target. More details than ever about company strategy and direction are being disclosed, and those details are more likely to be easily accessible from external sources.

Several sources provide a much fuller picture of a company's direction than can ordinarily be found on the company's intranet or through internal sources. Such sources include official documents, such as the company annual report; the Form 8-K filings to the SEC concerning material events and decisions by the company; and the analyst calls in which company officers brief analysts, investors, financial journalists, and others on company results, plans, and strategies. Reports and opinions by third parties can also be enlightening, including the reports from financial analysts; investor financial sites such as Yahoo! Finance, MSN Money, Hemscott, and The Motley Fool; or business and financial press articles.

Communicating the Scope

When you have spent time and effort defining the scope and context for innovation adoption, it makes sense to capture the key elements of context that you've uncovered in a simple written summary. This is particularly useful document for a central innovation group to create. Without a way to communicate the scope, others in your company who are tracking potential innovations will tend to operate in fragmented groups, each dealing with its own limited, local perception of need and direction. This summary might form an introduction to a broader trend and technology tracking document, which we will discuss in the next chapter.

The Hype Cycle of Management Strategy

A word of warning as we complete our discussion of scoping activities: corporate strategies and initiatives can themselves be subjects of a hype cycle. When a few pioneering companies apply a new strategy—or a leading academic writes a popular business book about one—many organizations start to embrace it as their own. For example, C. K. Prahalad's *The Fortune at the Bottom of the Pyramid* points to the huge untapped potential of selling low-cost items with low margins to "the next four billion consumers" in emerging nations and making large profits because of the scale involved.[33] Early movers to this strategy, such as Procter & Gamble and GE, are truly innovating in a way that will serve these markets, help their customers, and grow their corporate profits. However, the "buzz" around the approach also means that a growing number of companies will attempt to adopt a "base of the pyramid" strategy. Many of these companies will not really understand the type of innovation needed to address the requirements of consumers whose finances and physical infrastructure (transportation, power communications) are so different from those of developed nations.

Even key management processes such as strategy and innovation are themselves subject to waves of fashion that lead companies to adopt approaches that may not be a great match for them. Value curve or "blue ocean" strategies, open innovation, strategy maps, and other currently fashionable concepts all have important roles to play in many businesses, but will no doubt be overapplied in ways that will lead some to question their efficacy and thus cause a drop into the Trough of Disillusionment.

As an innovation leader who understands the force of the hype cycle, you may be in a strong position to temper blind enthusiasm for fashionable strategies by keeping a clear focus on the corporate core and on strategies that address enduring corporate goals. Not that we're telling you to second-guess your CEO—just that the goals and metrics easiest to disseminate along the lines of management may not be the ones most relevant for high-impact innovation. On the other hand, the average tenure of a CEO in the United States is less than five years, so you might be living with the consequences of your innovations far longer than your company's executives will.[34]

Seven

Track: Collecting the Innovation Candidates

To have a great idea, have a lot of them.

—Thomas Edison

L IKE MANY GOVERNMENT and military organizations, the Defense Information Systems Agency (DISA) has a clear statement of its scope. DISA is "the provider of global net-centric solutions for the Nation's warfighters and all those who support them in the defense of the nation." In its role as a core enabler of the nation's war-fighting ability, DISA needs to maintain a type A enterprise personality to stay ahead of its particular type of competition. Its army of employees need to operate on the leading edge of the communications networks, computers, and software that they deliver to support the U.S. Department of Defense (DoD).

In 2005 one of those employees, Fritz Schulz, returned from a year's assignment at National Defense University and proposed a strategic technology management initiative. Unlike other DoD groups such as the Air Force Research Lab (AFRL) or Electronic Systems Command (ESC), DISA didn't have a laboratory or research group to identify and disseminate information about leading-edge technology opportunities.[1] Innovation was happening all the time within individual DISA programs, but not in a coordinated way, leading to the risk of missed opportunities and duplicated effort. In line with one of DISA's core values—active partnering—Schulz proposed a function that would leverage the technology tracking activities and resources that already existed in the various DoD commands and interpret the findings for DISA's enterprise innovation needs. With the support and enthusiasm of his management, Schulz created DISA's "technology reconnaissance" group, named to reflect its goal of gathering intelligence about the future technology environment, in the same way that military reconnaissance teams are sent ahead to gather intelligence about the physical environment.

From the outset, the technology reconnaissance group has been designed to act as a hub to capture information from a broad range of sources, including other DoD commands, intelligence agencies, academia, commercial industry, and defense contractors. Within DISA, Schulz's core team is augmented by contributions from across the various disciplines and specialties. An internal Web site acts as the central repository of relevant technology updates and analysis. To help contributors stay focused on DISA's core mission, the portal includes pointers to relevant documentation and Web sites concerning strategic plans and road maps.

Within eighteen months, the technology reconnaissance group has constructed a pipeline of technology opportunities and has forged relationships with groups and individuals with similar roles in other agencies. Schulz credits much of the early success to their focus on partnerships. "This technology reconnaissance process is underdeveloped in most organizations," explains Schulz. "It's a specialty activity that needs to be resourced along with everything else. We've made an adaptation that relies on participation and partnership. The upside is that you get a lot of buy-in and understanding of what you're trying to do because you're out there trying to recruit people."

Why and When to Track

DISA's technology reconnaissance group focuses primarily on the track phase of the STREET process. The goal of tracking is to capture a broad range of potential innovation candidates, not just those that come to your attention because of media or seller hype. Tracking encourages you to seek out other opportunities that may turn out to be even more worthwhile.

A strong tracking activity seeks out both a broad range of innovation candidate types (business trends, process improvements, management approaches, technologies, and so on) and a broad range of innovation sources (external, peers, in-house experts, and so on). Your business value context and your risk context, as identified in the scope phase, act as a first filter on the huge range of possible innovations. Some ideas can be immediately discounted as irrelevant to your organization, no matter how fascinating they may appear. Others will be excluded because their time to maturity extends beyond your planning horizon, given your organization's tolerance for risk.

This first pass is a judgment call, frequently based on nothing more than gut feel. It's often the ability to conceptualize *use cases*—business situations where an innovation might be applied—that makes the difference between acceptance and rejection of an innovation candidate. For example, why would an insurance company be interested in robots, the stuff of science fiction? If, as Bill Gates and Honda seriously foresee, there will one day be a couple of android robots in many homes and those devices will be second only to houses and cars in value, then an insurance company might be interested for several reasons: to insure them for theft, damage, and liability; to link the robots' telemetry to their systems to monitor risk factors; or to offer discounts to homes and businesses that augment fixed alarms with mobile robot security patrols.[2] An innovative insurance company will watch developments in this area because of what might happen down the road. It's just that sort of radar watching that enabled Progressive to envisage and prepare for the "Pay As You Drive" opportunity (as mentioned in chapter 4) back when such an idea seemed equally outlandish.

Tracking is a continuous activity, as people are constantly exposed to new ideas. The challenge is to capture and record the relevant ideas before they disappear into the black hole of each individual's desktop files and e-mail archives. In addition, some organizations conduct a deliberate review periodically—typically once a year. This review forces people to make tracking activities a priority so that the organization can gather a critical mass of innovation candidates. By targeting a specific time period, people are more able to allocate larger amounts of time, energy, and enthusiasm to the exercise than with general background tracking. It's often timed to coincide with other strategy, planning, and budgeting activities so that selected innovations can be funded to the next stage of evaluation.

ExxonMobil is an example of a company that runs an annual cycle of technology scanning and screening, identifying hundreds of candidates with potential value. Activities include a number of opportunity workshops around specific business processes and themes such as manufacturing, supply chains, customer engagement, and home-based work productivity. The core technology innovation team organizes the workshops with representatives from across the business. The workshops start off with briefings about the initiatives and challenges of the business; then participants suggest technologies they are aware of that might address those challenges. After the workshops, the team distills down the hundreds of ideas into a manageable number of top candidates. According to Martin Kagan of ExxonMobil's IT architecture and integration group, and a project leader for ExxonMobil's technology scan, "Ongoing tracking is a wonderful idea, but if you don't focus on an annual publication cycle, it won't happen."[3]

What to Track: Products, Capabilities, and Trends

As you track down innovations within your scope rather than waiting for them to find you, the first challenge is to recognize that innovation candidates range from the very specific (products), through the moderately broad (capabilities), to the highly abstract (trends). The most effective innovators work along the whole spectrum, moving from products to capabilities to trends as necessary. By operating at a single level, you may miss potentially valuable opportunities (e.g., by focusing on a specific product) or fail to stay relevant to the business (e.g., collecting trends but not assessing their impact). However specific or abstract the innovations, identifying the innovations themselves is only one part of the work; the most import part is identifying the ways that the innovation can be applied within your organization.

PRODUCTS AND SERVICES

Products and services offer a tangible, shrink-wrapped, ready-to-use version of an innovation. A new product is often the first exposure that most people have to the innovation it embodies. For example, the concept of instant messaging developed in the 1970s among UNIX users, but it was the popularity of a specific product, AOL Instant Messenger, that introduced the idea to a much broader audience in the late 1990s. In the corporate world, demonstrations of a new software package are often the way that executives are first exposed to new business ideas such as customer relationship management (CRM) or supply chain management. Some companies are already creating software to measure and account for their greenhouse gas emissions—but it may be years before "carbon accounting" is fully packaged and made available to the majority. The fact that you can see (and buy) a packaged product and that it is actively marketed make this the most common way of identifying an innovation.

However, while products and services themselves are easy to see, their real value is sometimes hard to ascertain, particularly when they first appear. In many cases, the real significance of a new product is the deeper capability or trend it embodies.

To see how this works, let's visit Second Life, a 3-D virtual world created by San Francisco–based Linden Lab that caught the attention of thousands of users and the popular media during 2005 and 2006. In a virtual world, the user is represented by an avatar—an online character—that can explore the virtual world and see and talk to other users' avatars. Second Life users, known as residents, can customize their avatars and the online world through relatively simple tools, giving rise to a thriving virtual economy, whose virtual currency can be exchanged for real-world dollars, with real estate, clothing, furniture, and even extra body parts that can be bought and sold. By early 2007, the first Second Life millionaires were being lauded in front-page articles of the mainstream press. Businesses such as IBM bought up real estate and set up shop in Second Life to run client events, test new product ideas, recruit, advertise, and generally try to figure out what this new world was good for. But later that same year, the virtual world attracted the attention of real-world law enforcement. Threatened with legal action for unlicensed gambling, Linden Lab closed down all the casinos in Second Life, which cost the casino owners their hard-won clientele and associated income.[4] A run on the virtual bank followed, along with the first major devaluation of Second Life's currency against the dollar. For many residents, this was the first wake-up call regarding the fragility of virtual property. Along with ongoing corporate bafflement as to how to monetize their investments in the virtual world, it led to the inevitable Trough of Disillusionment for Second Life. At the same time, other virtual worlds started to get more exposure, as they developed tools that would let companies set up their own potentially more secure and manageable virtual environments. So, while Second Life may or may not maintain its dominance among virtual worlds, companies that became residents of Second Life to test various uses and benefits have actually been learning not just about this one product but about the broader lessons associated with the virtual worlds.

When faced with an innovative product, particularly a highly hyped one, remember that early entrants into a market are often not the ones that dominate in the longer term. Its easy to forget the long list of lessons like Commodore computers, DeLorean cars, and Betamax videotapes. Did you bet on HD DVD or wait for its contest with Blu-ray to resolve? You need to track and evaluate the innovation's potential independently of the functionality or fate of a single product.

CAPABILITIES AND TECHNIQUES

In general, the capability level, rather than a specific product, is a more appropriate level of innovation to consider as you move through the STREET process. A capability might be a technology category, such as virtual worlds, wikis, biometric identification, or RFID tags; or a management discipline or approach, such as Six Sigma, CRM, offshoring, or Balanced Scorecard.

Although it is fairly easy to distinguish products from capabilities (Second Life versus virtual worlds, Prius versus hybrid car), in some cases the capability itself can be described at varying levels of specificity. Sometimes specific product names get used generically, causing confusion—for example, MP3 is one specific audio digital file format, but people commonly use it to refer to all digitized music. In particular, the same capability can be delivered by different techniques. In part 1 we saw how capabilities typically survive the whole hype cycle but may use different techniques along the way, and we cited the example of broadband connectivity (capability) being achieved by cable modems or DSL (techniques).

In some cases multiple layers blur the line between techniques and capabilities. User identification is a capability required by companies wanting to provide secure access to their corporate applications and information. Biometrics is one approach to user identification that uses some unique physical aspect of an individual to determine identity. A set of common biometric techniques are used, such as fingerprints, hand geometry, voiceprints, or the patterns in the iris of the eye. However, each of these techniques may itself have multiple ways of being delivered; for example, fingerprint recognition can be performed by chip-based or camera-based scanning (see table 7-1).

You may first notice an innovation at any point along this spectrum from specific product to generic capability. For PC manufacturers, the in-

TABLE 7-1

Layers of capabilities and techniques for biometric identification

Trends	Need for stronger security
Capabilities	User identification
	Biometrics
Techniques	Fingerprint identification
	Capacitance chip, camera-based
Products	Product 1, Product 2

troduction of chip-based scanners as a new technique for fingerprint recognition was a catalyst to reexamine the potential for embedded fingerprint recognition in PCs, which led to the commercial availability of today's fingerprint-enabled PCs.

In an ideal world, it's best when the product, the technique, and the capability all survive the whole hype cycle. Having to switch techniques and replace the products that deliver them can create major costs and inconvenience. But for the purposes of innovation tracking, the trick is to track capabilities and alternative techniques and products in parallel, tying them all to relevant persistent business needs or corporate objectives.

Once we move into the world of business and management innovations, such as CRM or Six Sigma, we find that an innovation often involves a whole new discipline that combines concepts, processes, techniques, management skills, and approaches. Elements of the new discipline may be packaged into consulting services, frameworks, and training packages, but buying a product or service is certainly not the most important—or the most challenging—aspect of adopting these business innovations. The stories of failed CRM and other large corporate applications can often be traced to the belief that the company was buying a new software package rather than embracing new approaches and processes that the software embodied.

To derive value from business innovations, the new discipline needs to penetrate the entire organization rather than focusing on only one part, and it requires the broad supportive involvement of management and employees. In addition, many smaller innovations can fall under the umbrella of a new discipline. For example, call center voice recognition, customer analytics, campaign management, and automated e-mail newsletters can all be placed under the broad banner of CRM. When fully embraced, a management innovation becomes part of the new operational environment and forms a new persistent business need and a catalyst for further innovation.

TRENDS

This statement appeared in a 2003 Unilever earnings call transcript concerning one of the company's key products, Slim-Fast:

> This has been a disappointing quarter for Slim-Fast with sales well below the prior year, which has reduced Unilever's growth rate . . . Whilst part of this is to do with a tough comparator in the prior year as we expanded to new geography, the larger part comes from changes we have made to promotional plans and timing and through competition. The latter particularly relates to the current fad for low carbohydrate diets . . . This type of challenge is not new to Slim-Fast, but has occurred at a time when we have also had a relatively light innovation program, as we focused on rapid geographic roll-out, consolidating new market positions and as we brought new Ready-to-Drink manufacturing capacity on-stream.[5]

This was such surprising news that the next day Unilever's stock price dropped 8.5 percent, followed by an even bigger fall the next month as the story unfolded. Such is the sudden price of failure in today's high-speed and transparent economy. Happily, Unilever has since recovered, though the fortunes of Slim-Fast were the subject of public reporting by the firm for two years after this incident.

For our purposes, the question is this: why, in late 2002, did nobody in Unilever notice the fast-growing hype wave around the low-carb Atkins diet—including especially its uptake by Hollywood stars and its acceptance by hard-to-reach male dieters? Perhaps there's a clue in Unilever's admission that the wave "occurred at a time when we have also had a relatively light innovation program." We're not picking on Unilever. Missed opportunities and overlooked dangers like this happen to companies all the time, but most aren't this visible. This one had unusually high impact because Slim-Fast happened to be important to Unilever's growth strategy at the time. For whatever reason, Unilever was caught off guard. It moved quickly to develop low-carb products itself, and eventually low-carb alternatives became a part of mainstream nutritional varieties.

On a broader scale than diet fads, some social, political, and other trends are so massive that they change the way whole industries and markets operate. Consider, for example, how aging populations are beginning to force changes in the health-care systems of advanced nations, or how society's growing concern over climate change is pressuring individuals and corporations to change their consumption habits.

Seeing one of these megatrends coming should be easy, but because they're so enormous and slow moving, they are often barely perceptible. Future trends such as wars over water, rare metal depletion, and human genetic modification are already starting to be discussed. By the time they're obvious, as Unilever discovered, either it can be too late or there's a painful period of adjustment. To try to catch these game-changer trends earlier, many organizations now include a broad scan for trends in their innovation tracking, using categories such as political, economic, social, and technological (PEST analysis) or an expanded version that includes social, technical, economic, environmental, political, legal, ethical, and demographic trends (STEEPLED).

Abstract trends, particularly those in the political, economic, and societal realm, are only really "adopted" if they affect the organization's strategy. The trend of "globalization" or "climate change" or "emerging markets" cannot be adopted like a new computer system. While they may be picked up as part of the track stage, their significance is to drive change in the organization's scope. BP's early recognition of the environmental trend led to far-reaching corporate initiatives, including its marketing slogan of "Beyond Petroleum" and the launch of an Alternative Energy program to investigate low-carbon alternatives such as solar power. Marks & Spencer's recognition of the environmental trend led to the formulation of its "carbon neutral and no landfill by 2012" goal that we saw in chapter 6. The resulting changes in corporate strategy or objectives become part of the organization's scope for further innovation tracking.

Trends may impact at the departmental level too. For example, the HR department may need to innovate to adapt to societal trends such as the growing expectation of flexibility in work/life balance, or the legal department may need to create a new compliance group to deal with expanding legal requirements for corporate reporting.

For many executives, broader business and societal trends are playing a growing role in shaping their innovation strategies. As Nick Donofrio, IBM's executive vice president for innovation and technology, puts it, "The invention, the creation, or the discovery in the twentieth century was probably good enough in many ways to be called the innovation. That's not the way it is in the twenty-first century. This is much more about understanding the problem better—understanding the political issue, the societal issue, the business issue, the academic issue—so that you can take your technical knowledge and apply it in new and uniquely different ways."[6]

Where to Look: Working the Network and Innovation Challenges

The most successful innovation adopters expose themselves to a broad range of information sources from which they can draw their pool of innovation candidates. Sources include published information in business, industry, and trade press, online information feeds, and favorite blogs or Web sites. Conversations with customers, suppliers, other business partners, or venture capital organizations can yield new ideas, as can more formal visits to university, government, or industrial research labs. The statistical services of most governments and security agencies explore major trends in demographics and economics. Paid sources include innovation tracking services from consultants or industry analysts, or conferences that target leading-edge technologies and applications. Figure 7-1 shows the range of innovation sources identified by CEOs during a 2006 global survey by IBM. Note the importance that CEOs place on having sources both inside and outside their organization.

One of the best ways to stay well informed is to locate yourself at the center of a network of other people also performing innovation scans. This is the approach that DISA took with its technology reconnaissance group. In addition to its own innovation scanning, the group uses its partners elsewhere within DISA and in several other DoD organizations, along with representatives within one of their principal contractors, to identify new ideas and information.

This approach can work well in many corporate contexts—for example, a business leader who assigns to team members responsibility for monitoring specific information sources, or an information technology department that identifies domain experts responsible for tracking innovation within their various disciplines (communications, storage, PCs, etc.).

FIGURE 7-1

Sources of new ideas and innovation identified by CEOs

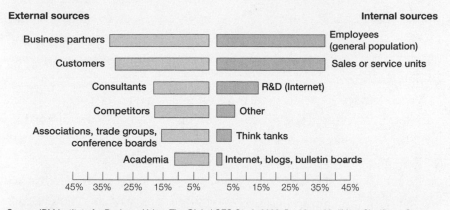

Source: IBM Institute for Business Value, *The Global CEO Study 2006,* fig. 10, p. 22, "Most Significant Sources of Innovative Ideas." Reprint Courtesy of International Business Machines Corporation, copyright 2006 © International Business Machines Corporation.

Large businesses with disparate and far-flung operations have further scanning opportunities. In spite of globalization, innovations still appear in different places at different times. For example, the ability to use text messages on mobile phones to pay for parking appeared in central Zagreb, Croatia, around 2002 but not in San Francisco or central London until 2007.

Erin Byrne, chief digital strategist for public relations firm Burson-Marsteller, stresses the importance of her international network in helping her stay current regarding client attitudes and trends. "I rely on my network of digital strategists around the world, who range in level from the most junior client executive up to director-level staffers," says Byrne. "I rely on them to be out in the marketplace working side by side with their colleagues every day and bringing back information."[7] Byrne conducts a monthly call with each region (for example, Asia or Latin America) to hear what is happening in other locations. The company has also developed a rich intranet platform as a knowledge-sharing tool, including a wiki, discussion boards, and internal blogging.

Competitive intelligence is one of the best places to look for inspiration as to what is possible. Look at how your competitors are using an innovation, but also look beyond your own industry at *comparators* (companies of similar size or with similar aspirations) for ideas that might be transferable to your own situation, particularly if you aspire to be an early adopter. Aetna, a leading health insurer, applied this approach to powerful effect when it became one of the first insurance companies to implement the business process improvement called *straight-through processing* that eliminates the need to reenter information manually several times into different computer systems.

"Aetna wanted to be an industry leader, and we realized early on that you could never lead if you were just looking at others in your own industry," says Frank Finocchio, strategic planning managing director in Aetna's IT strategy group. "You had to create something new, you had to innovate, and therefore you had to look outside the box at what other industries were doing."[8] Aetna saw the transformations that straight-through processing had delivered to the financial services industry, and determined that it could also bring value in health insurance, where it had not yet been implemented. In the 1990s, Aetna had gone through multiple mergers and acquisitions and as a result had a mix of different systems. Implementing straight-through processing enabled the company to streamline its claims process to such an extent that its rating in the industry for paying claims quickly (as measured by athenahealth PayerView) went from number four to number one. "Because of straight-through processing, we have actually been able to shorten the time that it takes to pay our providers, and now we're the best in the industry," Finocchio adds.

One way to draw deliberately on a broad population of contributors is through an "innovation challenge," which has become a popular way for companies to find innovative solutions from the world outside their corporate boundaries. In 2006, movie rental company Netflix offered a prize of a million dollars to anyone who could write a computer program that improved the personalized movie recommendations for Netflix customers by more than 10 percent. Thousands of engineers around the world have been working on the problem and providing Netflix with substantial improvements to its algorithms. In 2007, Netflix gave a team from AT&T Labs a $50,000 annual progress prize for improving performance by over 8 percent. As of early 2008, however, the grand prize has not been claimed.[9] The U.S. Army is offering its own million-dollar prize to the winning developer of a wearable, lightweight electric power system for soldiers.[10] Web sites such as InnoCentive and NineSigma operate as marketplaces where companies can launch their scientific or engineering "challenges" to scientists around the globe.

A similar approach can be used in-house by companies to leverage the creative potential of their employees (who are the largest source of innovation, according to the IBM survey shown in figure 7-1). AstraZeneca's Healthcare Innovation Center (HIC) was formed in 2006 to identify, design, and incubate new ways to improve the delivery and management of health care. The aim was not to create new products, but to enhance the value of the company's medicines—for example, by encouraging patients to fill prescriptions and take the medicines they have been prescribed. The HIC has run multiple innovation challenges on topics such as improving diagnostics for patients and improving AstraZeneca's own internal processes.

Unlike the "suggestion boxes" of an earlier management era, which collected discrete individual contributions, in-house innovation challenges aim to provide an environment where employees collaborate and build on each other's ideas. AstraZeneca's HIC provides a set of Web tools that support the collection and development of ideas, as well as the refinement and selection process that follows. The execution of selected ideas uses existing project and portfolio management processes, but is managed with the idea collection Web tools. The HIC announces the challenge to a group of selected participants (typically around 500, but it has been as high as 1,800) and lets the challenge run anywhere from three days to three weeks. The organizers ensure that at least a quarter of the participants are from areas of the business tangential to the topic of the challenge, because they have found that some of the more interesting breakthroughs come from such individuals. Participants enter ideas relevant to the challenge question and review and expand on ideas already contributed. The collaboration and refinement is an essential part of the value. "It's frequently in the building of an idea that the golden nugget of innovation actually appears," according to Fred Balliet of AstraZeneca, who has championed the innovation challenge approach at AstraZeneca and led several challenges.[11]

In most internal innovation challenges there is no million-dollar prize, although those originating or contributing to a successful idea often receive the option to work on the resulting project, which can significantly enhance their visibility in the company.

How to Capture the Results

All the hard work of identifying innovations and how they might be used within your organization is of little value unless those ideas are captured so that they can be reviewed and moved forward.

A brief written profile of a potential innovation is one way that organizations document the results of their tracking. An innovation profile typically includes a definition and description of the innovation, some assessment of its maturity and known risks, and a list of potential suppliers with approximate costs. Just as importantly, it captures the potential business opportunity within the organization—where and how the innovation would be applied, including any experience with it inside your organization already. Innovations with multiple distinct applications within the company—such as speech recognition for the call center versus speech recognition for dictation in the legal department—should have a profile for each application because costs, benefits, suppliers, and other aspects may differ significantly. Some companies have found that the simple act of adding images to an innovation profile—for example, supplier logos or a screen shot from a computer application—makes the profile much more likely to be read, particularly in printed form.

DISA creates brief innovation profiles it calls "nuggets." In line with its intelligence and reconnaissance theme, these are viewed as nuggets of intelligence from the front line, and can be submitted by anyone in the organization via the DISA portal. Submission of a nugget is triggered by a change in maturity of the innovation, as measured by the standard DoD Technology Readiness Levels (TRLs). TRLs are used in several different areas of the government as a common way to categorize a technology innovation's maturity. There are nine levels, with level 1 being the least mature and level 9 being fully proven technology. They are more fine-grained versions of the four stages of innovation maturity—embryonic, emerging, adolescent, mainstream—discussed in chapter 2.

Each nugget submitted to the DISA portal has a description, a "DISA impact" statement, the new TRL that has been reached, the name of the person who submitted it, and links to external resources for more information.

A number of companies have adapted the idea of TRLs to work within a commercial context. For example, GM's OnStar has created its own set of nine levels, ranging from paper studies at levels 1 and 2, through prototyping and validation at levels 4 and 5, up to pilot and production at levels 8 and 9 (see table 7-2). In adapting the levels, it has converted them from general indicators of the technology's overall maturity into guidelines of the specific level of readiness within its own organization.

In addition to the individual profiles, some organizations create and document higher-level categories for a set of related innovations. For example, the topics of RFID, geographic information systems, Google Earth, and location-based services could be collected under a theme of "location intelligence." As DISA's Schulz puts it, "You get a pile of nuggets on your desk, and it's a little hard to make sense of what's going on there. You're

TABLE 7-2

Technology Readiness Level descriptions from U.S. DoD and OnStar

Technology Readiness Level	DoD description	OnStar TRL name	OnStar description
1	Basic principles observed and reported	Think it	Basic research in emerging technologies and concepts. A product may not yet be available.
2	Technology concept and/or application formulated	Scan it	Research report documents the technology and product options
3	Analytical and experimental critical function and/or characteristic proof of concept	Prove it	Develop proof of concept to validate technology/product capability
4	Component and/or breadboard validation in laboratory environment	Fit it	Capability review and confirmation. Application is identified.
5	Component and/or breadboard validation in relevant environment	Try it	Prototype in relevant environment with key integration demonstrated
6	System/subsystem model or prototype demonstration in a relevant environment	Buy it	Select, standardize, and purchase
7	System prototype demonstration in an operational environment	Build it	Develop and test application(s) using the product(s)
8	Actual system completed and "flight qualified" through test and demonstration	Show it	Pilot application
9	Actual system "flight proven" through successful mission operations	Scale it	Full production

Source: U.S. Department of Defense, *Defense Acquisition Guidebook* (Washington, DC: U.S. Department of Defense, 2006); and OnStar's enterprise architecture group, communication with author, February 13, 2008.

starting to get into an area where the intelligence analyst comes into play. You take these fragmentary indications of what's happening, pin them to the wall and blur your eyes and drink a cup of coffee, and a pattern starts to emerge, and then you build up what the intelligence officers call a situation report."[12]

DISA's situation report is a longer document—around twenty five pages—that briefs people on the set of technologies and provides links to external resources on the topic. The report highlights five selected opportunities for DISA to apply the technology, along with recommended next steps.

The collection of innovation profiles constitutes a portfolio of innovation candidates. Some companies maintain the innovation portfolio on the company intranet so that all parts of the organization can see the status of innovation activities. Ideally, you should treat the innovation portfolio and the profiles it contains as a *living* document that is updated as you identify new candidates or uncover new potential uses. In reality, most companies focus on consolidating the candidates in an annual or semiannual update as part of the business planning cycle. This also helps the process of synthesizing multiple threads into coherent, relevant opportunities.

For example, the information technology department at AstraZeneca creates an annual "radar screen" document for its chief information officer (CIO). "We provide the CIO with a view of what we believe is important, things he should be aware of so that he won't be taken by surprise," explains AstraZeneca's Balliet.[13] The radar focuses on key thematic areas, with three or four key opportunities and impacts within each theme. At Aetna, the IT strategy group creates a "principal forces" document that examines market, regulatory, and technology directions. The document looks at how these areas are likely to unfold on the basis of political and industry directions, and how it may influence Aetna's future business processes and technology investments.[14]

Tracking activities provide you with a set of innovation candidates of potential value to your organization, gathered from a range of sources, and captured in a way that supports further investigation and decision making. The next task is to decide which of these are worth investing time and resources in and which must take a backseat for the time being.

Eight

Rank: Prioritizing the Candidates

Nothing is more dangerous than an idea when it's the only one you have.

—Emile Chartier

Y OUR GOAL IN THE RANK STAGE is to analyze what you have learned about each candidate in your innovation portfolio to select the ones that are most important to pursue. The rank stage acts as the second application of the scope filter in the STREET process (after the track stage filters the set of relevant candidates). Adding a ranking stage to your innovation adoption decision provides a powerful way (often the only way) to defend yourself and your organization against the tendency to be hype driven. If your organization had the resources to examine and act on everything that came along, then you wouldn't need to prioritize. But even a company with a strong balance sheet, a wealth of technical capability, and aggressive, highly capable management must do a certain amount of culling and ranking. There is a limit, even in such capable companies, to management time and attention and a limit to the organization's capacity for change. There are limits as well to the capacity of customers, markets, suppliers, and partners to change. If you cannot do everything, you need to make sure that what you do decide to do is established on the basis of potential value, not by hype alone.

Some innovation leaders take the short route to picking which innovation candidates to adopt: they continue to listen to the same gut feel that led them to start tracking the innovation in the first place. A minority of these leaders actually succeed with that strategy—usually those who have the vision, seniority, experience, and force of personality to drive the innovation to successful adoption, no matter what it takes. For the majority, the task is not so easy, and they find themselves challenged to justify their decision, gain buy-in from others, and defend against those with alternate gut feelings. Even if an innovation leader or team uses gut feel as their primary approach, it is worth recording briefly why other candidates being tracked did not seem important enough to pursue. This offers a small level of protection against market hype–driven adoption timing and helps validate a seemingly subjective judgment.

Beyond gut feel, there are more systematic ranking methods. These approaches fall into two groups: those that assess a single candidate in absolute terms against a predetermined set of objectives or goals, and those that compare candidates in a group against each other.

The individual ranking approach is useful when selection decisions are distributed throughout the organization and there are a relatively small number of innovation candidates in each area. It also tends to be used in autonomous and well-funded innovation teams that have the time, capacity, and independence to pursue a number of candidates before justifying their choices externally. Individual ranking involves answering a set of questions about an innovation to see whether it passes relevant thresholds of value and likelihood of success. If the questions are thoughtfully addressed, they provide a sanity check against hype effects and pet projects.

The group ranking approach is the stronger way to counter hype cycle influences, because looking at the relative value of candidates helps prevent being swept away by a single candidate. It also counters people's natural tendency to "satisfice" and go with the first good-enough alternative rather than trying to find the best choice. It is a particularly useful approach when an individual leader, team, or committee must recommend which candidates to pursue and needs to justify its decision.

Formal ranking activities are performed as the output of a periodic innovation scan (for example, annually or semiannually), typically to feed into broader organizational funding decisions. Midterm adjustments and additions in response to new opportunities are also common. You can find many different techniques for ranking and portfolios in the management literature. We outline a few of the most common and most useful here, followed by a discussion of how to balance the selection across multiple goals, and how to follow up and take action based on the results of the ranking.

Factors for Ranking

To start the ranking process, you need to collate a set of relevant factors and questions to ask about each innovation. During the ranking, you will assign a value or answer to each question. Depending on the level of detail of your tracking activities, much of this information may already be captured in an innovation profile. If you are taking advantage of some of the graphical models described later in this chapter, you will need to convert text descriptions into numeric or scale formats. An approximation or best guess is often all that is available at these early stages of the process but is enough to start the ranking process. You can gather additional information as needed to make a final determination—for example, more detailed cost information for two equally valuable candidates.

Relevant factors include the following:

Scale of benefit. How does the innovation contribute to the objectives identified in the scope stage? Will the benefits be transformational, high, moderate, or low? The higher the better.

Scope. Will the innovation be adopted companywide, or at a local or regional level, or within a specific function or department? The broader the better.

Current maturity. What is the current level of robustness and stability of the innovation? This can be represented as a numeric technology readiness level, as discussed in chapter 7, or using a simpler maturity scale, such as embryonic, emerging, adolescent, or mainstream, as presented in chapter 2. The farther along the maturity scale, the better, although some innovation groups may be deliberately scanning for early-stage opportunities.

Time to value/maturity. How long will the innovation take to reach the Plateau of Productivity from its current position on the hype cycle— that is, how far is it from the start of mainstream adoption? Note that this is different from *current maturity*—two innovations may both be currently "emerging," but one will mature in five years and the other will still be "emerging" for the next ten years. The faster a candidate is progressing toward maturity and predictable value, the more urgently it should be examined.

Risks. Are there major risk factors associated with performance, integration, penetration, or payback? The lower the risk, the better.

Costs. What are the estimated costs for development, integration, adoption, and roll-out? Higher costs are less desirable. For an otherwise attractive candidate, they make detailed evaluation (the next STREET phase) even more crucial, to make sure that the value justifies the high cost.

Sponsors/champions. Are there enthusiastic and influential people associated with a candidate? If so, it's more likely to succeed.

Current activity inside the company. Is there already investigation or adoption of a similar or related innovation that can be leveraged? If experience and skills are already available, the innovation is more likely to be adopted smoothly.

Spider Charts

A spider chart provides a simple graphic view of how well an innovation candidate satisfies objectives. It can help teams or individuals quickly analyze a candidate against six to ten key factors such as the ones listed above.

The chart has several spokes or radials, and each radial represents a factor expressed as an objective (e.g., high benefit, broad scope, low risk). The example in figure 8-1 has eight objectives. The innovation candidate is scored against each objective. Low satisfaction of an objective is plotted closer to the center of the chart. High satisfaction is plotted near the end of the radial, the outside of the diagram.

The result will look something like figure 8-1, in which the shaded area shows at a glance how closely the candidate satisfies the set of objectives that were selected. A large shaded area with no valleys indicates a strong candidate that should be pursued; a small shaded area, a poor one that should be dropped or tracked for a little longer. A lopsided shaded area

FIGURE 8-1

Spider chart of candidate innovation and cutoff threshold

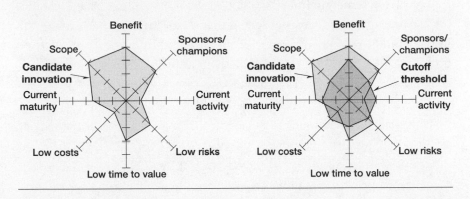

like the one in figure 8-1, or a large shaded area with deep valleys, indicates a promising candidate with potentially serious weaknesses; that is, there are objectives it satisfies well and objectives where it falls short.

Some organizations define thresholds below which an innovation candidate will not be selected for evaluation—one that is too immature, or too costly for current budgets, or below a desired level of benefit. The spider chart makes the relationship between an innovation and the thresholds easy to visualize. The right-hand spider chart in figure 8-1 shows how the innovation fails to achieve the objectives for costs and current activity, indicating that financial and resourcing needs are likely to be a challenge for this candidate.

While spider charts can be used to assess individual innovation candidates, they also can be used to assess quickly and visually a group of candidates. Prepare diagrams for each (using the same objectives for all of them), and then lay the diagrams side by side. The more promising will stand out visually, especially if color rather than shading is used in the diagrams.

Snapshot Hype Cycles

In addition to the timeline hype cycles we have shown in part 1, which track a single innovation over time, hype cycles can be used to show a snapshot of where a set of different innovations are at a single point in time. A snapshot hype cycle can provide an overview of a set of innovations within a particular topic area—for example, an industry such as insurance or automotive—or a particular technology domain, such as security or networking.

In addition to their current position on the hype cycle, we have found it useful to represent the varying speeds that innovations travel through the hype cycle. Innovations with relatively few inhibitors usually traverse the hype cycle to arrive at the Plateau of Productivity in five to eight years, although as we have seen, fast-track and long-fuse innovations operate at significantly different speeds.[1] To acknowledge the variability in timing, each innovation on the hype cycle is assigned to a *time-to-value/maturity* category expressed as "years to mainstream adoption."

Figure 8-2 is a snapshot hype cycle created by Gartner in 2007 for in-car information and communication technologies. It maps a set of technology innovations relevant to the auto industry and its suppliers, and shows the rate of progress of each innovation toward mainstream adoption at the Plateau of Productivity.

FIGURE 8-2

Gartner's hype cycle for vehicle information and communications technologies, 2007

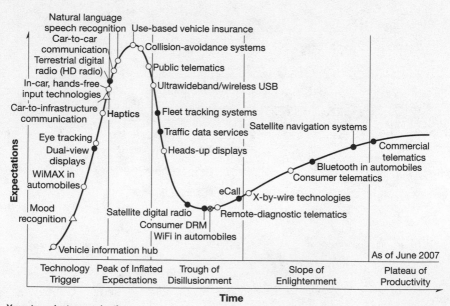

Years to mainstream adoption:
◎ Less than 2 years   ● 2 to 5 years   ○ 5 to 10 years   △ More than 10 years   ⊗ Obsolete before plateau

Source: Thilo Koslowski, "Hype Cycle for Vehicle-Centric Information and Communication Technologies (Vehicle ICT), 2007," Gartner, June 30, 2007.

Snapshot hype cycles are a useful starting point for discussion and prioritization of innovation opportunities, as their relative positioning and their "years to mainstream adoption" ratings both contain implicit assumptions that decision makers need to lay on the table. To determine a candidate's position on the hype cycle, use the indicators described in chapter 4 for each stage of the hype cycle, augmented by the type of quantitative analysis discussed in chapter 1 if available (for example, stock price of relevant suppliers, number of search hits, or tenor of new articles). Determining the speed involves tracking an innovation over a period of time, paying particular attention to the factors that lead to fast-track and long-fuse innovations (also discussed in chapter 4).

Some innovation leaders use snapshot hype cycles as a way to structure a discussion about their innovation candidates with their executives. At Michelin, the emerging technologies team draws on the annual hype cycle report from Gartner (which creates dozens of populated snapshot hype cycles across information technology topics, applications, and industries) to create its own portfolio of several hundred innovation candidates. It plots the most relevant on a snapshot hype cycle and divides the chart into two parts: pre- and post-trough (see figure 8-3).

For pretrough technologies, the team asks itself, "What's here that we should be researching?"—that is, where is it worthwhile for the organization to move out of its comfort zone and adopt aggressively? In the case of

FIGURE 8-3

Michelin's use of hype cycle for candidate selection

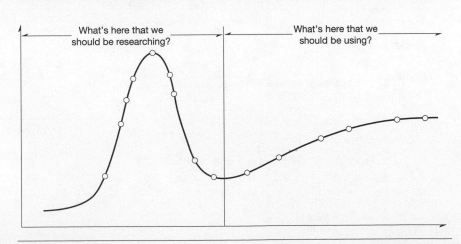

What's here that we should be researching?

What's here that we should be using?

RFID, for example, the company decided to move early, as it could see the technology would be important for its products. For technologies positioned after the trough, the team asks, "What's here that is transformational? Are we using it? If not, why not?" In other words, what are they missing, and do they need to do something about it? The insight from these discussions informs the emerging technology team's ranking and prioritization decisions.[2]

Radar Screens

A radar screen view of an innovation portfolio focuses primarily on the *time-to-value/maturity* factor—that is, it answers the question "How long before I need to pay attention to this innovation?" It uses the metaphor of a pilot's radar screen, with the measure of distance replaced by time. Figure 8-4 shows a radar screen that plots some of the technologies from the vehicle hype cycle in figure 8-2.

Some organizations segment the sections of the radar screen to group different classes of innovation together—for example, by business/process/technology or by technology domain. The size and color of the items on the radar screen can be used to convey additional information,

FIGURE 8-4

Radar screen with information extracted from Gartner's hype cycle for vehicle information and communications technologies, 2007

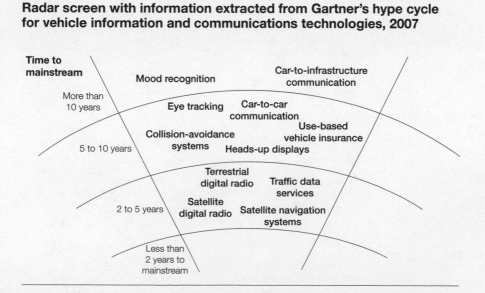

such as the level of potential benefit of each innovation or which candidates are recommended for follow-up.

AstraZeneca's annual CIO radar document includes a graphical depiction of a radar screen segmented into high-level streams of candidates they call "echos," such as business strategy, organizational capability, and enterprise architecture. "We wanted to lay the information out in a way that we could say—here are the things you should give immediate attention to, really home in on, because you are going to be hearing about this in the next three to four months," says Fred Balliet. "Then out at the other edge is stuff that we're hearing a lot about, but we don't believe will actually impact us for another three years. That's something you should begin thinking about or have someone look into a little more deeply."[3]

You can also add a visual indication of the level of interest in an innovation. By using various colors to show the number of groups that have potential applications for an innovation or that have expressed interest in it (e.g., red for high interest, green for low interest), the radar screen can act as a "heat map." High color intensity indicates a higher potential relevance and value for the candidate. A similar heat map approach can be used with other graphical models as well as the radar screen.

Priority Matrix

A priority matrix is a version of a risk/benefit graph that highlights where to focus innovation resources. The vertical axis shows the *expected benefit* of the innovation, while the horizontal axis shows some measure of the innovation's *risk*. Innovation candidates are placed in cells according to their risk and benefit profiles.

Categories for the benefit rating are:

Transformational. Enables new ways of doing business across industries that will result in major shifts in industry dynamics. It changes the game in some fundamental way.

High. Enables new ways of performing business processes that will result in significant revenue growth or cost savings.

Moderate. Provides incremental improvements in established processes that will result in increased revenue or cost savings for an enterprise.

Low. Leads to minor improvements that are difficult to translate into revenue growth or cost savings.

The risk rating can be made in several ways, ranging from a simple measure of the innovation candidate's *time to value/maturity* (with low maturity indicating high risk) to a complex analysis of its multiple risk factors. In its annual hype cycle special report, Gartner creates a companion priority matrix for each hype cycle, with the "years to mainstream adoption" value as the horizontal axis.

Figure 8-5 shows how to interpret a priority matrix. Candidates in the top left of the matrix deserve high-priority investment. These innovations are likely to have high impact and reach a reasonable level of maturity soon. Conservative (type C) companies will probably limit their focus to this area. More aggressive (type A and some type B) companies are probably already using innovations that will mature in less than two years. So they will be more likely to evaluate technologies farther to the right or lower on the priority matrix, innovations that will not be widely used for at least five years but that may provide a competitive edge in the interim.

Note that the potential benefit of an innovation varies significantly from industry to industry and even from company to company in the same in-

FIGURE 8-5

Priority matrix adoption profiles

Benefit	Years to mainstream adoption			
	Less than 2 years	2 to 5 years	5 to 10 years	More than 10 years
Transformational	Invest aggressively if not already adopted	Conservative (type C) investment profile	Moderate (type B) investment profile	Aggressive (type A) investment profile
High	Conservative (type C) investment profile	Moderate (type B) investment profile	Aggressive (type A) investment profile	Invest with caution
Moderate	Moderate (type B) investment profile	Aggressive (type A) investment profile	Invest with caution	Invest with extreme caution
Low	Aggressive (type A) investment profile	Invest with caution	Invest with extreme caution	Invest with extreme caution

dustry, according to the business models or the goals and plans of each. There may also be some intercompany and interindustry variation on the horizontal risk axis, but usually less than on the benefit axis.

A priority matrix is a particularly useful way to dampen the effects of excessive external market hype and can be used in conjunction with a snapshot hype cycle to juxtapose the expectation-driven view with a perspective based on value for your organization. By showing graphically the relative priority of the innovations, it's easier to justify why some innovations are being pursued and not others.

Another way to use the priority matrix is to divide it into quadrants showing the different actions that should be taken according to the risk/benefit combinations, as shown in figure 8-6.

The action for each quadrant is as follows:

Low-risk/high-benefit candidates should receive the most aggressive attention. These are the "low-hanging fruit" that all parties can agree are worthwhile.

High-risk/high-benefit candidates should be evaluated to understand better their risks, benefits, and timing. This type of candidate can present major opportunities once the risks are understood.

FIGURE 8-6

Actions resulting from a priority matrix assessment

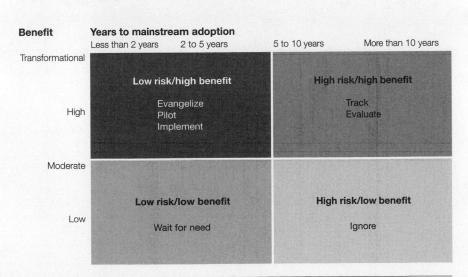

Unfortunately, it's also the type of innovation typically ignored unless there's a group specifically dedicated to evaluating and eliminating the risks.

Low-risk/low-benefit candidates are generally left until there is a distinct need or request for the innovation, or until continued nonadoption starts to increase the risk of being left behind.

High-risk/low-benefit innovation candidates are the lowest priority and are generally passed over in favor of other opportunities.

Innovation Scorecards

An innovation scorecard is a quantitative approach to ranking that offers a more detailed prioritization of multiple innovation candidates. The scorecard provides a format for assessing the relative value of the innovation when weighed against costs and risks. You'll probably find this technique particularly suitable for more careful ranking of fully developed innovation candidates that have already undergone some evaluation of benefits, costs, and risks.

To create a scorecard (see figure 8-7), list the factors contributing to the potential benefits, costs, and risks of the various innovation candidates. To each factor for each candidate, assign a score—for example, 1 to 10—such that favorable features (low risks/costs and high benefits) receive a higher

FIGURE 8-7

Rating scorecard

	Idea #1	Idea #2	Idea #3	. . .	Idea #X
Business objectives	8	7	8		8
Financial objectives	5	9	3		5
Risk factors	6	8	5		2
Business support	8	3	3		6
Score	27	27	19		21
Select?	Y	N	N		N

number, and unfavorable factors (high risks/costs and low benefits) receive a lower number. Then add up the numbers assigned to each candidate, and rank the innovations by their total scores. In more rigorous scorecards, factors are weighted to reflect their relative importance, so that scores for highly important factors count more than scores for factors deemed less important.

Note that some risks may be so important that they overrule all other considerations. For example, even a highly compelling innovation candidate with demonstrable business value can flounder because a single but influential manager opposes it, as shown in figure 8-7 under the factor "business support." (Note that this is the same principle as the cutoff threshold in a spider chart.) In such cases, it's important to remove or negate the risk, say, by delaying adoption until another test location with a strong champion can be found. Identify such risks on the scorecard, and note the score below which they trump other factors.

A note of caution about scorecards: they can quickly become complex as more factors, subfactors, and weighting algorithm variations are added. Once the spreadsheet or tool contains partially hidden formulas and calculations, the conversation among decision makers about real comparative features and issues can be impeded. A good practice is to keep the scoring model as *simple* as possible—don't allow the model owner to keep adding factors and weights beyond the point of diminishing returns.

Portfolio Balancing

Before making the final selection of which innovation candidates to pursue further, you need to make sure your portfolio of successful candidates is balanced. It may turn out, for example, that most of the candidates are focused in one area of the business. Progressing with all those candidates might overload that area's capacity for change and also upset people in other areas that feel neglected. Or the candidates might all tend toward high risk or low risk, toward long term or short term, toward one geographic region, or toward any number of other distortions. If the portfolio is somehow found to be unbalanced, you may need to reconsider some of the candidates.

One way to achieve a balance is to divide the portfolio into distinct categories and allocate each category a percentage of the overall portfolio.

For example, with respect to benefit, the categories of *run the business*, *grow the business*, and *transform the business* can be used as follows:

> *Run the business* applies to innovations that help keep things running smoothly. They are usually (but not always) relatively mundane, low-risk innovations with a fast but low value return. Typically around 20 to 30 percent of innovations fall into this category, although the percentage can be significantly higher among companies with a less aggressive enterprise personality, or when operating in an economic downturn when transformational innovation is hard to finance.

> *Grow-the-business* innovations are those with clear and substantial potential to help the organization improve its performance. They involve moderate risk, and pay back well within the framework of how the business traditionally operates and makes investments. These are usually the backbone of the portfolio and should make up around 40 to 60 percent of all candidates.

> *Transform-the-business* innovations break the mold. They force reassessment of how the industry works or challenge some aspect of the current business operating model. They might make up 10 to 40 percent of all candidates, depending on how eagerly the organization pursues radical change.

A benefit of segmenting the candidates in this manner is that you can compare like with like. By setting aside a portion of your budget for innovations that may transform the business, for example, you are not comparing a high-risk, high-return undertaking with one that is a sure but small win.

You may be tempted to add more levels to this—perhaps five or seven seems like a better number. You should resist this temptation in order to make sure that you stick with an organization-agnostic and abstract classification system. It can be easy for the categories to slide gradually through multiple revisions into departmental and functional proxies such as "market development" (subtext: marketing department autonomy zone) or "mandatory/regulatory" (subtext: chief legal counsel's budget), which can then end up just dividing investment equally or on established existing departmental pecking-order weightings—rather than making real innovation and change value-based decisions. This can impede some of the most valuable of innovations to adopt—those that offer value of a new type in areas that fall between existing organization structure and control lines. In the late 1990s those companies that stuck to the more abstracted analysis of inbound innovations changed their organizations to accommodate the Internet—for example, by creating a centrally governed Web site. Those that let their decision tools fall along existing organization structure lines ended up with many different company Web sites. Some of those are still cleaning up the mess today.

Taking Action Based on Ranking Results

In conducting a ranking of innovation candidates, you're likely to find that discussions around the values assigned to individual candidates are often more useful than the final ranking itself. In particular, breaking down the evaluation into distinct factors and objectives forces explicit discussion around all key factors and minimizes the risk that you'll overlook something important. This approach forces you and all others involved to be explicit about the reasons for your evaluations, which helps counter personality-driven decision making.

Needless to say, you should use such approaches as scorecards and priority matrices with care and judgment. They can become overly mechanical, and they can be gamed as participants try to bubble their favorite candidate to the top of the listing. According to Martin Kagan of ExxonMobil's IT architecture and integration group, "To be honest, we've got all kinds of ways of scoring, so we often end up with too many that score too high. So we formally acknowledge the need for tweaking, using a little intuition and a little judgment and bringing in other factors. There are many more good ideas than we have money to spend."[4] Intuition, especially when based on deep experience, can be a key input factor not measurable in any traditional way. As long as you ask the hard questions about how well each candidate meets organizational value and risk objectives, and respect the varying opinions that result, intuition and judgment are not incompatible with the more formalized ranking approaches discussed in this chapter.

The final choice of which innovation candidates will move forward to the evaluate stage is made differently in different organizations. It may be a recommendation from a central innovation team, based on the kind of ranking exercises we've just described. It may be a vote by members of an innovation committee. Or a key executive may decide unilaterally, on the basis of information, analysis, and recommendations presented to him or her.

One other set of decisions is still to be made at this point: what to do with the candidates not selected. In general, most will be placed on a list of candidates to watch, and a few of the least relevant will be dropped entirely. Organizations that maintain an active innovation portfolio update the entries for each candidate at this point, indicating the current status (e.g., inactive, tracking, evaluating) and incorporating any new information gathered during the ranking process.

Nine

Evaluate: Understanding Rewards and Risks

Never mistake a clear view for a short distance.

—Paul Saffo[1]

AFTER SCANNING THE HORIZON, capturing candidates that look as if they fit the needs of your company, and ranking those candidates, you're left with a number of innovations that look promising.

If the benefits, risks, and costs are well understood—for example, if you're adopting a mature innovation with a track record of successful adoption elsewhere—you may decide to proceed directly to adoption without further evaluation. However, skipping the evaluation phase does not mean dropping out of the STREET process. Even with a relatively straightforward adoption, many of the lessons and guidelines in the evangelize and transfer phases are still likely to apply, particularly if the innovation will be used by a broader community than just the person or group making the adoption decision. Most likely, though, the majority of your innovation candidates will need to be evaluated.

Your goal in evaluating an innovation is to reach a level of comfort that it will do what you want it to do. Will it deliver the value—in your specific organizational context—that it's supposed to deliver? To answer that question, you must come to terms with the real benefits and risks involved.

This is the third and final application of the scope filter in the STREET process. After the track stage determines which innovations are relevant, and the rank stage determines which candidates should be evaluated as a priority, the evaluation stage determines whether an innovation is worth moving forward into adoption at this particular point in time. There may be multiple substages in this filtering, particularly for innovations requiring a large investment, as the innovation moves through more detailed and more costly evaluation before a final decision is made.

At the end of the evaluation, one of the following four decisions will be made, as shown in figure 9-1.

1. *Proceed to next stage.* Move to the evangelize and transfer stages as the first step of deploying the innovation.

2. *Reevaluate.* Revisit the evaluation in a revised form—for example, with a different application or an alternative product.

3. *Return to tracking stage.* Delay further consideration of adoption until the innovation matures further and can be reevaluated.

4. *Drop from consideration.* Remove the innovation from the portfolio being tracked.

Planning the Evaluation Project

The scale of an evaluation project may range from an individual downloading free tools from the Web to try them out, to informal in-house prototyping, or to a multimillion-dollar trial involving thousands of people in

FIGURE 9-1

Decisions in the evaluation stage of the STREET process

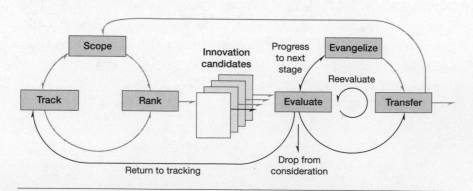

multiple locations. The size of investment required to fully adopt the innovation drives the overall weight and formality of the evaluation activities. An evaluation project should perform the minimum necessary to obtain the information and insight you need. For large and disruptive innovations, you may want to break the evaluation into multiple stages to lower the initial level of commitment.

One company uses the guideline $3 \times 3 \times 3$ for its initial evaluation projects—they should take no more than three people working for three months at a cost of $30,000. At ExxonMobil, evaluation projects range from $50,000 to $100,000, taking several months of effort. ExxonMobil's IT architecture and integration group is responsible for an "alpha phase" of mainly paper-based information gathering and a "beta phase" that involved hands-on proof-of-concept and usability testing. In other organizations, depending on the size and scope of the various groups involved in an evaluation, different stages of the evaluation may be performed by different teams. At DISA, for example, the technology reconnaissance group creates recommendations for other parts of the agency to follow up on.

The most useful evaluation projects focus on a specific application of the innovation, not on its potential in the abstract. If there is not yet a business champion for the innovation, you should identify one during evaluation, because the availability of a strong advocate is a key factor in the decision to proceed or not. In addition, think about how to involve ultimate end users in the evaluation, to begin the transfer process and ensure a path forward if the evaluation is successful.

The project plan for an innovation evaluation project should contain the normal planning components: a work breakdown, milestones, staffing, timeline, cost, deliverables, decision points. Your plan should include the explicit goals for the evaluation, and the criteria by which success will be determined. You should include an initial indication of longer-term plans, particularly staffing and funding, to ensure that a path to further development exists if evaluation leads to a decision to proceed.

Getting to the right go/no-go decision is important, but it's not one that should be made by technical specialists and consultants in the innovation alone. Specialists on their own are not always good at judging how end users will take to an innovation. Those end users should be a big part of the evaluation phase. The question is not only what benefits an innovation will deliver, but what will be required to make that innovation actually work in your organization (penetration and payback risks). The goal is not simply to get the innovation in through the door but to roll it out to full adoption. Understanding how to do that should be a key part of your evaluation project.

What to Evaluate: Benefits, Risks, and Costs

An evaluation project begins the process of determining whether there is a business case for the innovation, although it does not typically produce the same detailed financial plan required for a full-scale deployment and rollout of the innovation. Depending on the nature of the innovation, creating this level of detail may itself be a large project that will follow the decision to adopt. At this evaluation stage, there will be too many unknowns for you to specify benefits and costs in detail. For example, you might not know how much it will cost to roll out a wireless e-mail device until you ask all management teams to forecast their usage. Or you won't know the cost of consulting needed to install a Six Sigma development program until you've requested proposals from several consulting organizations. What's most important at this stage is to convey the big picture rather than precise numbers. Your aim is to estimate benefits, costs, and risks to a level that enables a decision to be made.

Evaluating Benefits

Determining the potential benefits of an innovation is particularly challenging during the early stages of the hype cycle, as there is little evidence from other organizations about the real value gained once the innovation is deployed. Even once an innovation is better understood as it climbs the Slope of Enlightenment, there are still two major challenges: the value may be not be easily expressed in numerical terms, and the experience of other organizations may not be applicable to your environment. You need to find ways to explore a candidate innovation's value proposition that are appropriate to the innovation itself and to the impact on your organization.

Like most government and not-for-profit organizations, the Ohio Bureau of Workers Compensation is driven not by competitive advantage but by the need to help its clients. Its mission is to support workers in the state of Ohio and help them suffer as little as possible in the event of work-related injury. In this situation, traditional return-on-investment measures are of little value. Jim Wasil, the director of advanced technology information services at the Bureau of Workers Compensation, stresses the need to focus on intangible returns. "We're trying to move beyond the perspective of a strict, pencil-sharpening chief financial officer," says Wasil. "If you can cut a week off somebody getting a check, that if they didn't get they might lose their house, how do you place a value on that?"[2]

In looking at the particular challenges of business cases for early-stage innovation, a useful way to structure discussions and investigations is to consider four sources of value: solving a *problem*, creating an *opportunity*, making someone *feel good*, and making someone *look good*.[3] The first two are the type of value propositions that fit well into traditional business case analysis, but the second two—making someone feel good or look good—are a valuable addition to acknowledge the "softer" benefits that are often overlooked in metrics-driven organizations. Delivering an injured worker a check that lets them keep their house is a clear example of making someone feel good.

You need to allow yourself a certain amount of creative freedom to explore the full range of benefits an innovation has to offer. Often an innovation is identified and taken to evaluation for one fairly narrow reason. Even where that reason seems compelling, you should still try to expand the list of benefits within and across the different types of value. For example, a pharmaceutical company may decide to evaluate Tablet PCs to improve the productivity of its sales force by removing the need for them to manage piles of marketing brochures. The initial trigger is solving a problem for the sales force, but additional value may come from improved customer retention of the product information (creating an opportunity), improving the customers' opinion of the sales force (making someone look good), and increasing the free time of the sales force (making someone feel good).

Table 9-1 shows examples of benefits organized according to whether they affect your organization's people, processes, business, or infrastructure.[4] They include examples from all four sources of value—for example, minimizing errors to solve a problem, enabling strategic partnerships as an opportunity, improving employee morale to make them feel good, and improving your company's brand image to make it look good. Use this as a checklist when you are considering the range of benefits that an innovation can bring, but don't limit yourself to these if you think of other ways to express the value.

TABLE 9-1

Example benefits of an innovation candidate

People	Processes	Business	Infrastructure
Improve training and career development	Reduce transaction processing times	Improve brand image	Increase reliability, quality, and integrity
Improve employee morale	Shorten product development	Create new revenue sources	Reduce complexity
Remove obstacles to productivity	Eliminate non-value-added tasks	Improve decision speed and quality	Lower future development costs
Repurpose employees to more value-added tasks	Minimize errors/rework	Enable premium pricing	Reduce software purchase prices and license fees
Develop process experts	Standardize processes	React faster to business change	Reduce ongoing support costs
Reduce personnel costs	Implement self-service	Improve customer service—quality and response times	Increase future scalability, flexibility, and agility
Reduce headcount	Implement best practices	Reduce risk	Decrease facilities and management costs
	Centralize customer service	Grow market share	Eliminate redundant information storage
		Enable strategic partnerships	
		Comply with regulations	

Where possible, the benefits should be related back to the work that you did in the scope phase to identify your business value context. By figuring out the impact of an innovation on specific business goals and metrics that matter to leaders and stakeholders in your company, you'll be better able to predict and evangelize the improvement the innovation will bring.

With innovations that involve change on multiple levels, it's important to identify clearly where the various benefits are actually coming from. For example, it's common for a process change and a technology to be confused. The innovation value more often arises from the process change enabled by a new technology. However, in marketing technologies, vendors often tout them as enabling changes that, in fact, could be made in other ways. This was the case with many of the RFID initiatives undertaken in response to the Wal-Mart mandate to its suppliers to use RFID. Companies found that significant benefits, which were at first thought to be enabled by RFID-based process change, could in fact be achieved by reengineering the process but still using the old bar code approach.

Similarly, in the middle 1990s many uses were proposed for contactless smart cards. These were credit card–like devices that used a chip and an antenna buried inside it rather than a magnetic strip on the back. When they were placed near a reader, information flowed wirelessly between the card and the computer network attached to the reader. This was great technology for implementing "electronic purse" concepts such as the London Underground Oyster card travel pass, where value was stored on the card and decremented with each journey taken.

However, in the early days many other uses were suggested for the technology, such as tracking people. When this technology was first offered to the travel industry, a number of unwarranted uses were proposed and indeed evaluated by some companies. These included tracking people in an airport in order to round them up when they failed to appear at a departure gate on time. While on-time departure was a key airline metric, and so an innovation that improved it was considered significant, the problem was actually much simpler to deal with in other ways. For example, airline personnel could enforce a policy of closing the airplane doors fifteen minutes before departure. Another use suggested for smart cards was automated access to facilities such as lounges, but that task could be accomplished with a much cheaper conventional magnetic stripe card. The smart card, with its greater memory, could be used to hold information of value to the customer, such as frequent-flier mileage. But it turned out to be easier and cheaper to provide access to that information via the Web.

New technologies and other innovations often initiate fresh conversation about a tired or ineffective process that could be improved in other ways more easily and cheaply. Be clear about what an innovation can *uniquely* offer, and keep that as the foreground proposition in evaluation.

Evaluating Risks and Costs

In addition to assessing the potential benefits, evaluation needs to focus on learning, understanding, and minimizing the different types of risk associated with an innovation. Gaps or weak areas in the innovation profile can highlight where you should focus your investigations. It can help you plan an effective evaluation project if you think about the four types of value gaps we discussed in chapter 2.

Performance. Does the innovation work reliably as expected?

Integration. Does it perform within cost and time requirements in a real, working environment? Do you know how to incorporate the adoption into an existing environment?

Penetration. Will the ultimate users of the innovation embrace it and assimilate it into their daily work? For the innovation to provide value, must all or most of its users adopt and use it?

Payback. How confident are you that the projected business value will materialize as expected and on schedule?

Table 9-2 shows potential risks associated with an innovation, structured according to each of the value gaps, along with some pointers on how to mitigate or defend against each risk.[5]

Along with benefits and risks, estimating costs is the third key element of the evaluation. Most innovations of substance will involve some upfront costs to purchase and deploy. These costs should be treated as an investment like any other and should conform to your company's general methods and approaches, such as return on investment (ROI), net present value (NPV), or other standard financial assessment techniques. When you're assessing an innovation's financial impact, it's often useful to ask, "What increase in cost would cause me to abandon this investment?" If the answer is only a small percentage, then the investment may be excessively risky.

You should assume that the return on adopted innovations will be lower and later than initially expected because of costs and risks not identified. Returns substantially greater than forecast do occur but they're rare.

How to Evaluate: Prototypes, Pilots, and Champion/Challenger

Evaluation of an innovation candidate involves a range of activities, including meetings with vendors, competitive analysis, financial calculations, team brainstorming sessions and discussions with others in your organization with a business, process, or architecture perspective. It is also common to conduct more hands-on, experimental evaluations of the innovation, in the form of prototypes, pilots, and champion/challenger testing.

Prototypes

Prototypes are a rough-and-ready version of an innovation used for internal investigations. They are used primarily as a risk-reduction tool to explore areas of high uncertainty, particularly those relating to performance and integration risks. Prototypes might be used, for example, to:

TABLE 9-2

Example risks of an innovation candidate

Type of risk	How to mitigate the risk
PERFORMANCE RISK	
Innovation doesn't meet performance levels in real-world setting	Solution selection due diligence; phased implementation; pilot programs
Performance is inconsistent or unreliable	Extended pilot programs and trials
Innovation is superseded or fails in the marketplace	Innovation maturity analysis; industry outlook; mainstream/late adoption
Innovation is dependent on another system that fails to deliver	Risk assessment of other projects where dependencies exist
INTEGRATION RISK	
Unable to manage solution complexity	Phased implementation; pilot programs; additional parallel testing; custom training program; hire new skills
Lack of skills in the marketplace	Custom training program
Unable to maintain project schedule	Third-party independent validation and verification program; best project managers assigned
Inability to integrate with current systems	Solution selection due diligence; pilot programs
PENETRATION RISK	
User resistance to change	Change management and communication programs
Users do not see personal benefit	Evaluation of individual, not just corporate, benefit
Users use occasionally or superficially	Training, seeding power users
PAYBACK RISK	
Business requirements are inaccurate	Comprehensive requirements gathering
System does not meet business requirements	Solution selection due diligence; pilot programs
Business requirements change	Business accountability for requirements and formal sign-off; phased implementation
Project costs more than anticipated	Total cost of ownership analysis; contract minimizes risk of cost increases
Supplier stops selling/supporting the innovation or goes out of business	Supplier outlook assessment; contract terms
Benefits are elusive or less than anticipated	Conservative benefits estimation, pilot programs, adoption plan with key benefits milestones and dependencies
Lack of full success leads to reputation damage	Detailed pilot evaluation; mainstream/late adoption

- Assess the robustness, performance, or accuracy of the innovation.

- Determine its impact on established architecture and infrastructure.

- Explore alternate process options created by the innovation—for example, through the use of simulation and modeling tools.

- Refine the scope of how the innovation will be used.

- Estimate the costs of deploying a pilot or full-scale rollout.

Prototypes are also sometimes used as a marketing tool to increase internal awareness of an innovation's potential and to inspire management and users by demonstrating potential business benefits. Marketing prototypes should focus on showcasing the new business capabilities that the innovation will drive.

You may also use prototypes in a more exploratory manner—for example, to gauge market reaction or to be perceived as a market leader. In 2006, Volkswagen (VW) demonstrated a new prototype in-car navigation system at trade shows. The prototype used the Google Earth 3-D maps and a 3-D graphics processor. Both, as well as in-car GPS navigation, are common, easily available technologies. But VW was constructing a new combination of these technologies with more advanced features and was using a prototype to test market reactions. "What we're doing here is to prototype an application where we show photorealistic 3D graphics in the vehicle with an online connection," said Daniel Rosario, a senior project engineer at VW's Electronics Research Lab in Palo Alto, California.[6] The full value of such a system would require Internet access from the car—something that, while possible, was still uncommon. So this innovation might take five years to bring to market in full, according to Rosario.

It's important that you clearly define the role and function of a prototype in advance, because some goals may be incompatible in a single prototype. For example, a technical prototype might uncover performance issues but would be unsuitable for a high-impact management presentation, while a proof-of-concept screen show could highlight changes in business processes but would not test an innovation's limitations.

You should be clear from the outset whether a prototype is intended to morph into operational use or whether it's a "throwaway" version. With innovations requiring significant in-house development or customization, it's usually unwise to allow prototypes to creep into operational use, even if there are enthusiastic and urgent requests to do so. The goals of a proto-type and of an operational innovation are frequently incompatible. The levels of robustness, security, quality testing, and so on required for opera-tional deployment usually exceed those for a prototype. Trying to incorpo-rate them into a prototype would significantly slow down delivery of the prototype and hence the decision as to whether operational deployment is even warranted.

Prototyping can serve as a vehicle to begin the process of transfer that the innovation will require. For example, business unit representatives might be brought in to help define requirements for the prototype of a new workflow based on a new technology. Or an IT architecture group might be involved in assessing what upgrades would be required in the corporate network if a new technology were to be deployed.

Pilots and Trials

A further way to investigate unforeseen problems, particularly with user penetration issues, is to develop pilots and trials for use in a live op-erational environment. The focus of a pilot is to evaluate the usability and effectiveness of an innovation with a small number of users, before a wider introduction. This is a big step beyond a prototype, which typically only demonstrates basic feasibility under controlled, laboratory-like conditions.

To fully assess an innovation's potential benefits and issues, pilots must be evaluated by typical users trying to perform their normal tasks. The evaluation should include staff or customers new to the innovation, not just those involved in the pilot development, because they will have differ-ent preconceptions and prejudices.

You should use both quantitative and qualitative evaluation criteria to determine the extent to which the innovation is likely to improve a process—for example, by reducing transaction time or increasing effi-ciency. For example, in the aftermath of 9/11, aviation authorities around the world scanned the horizon for new ways to tighten aviation security. One innovation, biometric identification, had been evolving for a while. It seemed promising but had never been seriously tried.

After ranking various alternatives—including facial features, hand geom-etry, fingerprints, and even gait recognition—airline industry groups se-lected iris and fingerprint recognition as approaches that might work well.

Using prototypes, different trials were conducted in different countries. For example, the company running Amsterdam's Schiphol airport tested a system for speeding business frequent fliers through security. Airport authorities registered 1,500 willing volunteers for a test scheme called "Privium," which seemed to go well. But aviation authorities across Europe and beyond knew that widespread use of biometrics for all or most fliers would be more problematic. It would involve children, the elderly, the handicapped, and a wider span of age and other physical characteristics than those of a small group of travel-savvy businessmen.

More detailed trials were conducted for the Netherlands and British governments and others. The trial reports reveal the sort of awkward practical details that all innovations must overcome. For example, from a U.K. report: "A small number of participants with glasses failed verification when they wore their glasses and passed when they took their glasses off."[7] And an example from a Netherlands report: "In children who suck their thumbs a lot the skin of the finger is very soft, and it is often impossible to take a good print from such fingers."[8]

If such problems were not caught at an early stage by thorough piloting work, full projects might be approved without understanding the risks or designing or budgeting for them. In this case, delaying elderly people and small children at airport security checkpoints could have been damaging at a time when confidence in security competence was paramount.

A pilot also represents a critical phase in the technology transfer process when an innovation team and business unit staff members work together. By the end of the pilot phase, the organization ultimately responsible for the rollout must be prepared to lead the development, deployment, and ongoing support of the innovation.

Champion/Challenger Testing

An additional purpose of a pilot may be to evaluate the relative benefit of a new approach using the innovation. This test is a statistical real-world comparison that pits an already-established way of operating (the champion) against the innovation (the challenger). Because changes to an operation process or system can be risky, a champion/challenger test can reduce the risk of exposing the entire current business operation to the new approach. It typically involves running a trial with a recruited group of test users and perhaps a control group for comparison over a defined period.

A similar approach can be used to test multiple variations on an innovation and see which one generates the best response. This approach is well established in marketing campaigns (e.g., which version of a direct mailing, each sent to a different group of consumers, generates the best response). This can be set up as either a champion/challenger to see the value of the innovation or as multiple challengers.

The perpetual beta world of the Web discussed in chapter 1 is a natural test bed for evaluating alternatives. The Web may make it more challenging for adopters to stay on top of the range of available innovations, but it helps providers of an innovation obtain rapid feedback on the best way to deliver their capabilities.

For example, four days before Google launched its Google News service, the development team had to decide which of two functions they should add before the service went live.[9] The choices were to rank news by date (most recent first) or by location (local news first). The team members couldn't agree on which would be more important to users. They decided to launch without either feature and see what users requested. By the end of the first day, the requests to sort by date outnumbered requests to sort by location by one hundred to one. By saving its development effort until after its users had spoken, Google was able to focus its resources where it mattered most.

Challenges and Best Practices in Evaluation

In the summer of 1992 the St. Francis Winery of Sonoma Valley, California, decided to evaluate a radical innovation: plastic corks.[10] A lot was at stake. The technology might reduce the 3 percent wastage rate typical for wine producers at that time, but it could seriously irritate customers of a product in which traditions and standards are important attributes. They launched a trial of plastic corks in 2,700 cases of wine to determine whether the technology would be worth adopting. They had to test consumer acceptance, leakage rates, returns, and many other factors. The cork insertion failure rate in the bottling process was found to be comparable to that of natural cork, and some customers didn't even notice the synthetic substitute. Because of the positive evaluation findings, the company stepped up its use of plastic corks the following year.

But *sixteen years* later, plenty of vintners around the world are still hesitating about this wine packaging innovation, and screw caps, and Web direct selling, and organic production. They are doing more tests, debating, and continually watching market developments. This type of analysis paralysis is an enemy of innovation. Without defined and time-boxed organized processes for candidates, innovation evaluation can become an ongoing and indeterminate consumer of corporate resources. You need to identify and mitigate all the major obstacles that might cause the innovation to fail, but you have to accept that you cannot know all the detailed risks in advance or how they will play out.

Analysis paralysis is a common challenge in evaluation activities. In observing the way many organizations go about the evaluation phase, we've identified a number of similar challenges, and best practices in dealing with them.

Avoiding Errors and Traps in Evaluation

If we could be 100 percent confident in our estimates of risks, costs, and benefits and how they will change over time, the adoption decision would be much easier. But we exist in a world of uncertainty, and as we explored in chapter 2, our brains and culture have evolved ways to keep us from being overwhelmed by the unknown and help us make decisions in the face of uncertainty.

Many biases in the behavior of organizations and in your default behavior as an individual create the sort of traps that lead to either missed opportunity or wasted effort. Understanding these biases can help. There are also practices that can help counter them.

SATISFACTORY VERSUS OPTIMAL

One way we all avoid analysis paralysis is by collecting enough information to arrive at a satisfactory but not necessarily optimal decision. Given that you know you will be operating with incomplete information, one of your main challenges in evaluating an innovation is knowing whether you have found out just enough to make the decision to commit or whether you are risking too much because the evaluation has not gone deep enough. One approach is to limit the length of the evaluation project to, say, a few weeks or up to three months, depending on the complexity of the innovation. Even though you may need to do further evaluation, keeping each project short will force you to focus on the most important points and arrive at a high-level determination of risks, benefits, and timing.

UNDERESTIMATING TIME AND EFFORT

In the field of artificial intelligence, researchers have argued for forty years that computers with "true" artificial intelligence will become feasible once faster computers are available and ten to fifteen more years of research is done. Slow-maturing technologies such as artificial intelligence, machine translation, biometrics, and speech recognition progress endlessly toward maturity but never seem to reach the long-promised point of producing significant value. On a smaller scale, as your investigation proceeds, note whether you feel you're getting closer to the resolution of performance, integration, and penetration issues or whether more complexities and concerns just keep cropping up. Keep Hofstadter's Law in mind: that the time and effort required to complete a project are always more than you expect, even when you take into account Hofstadter's Law.[11]

OVERESTIMATING ADOPTION CAPACITY

There is a natural limit to the number of innovations that can be absorbed by individuals and organizations in a given period of time. So, independently of the specific innovation itself, you need to examine the organization's ability to absorb further change, particularly if this innovation will create major disruption in existing work patterns. Understanding user behavior is becoming increasingly difficult because technology is changing long-standing habits of communication, collaboration, entertainment, shopping, payment, and information seeking.

OVERCONFIDENCE

Most people are overconfident in their own ability and the likelihood that their decisions will be correct. Even experts find it difficult to assess how confident they should be in their own predictions. Experiments have shown that as professionals gain more experience, the rate at which they improve slows down. However, their confidence continues to grow and so loses touch with their actual ability. The same is true with research and experimentation. More and more research and evaluation may not generate real additional value, but it can lead you to feel disproportionately more confident in your conclusions.

Large amounts of performance feedback can help people calibrate their ability to know when they should be confident in their predictions. Studies of several professions, including doctors and lawyers, have revealed mete-orologists to be the best at knowing when to be confident and when not. It's no coincidence that they are the group receiving the most constant and rapid feedback about their often public predictions.[12]

Listing reasons for and against a decision can also help you calibrate confidence with accuracy. The crucial step in creating such lists is creating the list of opposing reasons—that is, the list of reasons that your preferred answer might be wrong. A simpler method is to adjust downward any as-sessments of confidence automatically—10 to 20 percent is a typical error range. In particular, high levels of confidence are especially unwarranted when predicting how people (as opposed to technology) will behave.[13]

CONFIRMATION BIAS

When you're examining an innovation, it's natural to look for evidence that it's improving, gathering pace, and likely to succeed (and as we saw in chapter 2, this is one of the factors leading to the Peak of Inflated Expecta-tions). However, this search for confirming evidence can lead to a blink-ered perspective. Armed with four or five positive cases—for example, about an innovation's success in other organizations—you can convince yourself and others to proceed. A tougher test might be to invert the evidence-gathering mechanism. Force yourself to gather evidence that the innova-tion doesn't work, won't work, and that those who try to adopt it will fail to find value in it. This may seem odd behavior for a believer and evangel-ist, but it's a necessary discipline. For example, researchers Edward Russo and Paul Schoemaker point to an investor, Jay Freedman, who applies this approach when gathering intelligence on a company: "He deliberately asks questions designed to 'disconfirm' what he thinks is true. If Freed-man thinks the disposable diaper business is becoming less price compet-itive, for example, he will ask an executive a question that implies the opposite, such as 'Is it true that price competition is getting tougher in dis-posable diapers?'"[14]

CONSERVATISM

Once people have formed an initial judgment, they don't easily change their view in light of new information. Some psychologists claim that "it takes anywhere from two to five observations to do one observation's worth of work in inducing the subject to change his opinions."[15]

This inherent conservatism is exacerbated in group settings by the perceived need to look decisive and remain firm. As an innovation leader, you may be reluctant to change your opinion about an innovation, even in light of discouraging evidence. As a result, you might be prone to stick with an innovation when evidence suggests you should let it go. One way to overcome this aspect of human nature is to explicitly espouse neutrality from the beginning about all innovation candidates. Expressions such as "looking at a promising innovation" can imply support, while "under investigation" is more neutral. Consider standardizing the terms used to describe innovations under assessment to keep them neutral.

FRAMING

As you discuss options and try to arrive at a recommendation, you need to be aware that how a proposition is presented makes a significant difference on whether people choose to accept it. For example, asking, "Shall we go ahead with this project?" versus "Shall we put this idea on hold?" can make a significant difference in the answers you get, because "yes" is likely to be the preferred answer to each to a certain degree. People like to respond positively, and that preference may swing the decision in borderline cases.

Overcoming Estimation Problems

As you proceed through evaluation, you will be making estimates and predictions and basing judgments on them. Here are several steps you can take to make sure your estimates are reasonably accurate and free from basic biases:

Include different views to remove estimator's bias. Soliciting advice from several sources can reveal very different perspectives on the same subject. Note, though, that others may have their own hidden agendas and biases.

Understand the assumptions. To base an estimation on more than gut feelings, you need some foundation for it in the real world. The drivers and potential obstacles or inhibitors behind your predictions should be clear. Making those assumptions explicit will be useful both in evaluating the estimate and in modifying it on the basis of new information or environmental changes.

Examine different scenarios. You should consider a range of possible futures to uncover and avoid potentially disastrous decisions. This can be accomplished by doing some limited scenario planning.

Learn the subject matter. The most important qualification of a decision maker is that he or she know enough about the business, innovation, and related subjects to make insightful and accurate judgments. Ignorance of relevant matters can easily lead to misinterpretation, poor decisions, and misguided implementation.

Exploiting External Sources of Evaluation

In addition to your own estimation and evaluation efforts, you might find a wealth of external information that can be used to inform the adoption decision. Other adopters who are farther ahead in their cycle can be a valuable source of knowledge and are often willing to share what they've learned if they're not direct competitors. Even in a competitive environment, sharing of experience can still take place for innovations not tied to immediate competitive advantage.

If you're working with one or more suppliers of an innovation, you can ask them for referrals to others who have already adopted. Even contacts provided by a supplier are usually surprisingly blunt about their experience with the innovation and the supplier.

Dealing with People and Change Management

One of the biggest risk assessment mistakes innovation adopters make is to underestimate the effects of the innovation on people. Changing the way people work or define themselves and their roles is not trivial. Resistance may be due to factors such as personality (some people are naturally less innovative and more prone to resistance), incentive conflicts, lack of understanding of the rationale for adoption, and skepticism about the usefulness of the system and whether it will "take" (and, hence, whether it's worth learning).[16] Fear also plays a major role, including fear of job change, loss of power and influence, and loss of prestige and of "being an expert" in the old way of doing things. If an innovation requires widespread change, you must identify the changes required and their effects on the individuals and groups involved.

People's resistance to something new can be subtle, and their reasons not immediately obvious. For example, observations of trials of computerized information kiosks and ticket machines in public spaces have often revealed people hovering in the vicinity of the machine but not using it. Fear of not being able to cope, holding up others in the line, or looking silly are often the root cause. But only careful and open questioning of participants will reveal such important subtleties. When people see others walk up to a device and use it easily, they're more likely to use it themselves. So, hosting a kiosk for a while with coaches who can help seed the population with confident users can make all the difference.

Assessing change involves digging deeper than the obvious changes to process and infrastructure. You will need to look at whether the innovation has an impact on organizational structure and responsibilities and, perhaps hardest of all, how it affects people's mindsets. What beliefs and behavior codes do people have today? What new beliefs and behaviors will people espouse once the innovation is adopted?

For example, in the early days of the Internet, people tended to focus on technological aspects such as Web browser software, e-mail, and explaining what hypertext was. But consideration of other factors turned out to be equally important, such as understanding which department was responsible for the Web site (structure), how content would be produced (process), and how open and responsive the organization should be online (mind-set).

Think about cultural, business, and economic impacts on the innovation and its adoption over time. These can have double-edged effects. For example, in late 1990s, earpieces for cellular phones were widely available at a reasonable price, but people weren't using them for fear of looking "geeky." Two factors helped create change: first, emerging health concerns that holding a cell phone next to your head might cause brain damage caused people to overcome the social fear. Second, various countries and cities introduced laws banning the use of handheld mobile phones while driving. Health and safety concerns ended up being the catalyst that overcame the more subtle social fear about appearances.

Documenting the Evaluation Results

Innovation evaluation reports present the results of evaluation efforts in a way that facilitates making an adoption decision. An evaluation document typically follows a structure similar to that of the original innovation profile prepared back in the track stage, but contains significantly more detail on each topic. In particular, it should include more detailed assessment of benefits and costs as input to a full business case. Also, it's important to highlight remaining areas of risk. The report can incorporate the results of ad hoc experimentation, surveys, competitive analysis, user or business model analysis, or prototyping and pilot activities as outlined above, although you may not want to include all the details in the main report.

The report should also examine alternatives to the innovation by asking the question "How might you achieve the same benefits in a different way?" Perhaps there is a work-around using your organization's current capabilities and assets, or maybe an alternate innovation. And what would happen if you chose to do nothing for now? Consider in particular the staying power of existing methods and devices before moving on to new ones. Organizations can get hooked on implementing the next thing and the next and the next without milking the current environment for all its potential benefits. Look farther into the future. How many versions of an innovation will there be over the coming decade? Do you need to adopt each in turn, or could you skip some deliberately in order to maximize returns from those you do pick while holding down overall costs and risks?

If you haven't created a hype cycle for the innovation candidate, now is a good time to assess where the innovation is currently, and how fast it is moving through the hype cycle, using the guidelines and indicators in chapter 4. This will help determine how confident you should be in your estimates of benefits, cost, and risk (the earlier the innovation is in the cycle, the less confident you should be). It will also alert you to potential issues or opportunities with respect to user acceptance and management buy-in, depending on the level and tenor of hype in the external marketplace.

The report style will vary according to the scale of the innovation and the target audience. For example, evaluating a simple new add-on device for company mobile phones might only require a short three- or four-page write-up. But deciding whether to introduce biometric passenger security into an international airport will require far more substance. Bear in mind that the formal, detailed, technical style of reporting an engineering team might prefer will differ from the visual "net it out" style a marketing team likes.

The evaluation report must tread a fine line. It must remain—and *appear* to remain—neutral, unbiased, and analytical as it presents its recommendations. Yet, in practice, it will often be used to promote and evangelize the innovation. The trick here is to recognize that thorough critical analysis will help sell the idea. The more confident readers feel about the risks and the more they understand the issues, the less threatening and unknown the innovation will seem to them. Most decision makers aren't naive enough to expect an innovation to be perfect and without rough edges. Simply providing the richer level of detail will reassure them that you have done your homework and know what you're talking about. Table 9-3 shows a few important but often ignored best practices.

Conclude your evaluation report with a recommendation supported by evaluation data. In most cases, the recommendation will be to adopt. After all, much careful judgment preceded the decision to evaluate the innovation. As Jim Wasil from the Ohio Bureau of Workers Compensation puts it, "Often once we've made the case to go forward with evaluation it's crossed over so many different hands and so many people have been involved and it's been scrutinized to the point where people have pretty much made up their mind that it's the right technology. Most times the evaluation ends in 'let's continue' rather than 'let's put the brakes on it.'"[17] But in those instances when your decision is not to adopt, you should still record the evaluation process and final decision. Corporate amnesia is a reality. Even six months after an unsuccessful trial, someone in an adjacent business unit will come across the same innovation or something similar. A thorough no-go report can save a company from duplicating effort. Simply saying "We tried that last year and it didn't work" is unlikely to dissuade people from going ahead.

A frequent reason not to adopt is timing rather than the inherent value of the innovation. So in your report, it's worth noting the timing and situational factors that led to rejection. That information will help others reviewing the same innovation a year or so down the road to see whether

TABLE 9-3

Best practices in formatting an evaluation report

Do	Include summary charts	Don't	Include pages of data
Do	Include innovation trial pictures	Don't	Turn it into a magazine
Do	Include user/customer quotes	Don't	Fill it with technical jargon
Do	Provide a management summary	Don't	Write a tome
Do	Give a clear recommendation	Don't	Exclude or hide the weak points

the same challenges still exist or apply to them. If possible you should note explicitly what problems must be solved for the innovation to be adopted, because a decision not to adopt is rarely an absolute decision. It often is one that will be revisited periodically. It will help to have identified the conditions that will make the innovation attractive in the future. This information can also help others determine whether the innovation might be applied to a problem or in a setting different from the one originally tested.

Making the Decision

The key deliverable from an evaluation project is not a report, a recommendation, a demonstration, or a prototype of the innovation, though all those may be important parts of the evaluation. The key deliverable is the *decision* to proceed or not, or to return the innovation to the tracking or evaluation stage.

Before embarking on an evaluation project, you should make it clear that a decision will be required. You should also establish how the decision will be made and who will make it. The decision maker might be a business process owner, governance committee, or an individual such as the chief information officer or chief marketing officer. If the evaluation has been performed by a central innovation team, they will need to make the decision together with the business sponsor.

It's worth reiterating that *not* proceeding should be considered as successful an outcome as a decision to go ahead. It's not the goal of the evaluation phase to proceed with the innovation. The goal is to make the right decision, and a clear decision not to proceed can be a valuable thing.

Such a decision may save the company considerable expense. It's preferable that rejection occur early in the evaluation process rather than later because it's harder to stop development of an innovation after significant investment has been made. By making a small investment in a number of evaluations, a company can identify innovations with high chances of success, in the same way that a venture capitalist invests in many companies, most of which will fail, for the sake of the few that will generate high returns. Some companies actually plan for a specific amount of failure in the evaluation stage. They might expect, say, 50 percent of innovations evaluated not to move forward. They feel they're not being aggressive enough if all their candidates progress into deployment.

Whichever action is chosen, it should be a conscious, explicit decision. In some situations, you may be tempted, perhaps for political reasons, to say something like, "Well, nobody seemed very interested, so we shelved it." Such an indeterminate outcome does not extract full value from the often costly evaluation work.

The decision to adopt, in spite of all the work that preceded and supported it, is really only the first step in the adoption process. Now begins the process of actually bringing in the innovation and inducing the organization to weave it into the fabric of its everyday work. For that process, we move to the final two stages of the STREET process: evangelize and transfer.

Ten

Evangelize and Transfer: Making It Happen

When it comes to innovation, a company's legacy beliefs are a much bigger liability than its legacy costs.

—Gary Hamel[1]

I N THE EARLY 1990s, executives at CEMEX, a cement company headquartered in Monterrey, Mexico, started receiving puzzling phone calls from their CEO. "Have you looked at your email?" he asked.[2] Unable to ignore the prompt from their boss, they took a look at this new way of communicating. Initial reactions from the executives were mixed: some asked him why he was wasting his time typing in messages when he had a secretary to do it for him.[3]

The e-mailing CEO, Lorenzo Zambrano, was spearheading the early stages of what would become known as "the CEMEX Way," a set of pioneering business processes delivered on the foundation of information technology. Zambrano knew that dramatic transformation would be necessary for the company to differentiate itself from its competitors in a commodity business and avoid being swallowed up by a larger company. "At CEMEX we strive to transform knowledge into profitability. The CEMEX Way is our tool to accelerate and intensify that process," said Zambrano at an analyst meeting in 2001. "We are aiming at nothing less than to reinvent our company and our industry."[4]

At the heart of the CEMEX Way was a drive to identify and capture the company's global best practices and standardize them into business processes across all their operations. Through this standardization, CEMEX was able to save hundreds of millions of dollars in areas such as logistics, maintenance, procurement, online channels, and data centers. At the same time, the processes were designed in a way that allowed each region to customize them to its local market and encouraged continuous improvement and innovation. As well as cost savings, the changes drove higher customer satisfaction and loyalty from the simplified business interactions and improved reliability of service. For example, inspired by visits to military assault teams, overnight delivery services, and 911 emergency dispatch sites, CEMEX so improved its approach to ready-mix concrete delivery (a highly time-sensitive logistical challenge) that it could offer discounts if the delivery wasn't made within twenty minutes of the scheduled time.[5] By 2005, thanks to the CEMEX Way, the company was the world's third largest cement maker and the largest ready-mix concrete producer.[6]

From the outset, Zambrano understood the need to engage his thousands of employees around the globe if the CEMEX Way was to take hold in the company. When he became CEO in 1985, the company was designed around the ready availability of low-cost labor rather than the efficiency of real-time information. But that would need to change. "A smart organization not only empowers, but also encourages its employees to use that information in creative ways," explained Zambrano in a presentation to analysts in 2001. "And CEMEX is a smart organization. Implementing the CEMEX Way will produce an important cultural shift within our organization."[7] Zambrano knew that such a major shift had to begin at the top and that the leaders of the organization had to set an example. Zambrano explained the rationale for his phone calls: "When I became CEO, I began using email as a way of communicating. When I didn't get an answer quickly, I would grab the phone and ask: 'Have you looked at your email?' It soon became used by everyone throughout the organization."[8] By using the new technology himself and setting the expectation that his managers would also use it, Zambrano was both pushing its adoption and setting the tone for a much broader shift. The early adoption of e-mail was one step in Zambrano's relentless drive to integrate technology adoption into every aspect of the business.

Making sure that new ideas take hold in an organization can be as challenging as the most complex technology implementation. As with the earlier stages of innovation adoption, this stage requires discipline and explicit focus. Without addressing the difficult challenges here consistently and thoroughly, all your prior hard work of tracking and evaluation will result in nothing but another report for the corporate archive. You must make it happen—think of Zambrano's hectoring phone calls—because it rarely, if ever, happens by itself.

This activity has two main parts: evangelize and transfer. Evangelizing involves explaining the good news about the potential of the innovation and getting others to believe it can work for the company. It might range from demonstrating the value of a new mobile gadget to, as in Zambrano's case, inspiring a new mind-set as the future direction of the entire organization. Transfer is about getting others to own the adoption themselves. In some cases it's a formal rollout project to a massive organization; in others it's just about incorporating a tool or technique into local, everyday practice. Transfer drives acceptance of the innovation to a point where further development and adoption become self-sustaining within normal business processes and practices. Projects may still need to be defined to implement the innovation, and users may still need to be trained in its use, but it no longer requires special attention as a risky and uncertain proposition.

Evangelize and transfer complete the STREET process. Although they have different goals and outcomes and so form two distinct stages of the STREET process, evangelize and transfer require so much in the way of common skills and best practices that we treat them together in this chapter. Both evangelize and transfer need to start early in the STREET process, in some cases while an innovation is still being tracked, and at the latest during evaluation activities. Like the other adoption stages, successful evangelizing and transfer involve being proactive about defining and following through on a distinct set of activities and best practices. Both require strong people and organizational skills. Mastering the hype cycle is as much (if not more) about these people and organizational skills as it is about understanding the technicalities of an innovation or being adept at preparing business cases to quantify its value.

As one manager, Nick Riso at Nestlé USA, said when trying to drive change as leader of the company's e-business initiative in 2001, "Putting these technologies into place is the easy part. It's much, much harder to get 17,000 people to change their behavior and really incorporate this stuff into their thinking."[9]

Evangelizing the Adoption

Evangelism is a relatively new management term coined sometime in the early 1980s and first popularized through the work of Guy Kawasaki at Apple. Kawasaki's role was to create passionate Apple advocates who would talk up the brand. His efforts are regarded as one of the reasons the Mac computer became such a success. His 1992 best-selling book, *Selling the Dream*, helped popularize the concept of technology and other nonreligious evangelism as a business technique.[10]

Kawasaki suggested five building blocks of evangelism:[11]

1. *Believe in the vision.* Whether it's the pursuit of aesthetics in great design, the aspiration to conquer a disease, or simply the drive to create a better mousetrap, belief in the endeavor is a key ingredient in evangelism.

2. *Understand the vision.* Evangelists continue to sustain and explore the vision, adapting it as necessary to support developing needs.

3. *Believe in people.* Evangelists are social leaders. While they may be involved in creating new management processes or filing patents, it is their ability to inspire and motivate others that sets them apart.

4. *Set an inspiring example.* Like Zambrano, good evangelists lead by example, not just exhortation. Peers and juniors are motivated by the personal behaviors and achievements of the evangelist.

5. *Share the cause.* There is no such thing as autocratic evangelism. Openness to ideas and allowing fresh contributions in to build the vision are essential traits. Without some sense of shared ownership, others will not follow.

This humanistic list contrasts markedly with the somewhat more analytical mind-set that sometimes dominates the evaluation stage. But like many other so-called soft skills, this people-oriented approach can determine the hard reality of whether your innovation succeeds or fails.

The reason such people and organizational skills are so key is that, in many cases, those responsible for uncovering, evaluating, and recommending innovations do not have the authority to *require* the adoption of their recommendations. So the driver of an innovation must inspire and influence those in a position to put the innovation in place. Even someone like Zambrano at CEMEX can only encourage, not require, managers throughout his organization to act as innovation leaders. Whether they have formal authority or not, most people at some point must market the idea of adopting what they believe is a critical innovation.

The goal of evangelism is to make sure that everyone who must be involved is exposed to an innovation and understands its value. Modern business organizations live in compartments of regional offices, remote workers, departmental functions, professional specialties, 24/7 operating shift patterns, and widely disparate generational subcultures. Even in so-called flat organizations, the number of sections and subgroups can be high. You cannot assume that most people will have heard of an innovation, especially early in the hype cycle. Even when the hype hits hard, it often hits only in one specialist area. Human resources may never have heard about a hot new technology innovation, and the IT department may be unaware of the latest approach to employee engagement. Even those who have heard of an innovation may have only a hazy idea of it. Jim Wasil of the Ohio Bureau of Workers Compensation explains, "You can tell people about a technology and they can nod their heads, and they can be very polite about you making them believe that they understand the technology. But then when you turn around, they don't understand it. And if they don't understand it, then they don't buy in. And if they don't buy in, they don't support it. And if they don't support it, there's no priority for it and there's no money for it."[12] You should assume that any innovation of significant scope will only be known to a small proportion of the stakeholders whose support will be necessary to bring it on board, and deeply understood by an even smaller number.

One of the subtle challenges with evangelism is that not everyone realizes what a distinct and essential part of the adoption process it is. In fact, it's one of the most important and time-consuming parts. There's often an assumption that once scientific management has logically revealed the need for an innovation, everyone will see the light and simply proceed to adoption. This faulty assumption infects the thinking in many companies to some degree because those departments through which innovations enter are often the more technical. Whatever logicians might think or hope, human frailty does play a big part in the success or failure of adoptions. We all resist change sometimes. We all have prejudices and the kind of biased thinking described in the last chapter. We all identify with the groups we belong to, and we all fall into ruts that exclude new ideas. Not to acknowledge and deal with those human realities can only create problems.

Some organizations address the challenge by following Apple's lead, giving someone a full-time job as "chief evangelist." Google has a chief Internet evangelist, IBM has a metaverse evangelist, and Microsoft has many technology evangelists. Even smaller companies, such as Six Apart, which provides blogging services, retains a dedicated evangelist to move innovations forward. Those in this role not only explain and market concepts to customers but also sell big ideas within their own firms. Most of the companies that have created evangelist roles are technology providers. In the white heat of high tech, it is perhaps most important that innovative ideas are quickly taken up.

While a full-time evangelist may not be required in most cases, the activity is nonetheless essential in virtually every adoption. A line manager pushing forward one innovation only needs to do a little of it, whereas a formal innovation head working across a large organization must do much more.

During the early stages of evaluation, the evangelist activity should be light because you must both maintain and *appear* to maintain an open mind. However, just by asking questions and opening up dialogue about an innovation, you will convey the idea and move it forward. During later stages of evaluation, however, as you close the value gaps and grow more confident, you may actively begin preparing key decision makers to fully understand and embrace the innovation.

After the evaluation phase, once a decision to proceed has been made, the activities of evangelism kick into full swing. These include inspiring and educating key decision makers, stakeholders, and participants to understand the opportunity, while exploiting or countering the effects of the external hype cycle as necessary.

Evangelism Activities

One manager refers to his evangelism activities as "hand to hand combat," stressing the importance of direct contact with key individuals. You should treat informal networking as a distinct activity and recognize that it can take a surprising amount of time and skill to do well. In fact, one of the most important success factors for innovation leaders is the strength of their personal credibility and connections with key decision makers in their company. An innovation leader needs to be politically aware, for, in the end, no amount of technical knowledge or analytical capability can compensate for organizational naiveté or a lack of people skills. Allocating specific time and effort for hallway discussions and other impromptu meetings with key players is an essential part of preparing for the inevitable point at which an innovation leader must *transfer* responsibility to other groups. In most organizational cultures, this type of face-to-face communication succeeds far better than lengthy work-in-progress reports and memos. Networking needs to go well beyond a single business champion for an innovation because, in many cases, multiple groups are affected by funding and staffing requirements. Where there is a centralized innovation group, its staff can also help forge connections at various levels throughout the company. Many such groups we know assign specific group members to create and maintain relationships with key managers.

The need for such a high level of interpersonal skills, in addition to the technical skills needed for most innovation evaluation, raises the question of whether a single person can do both equally well. Some can, but it's an uncommon combination of talents. Perhaps that's one reason companies struggle so much with innovation adoption. In a team, roles can be split among members according to their particular talents. It may also be possible to outsource evangelism activities to someone other than the originator of the idea; for example, if you identified a champion to support an innovation as far as the evaluation phase, that same champion can be the most powerful advocate to share the vision with others. Note that the innovation champion plays a different role from the innovation leader. The champion usually attends to just one innovation at a time and does so within the context of his or her existing role, whereas an innovation leader is often a "serial innovator" who has to work outside of his or her direct lines of authority. An effective champion serves as a critical thinker regarding how the innovation will be adopted and used within the user community. The champion may be the manager of the people who will use the innovation, but not always. A lead user—a well-respected representative of the user population who enjoys being an early adopter—can be highly effective in the role. Champions are quite often self-selecting. Their motivation for volunteering will vary, but learning and personal development or career advancement are common drivers. Champions distinguish themselves by their higher-risk orientation and intrapreneurial drive.

The Role of Training

Sometimes evangelism resembles an educational process. You may target key executives to keep them apprised of promising innovations so that they can recognize when one of the innovations matches their specific business needs and opportunities. The process of educating executives typically involves preparing a position on an innovation that is generating interest, followed by face-to-face sessions with supporting materials. Gaining the early trust of decision makers through often private and confidential briefings can give an important innovation a useful foothold that will help ensure its later progress.

More speculative educational sessions might consist of seminars or lunchtime sessions in which an internal expert or external speaker presents a tutorial on an area of interest. The profiles and evaluation white papers created by an innovation team for innovation candidates can also be made broadly available as an educational resource. Some groups publish regular updates and distribute them on paper or through e-mail, or store them on an internal Web site.

PR company Burson-Marsteller has a strong focus on internal education and training of its professional workforce. The company takes a two-phased approach, where the first stage is to build awareness of new tools or opportunities, or work the company has done that can be applied more broadly. The idea is to make everyone conversant with the language and concepts around the innovation, to help them understand the implications and to give them time to internalize what it means.

In 2007 the company delivered a global training program called Digital Boot Camp to every office around the world. The aim was to explain to employees about digital tools, some new and some not so new, and the larger cultural shift that was happening to make the tools so relevant. "We needed to explain that it's not really about blogging, it's about consumers having a voice, and it's not really about YouTube, it's about people being able to broadcast themselves and become citizen journalists," says Erin Byrne of Burson.[13]

The second phase of training at Burson is about moving from awareness to action. Byrne views this as creating the rational and emotional drivers that make individual employees willing to own an innovation. "It's how you move them from compliance, from them saying, 'I'm going to talk to my clients about blogs because the firm told me I have to,' to them saying, 'I'm going to talk to my clients about blogging because I understand it, and it's relevant and important to my clients,'" says Byrne.

In 2008 Burson launched its second phase of digital training, called Digital In Action. Each training session included a two-day program that covered a framework for understanding what companies can influence versus control online. This was followed by a day and a half during which the employees went out and did some work on behalf of their clients. "At the end of the training session, they've not only heard lectures, and heard our point of view, but they've done work. So now it's internalized for them," says Byrne. Burson found that once its employees started presenting their own work to the clients, it became personal, something the employees wanted to drive because they believed in it rather than because they were told to do it. Several new ideas and assignments have already arisen out of the working sessions performed as part of the training course, and Burson aims to extend this training approach to other areas of innovation.

Presenting the Innovation in Business Terms

Even during the early stages of the adoption process, evangelizing a particular idea or concept is most influential when the innovation is showcased in a specific business context. This is particularly true in cases where innovation leaders have identified a promising new candidate and want to "push" it into the business (as was the case with Burson-Marsteller), as opposed to situations where business units have requested an innovation they want to "pull" into their own department. In "push" cases, the innovation leader must take the extra step of identifying potential business impact points and presenting the innovation in terms of its business benefit. For example, to build interest in grid computing (a way of using idle computers, such as employee PCs, to increase available computing power), an innovation leader could begin with "Let me show you how we could calculate the value of our derivatives trading portfolio in less than half the time," rather than "Let me tell you about grid computing." This often involves tapping back into the scope phase to reaffirm the context and motivation for the innovation. By the time an innovation is undergoing serious evaluation, the business scenario should be well developed.

An effective way to generate enthusiasm for an innovation is to create an "adoption story" that showcases how the innovation would operate and add value in a specific business context. The purpose of an adoption story is to show the innovation's real value, apart from hype, in terms of the organization's specific needs. The story must be simple, clear, and concrete as to results and benefits in order to make it memorable. A related approach is to create a model or mock-up of how the business will function after the innovation is in place. The mock-up could be a series of computer screens showing a new workflow or a video showing "a day in the life" of an employee or a customer with the innovation in place.

As one example, during the early days of a major initiative to integrate the disparate forms of customer contact—touch-tone, live agent, and Web channels—an insurance company developed a video showing how the interaction between a call center agent and a customer would look once the new integrated system was in place. Members of the company's innovation team and some colleagues played the roles of the agents and different types of customer. Professionally produced, the video was shown by enthusiastic executives at many internal company events. Such demonstrations can create a unifying vision for a major innovation initiative. However, timetables and expectations must be set carefully when laying out the vision, because a common response from those who saw the video was, "Why can't we have this now?"

In evangelizing an innovation, it's also valuable to allow your audience to contribute ideas. Often an innovation will have multiple uses beyond the original purpose you have identified, and uncovering these additional uses will create even higher value than first anticipated. One way to get the discourse going is to call for contributions and constructive critiques in a small-scale version of the innovation challenges we discussed in chapter 7.

A good way to present innovation candidates and gather new ideas is to organize an innovation fair that showcases a major innovation initiative or a set of innovations. This is an exhibition-style internal event operated much like a mini–trade show with booths or tables, demos and display boards. Innovation specialists or project champions man the booths, and a wide community of company managers and employees are invited to drop in. Sometimes an innovation fair might be operated as a sidebar to major management or "all hands" off-site meetings. Sometimes they're set up in the lobby or another high-traffic area of a large company headquarters and then toured around other company sites.

Working Within Internal and External Hype Cycles

So far we've talked mostly about external hype cycles—that is, those that occur in the wider world outside your organization. But there is also an internal hype cycle of expectations that rises, falls, and then rises again *inside* your organization when it adopts an innovation. Through the cycle, the prevailing organizational attitude toward an innovation will change, so what's required of the leader to move the adoption process forward is likewise different at each step.

To start with, for the first half of the internal cycle, an innovation is likely to be a net *cost* to a company. Call it an investment, but in that period it's costing more than it's delivering. Only in the second half, from the rise up the Slope of Enlightenment, does it clearly return obvious net benefits, which then grow over time.

Besides the many skills needed to lead in the first half, leadership at that stage requires a set of personal characteristics—courage, persistence, and so on—that enable the leader to take the arrows that come with carrying the entrepreneurial (or we should perhaps say intrapreneurial) burden of this early stage. Compare those with the different characteristics—collaboration, attention to detail—needed in the leader who follows on and brings the innovation home to full assimilation, with its benefits and revenues.

An innovation leader who guides the innovation through every step will need to vary their approach to deliver the following types of support (see figure 10-1):

Incubate. Around the Innovation Trigger, the innovation may seem exotic and either threatening or resource wasting. The leader's role is to protect and nurture it. Many innovations wither and die early for lack of good husbandry at this stage.

Orient. Rising up toward the peak, the innovation may have been an abstract idea, an R&D project, and often without real focus or direction. Here the leader's role is to orient the innovation. That means aligning it with business goals, generating and testing various possible uses, and sometimes cutting off variations that are likely to be fruitless.

FIGURE 10-1

Role of the innovation leader through the internal hype cycle

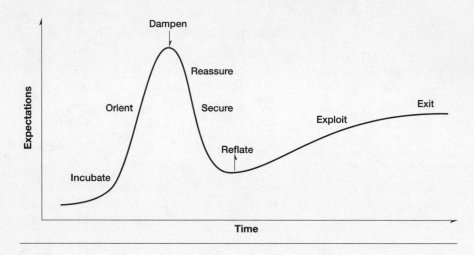

Dampen. Around the Peak of Inflated Expectations, the excessive zeal needs to be moderated. At this point, the leader should not get carried away, but should be damping down any overoptimistic expectations. This is the time for realism and pragmatism and a quiet, steady hand.

Reassure. Falling from the peak, as excitement around the innovation starts to fade, when the inevitable backlash hits, the leader's task is to reassure all stakeholders. This the time the leader must switch from calls for moderation to calls for keeping the ultimate goals and benefits in mind, in spite of the crowd's current disenchantment.

Secure. As the innovation continues down the descent toward the trough, it may be attacked and seriously challenged. Budgets may be chopped and key staff pulled away. The role of the leader at this time is to set up clear lines of defense around the innovation. This is one of the moments when personal reputation may need to be put on the line.

Reflate. In the trough, team morale and faith in the innovation are low. Some of the people involved are wondering why they got caught on such a loser project, while many outsiders are saying, "I told you so," thankful they dodged a bullet. The leader must take planned and mea-sured steps to reflate confidence, which may take the form of a series of small milestones and successes showing progress and reigniting the vision.

Exploit. As the innovation rises up the Slope of Enlightenment, the leader's job is to make sure it gets fully exploited as quickly as possible. This is transfer, rollout, road show time. It's a time when early success stories get packaged and told and retold. It's the time for engaging communications and personal awards. It's a time for making units and people not taking advantage fully aware of what they're missing, even embarrassing them if necessary. It's a time for self-congratulatory presentations to the board.

Exit. At the plateau, the leader must let others move to the forefront in terms of ownership, but maintain a level of connection with the course of the innovation, to catch any potential problems with broader adoption and assimilation, and to make sure that the leaders of the operational efforts are moving the innovation forward appropriately.

In many cases the leader's task can be complicated by the interaction between the internal innovation project hype cycle and the wider external hype cycle for the innovation in the market. How these two curves, external and internal, interact—whether they're in sync or not—will impact the nature and timing of your evangelizing activities.

To understand the interaction and its effect on you, you first need to construct an *external* hype cycle for the innovation you're adopting, if you didn't do this already in the evaluate phase. Think forward and plot out the milestones of when the external curve will climb to the peak, drop rapidly into the trough, and then climb again to the plateau. (Depending on when you adopt, some of these stages may already have occurred.) You might try to estimate when future generations of the innovation will come out, what prices will be charged, what others will be doing when, and so on.

Second, plot out the hype cycle of *internal* enthusiasm, disillusionment, and subsequent enlightenment within your own organization for the specific innovation you're now adopting.

Third, align these two curves so their timelines match up. You'll be able to see immediately how the curves relate and interact. The key feature to note is how the up and down slopes of each match up and whether they are in sync or out of sync.

Here are some guidelines for what to do as the curves interact.

WHEN THE CURVES ARE RISING TOGETHER

If they're both rising to the peak at the same time, the external curve will turbocharge internal expectations around the peak, which will only make the subsequent internal trough more painful. So you'll want to moderate internal expectations at the peak in order to reduce the subsequent trauma of falling into the trough. You might even talk about the coming trough, so that when it inevitably arrives you can say, "We predicted this, and we predict the curve will rise again." You certainly shouldn't be adding to the inflated expectations of the outside world. Instead, your evangelist voice should be soft, calming, and encouraging, but tempered with a note of caution. For example, here is the CTO of General Motors, talking about Web 2.0, a promising collection of innovations that was around the external peak at the end of 2006: "We're seeding the company with Web 2.0 pilots to help us understand how such technologies get used within the company and to allow us to see what challenges we have from a change management standpoint—we recognize that there's a significant amount of communication needed in order to educate users on how to use these technologies and how to engage with them."[14]

If your internal curve is rising toward the peak while the outside curve is rising up the slope, it means that you are adopting in the external trough. So, first, be prepared to explain why you are adopting when the outside world is turning sour on the innovation. This is where you need a good adoption story. However, as the external world soon rises up the Slope of Enlightenment, you can use success stories there to bolster your adoption story and push your organization toward its internal peak. In this situation, you will have a moment of dissonance when your internal trough coincides with the external Plateau of Productivity. Here you can use the spreading optimism and acceptance of the innovation in the outside world to mitigate the effects of the internal trough and pull your organization more rapidly up its own slope.

WHEN THE CURVES ARE FALLING TOGETHER

The big question here is what to do as the internal and external cycles both crash into the trough. This is where you will need a truly powerful adoption story and great persuasive skills, because the disillusionment of the outside world will magnify the despair inside your organization. You will need to pull every evangelizing lever at your disposal and remind your people constantly of the coming benefits. This may be where you put your role as innovation leader, and perhaps even your job, on the line. If your organization set out to innovate as a competitive differentiator, now is the time to point out that sheep will all run away as a flock, without really knowing what they fear. Being different means having the confidence to stay the course.

WHEN THE OUTSIDE CURVE IS RISING WHILE YOUR INTERNAL CURVE IS FALLING

If your organization is falling into its own trough while the outside world is rising up the Slope of Enlightenment, your strategy should be to talk about the increasing number of success stories around the innovation in the outside world. "If others can make it work, so can we." In fact, this confluence of the two curves should help you soften and shorten your time in the trough.

WHEN THE OUTSIDE CURVE IS FALLING WHILE YOUR INTERNAL CURVE IS RISING

If you adopt at the peak and internal expectations are rising while external expectations start dropping, the outside curve will probably weaken your peak and pull you into an internal trough faster than would have occurred normally. This is another situation that calls for a strong adoption story, persistence, patience, and constant reminders of the benefits ahead. Demonstrate that you have already learned from the mistakes of other, earlier adopters. It will help that as you fall into the trough, the outside world will soon be starting its rise up the slope, which should shorten your time of internal disillusionment.

Finally, be aware that in very large organizations there may be multiple internal hype cycles as various internal divisions or business units take up the innovation in sequence. At any given moment, different internal groups may be at different places on their internal hype cycle. Innovation leaders need to manage the various internal and external hype cycles appropriately, sometimes aiding and abetting the hype and sometimes dampening it as needed.

Transferring for Rollout

Transferring knowledge and responsibility from those who assess, introduce, and pilot an innovation to those who must make it a reality is a common point of failure in innovation adoption. It's not enough to write a white paper, give a presentation or a demo, or make a recommendation, and then wait for someone else to run with the idea. For a process improvement to become part of mainstream operations, or for a new device to be rolled out to the sales force, those who drove the early stages of adoption must determine how to transfer ownership to another department or project team to roll out. Transfer between management or development teams is a challenge similar to, but distinct from, having the innovation adopted by the ultimate end users. For the purposes of this discussion, we will call the people on the receiving end of responsibility for the innovation the *adopters*, even if they're not the actual end users.

Of course, if the decision to adopt is made by the group or individual who will actually be driving adoption, then no formal transfer phase is needed. However, some of the lessons in this section on overcoming organizational resistance may still be valuable for rolling out to the end users and encouraging deep assimilation. But frequently, innovations in organizations are evaluated by one set of people on behalf of others. When that happens, there will need to be an explicit transfer process.

As with the evangelize phase, the transfer phase is a process that best begins early in evaluation but becomes particularly important as an innovation migrates to operational development or deployment. A best practice is to evolve and document a repeatable method that forces you to plan early for transfer. Martin Kagan at ExxonMobil explains, "When we transition from an incubation to a formal project, there's a tendency on the part of project managers to want to redo things and do it their own way. To overcome that, we worked with the owners of our IT project methodology to document a philosophy and set of guidelines for transitioning between what we do and what a formal project does. To facilitate the transition, we try to make sure that the people involved in the innovation projects are a mixture from the central technology organization and the units that are going to actually do the service implementation work in the end."[15]

Knowledge Transfer Is Through People

While briefings and reports can help raise awareness of an innovation's potential, the only effective way to transfer an innovation is to create a process in which the necessary knowledge—and, more importantly, the enthusiasm—is transferred between people working side by side. The best approach, we've found, is to make sure that the people ultimately responsible for driving the innovation forward are involved in the early investigations and decisions, as in ExxonMobil's process. Starting the transfer process early will increase comfort with the innovation and foster a sense of co-ownership. The true mark of success is that the adopters of the innovation think it was their idea to start with. On the other hand, nothing is more likely to meet a brick wall than an innovation foisted on a work group seemingly out of the blue, no matter how carefully it was centrally reviewed.

One highly effective way to transfer knowledge and enthusiasm is to phase the responsibility of ownership. This is most appropriate when an innovation is introduced through phased evaluation or development—for example, as follows (see figure 10-2):

Early evaluation (papers and prototypes)—led by innovation leader, supported by adopters

Late evaluation (pilot system)—led jointly by innovation leader and adopters

Rollout—led by adopters, supported by innovation leader

Depending on corporate culture and resources available, a number of scenarios are available for transferring innovations through staff assignments, including assigning adopters to the evaluation and assigning innovation leaders to the rollout.

FIGURE 10-2

Transfer through changing roles of innovation leaders and adopters

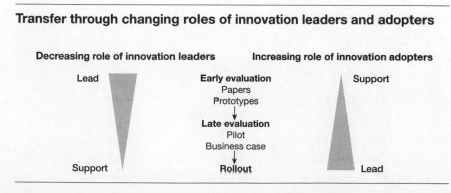

Decreasing role of innovation leaders		Increasing role of innovation adopters
Lead	Early evaluation Papers Prototypes	Support
	↓	
	Late evaluation Pilot Business case	
	↓	
Support	Rollout	Lead

ASSIGNING ADOPTERS TO THE EVALUATION

Even when an innovation team initiates prototype and evaluation projects, it must involve key staff from relevant support functions (HR, legal, purchasing, properties, IT, finance, and so on), as well as the relevant business operating units, at all stages of evaluation. A common way to achieve this is by assigning support or business unit personnel to work as part of the project team, often part-time or even full-time, for short periods. These personnel will learn the required new skills during the early stages and be able to take a leadership role during deployment when the innovation leaders draw back to a consulting role. Some companies deliberately bring in naysayers as well as enthusiasts at this point, to try to uncover objections to the innovation and to hopefully turn the naysayers into supporters. Note that knowledge transfer actually works in both directions: the support function or business unit staff come to the project with specialist knowledge or business skills that are an asset to the project from the time they first join it.

This is true as well with "bottom-up" adoption of an innovation that has been brought in by employees and now needs to be adopted more broadly in a enterprise-friendly way (i.e., scalable, secure, and compliant). The knowledge and experience of the early adopters can be a strong asset, and involving them can help temper their personal enthusiasm with consideration for the broader organizational implications.

ASSIGNING INNOVATION LEADERS TO THE ROLLOUT

Innovation leaders can be temporarily assigned to help with initial implementation and the first stages of rollout, usually for several months, in order to transfer specific skills and ensure that issues uncovered in the early phases of evaluation are properly addressed. Once the deployment is well under way and other team members are fully up to speed, the innovation leaders will rejoin their central team (or whatever their previous role was) to work on new assignments.

In driving the CEMEX Way into current businesses and into a stream of international acquisitions, CEO Zambrano used employee assignment as one of multiple approaches that helped ensure innovations could be deeply and permanently assimilated across a range of geographies and cultures. For example, in the case of acquisitions, an integration team of experienced managers went out to the new company to install the physical information technology systems and associated business processes that were the CEMEX standard. But instead of installing the system and leaving, the team stayed for months—up to a year if necessary—to transfer skills, recruit personnel, and conduct training. Adoption was mandated, and the new processes were incorporated into the acquisition's business software, but CEMEX knew that working alongside the receiving team was still essential. Ongoing online training was expected of each employee and was a part of each employee's annual performance appraisal. Many employees were required to develop additional training modules. CEMEX's CIO at that time, Gelacio Iniguez, explained, "Assuming individuals will use technology or data because it is available is a mistake. Unless management devotes the required resources for training . . . the integration will be superficial."[16] Along the way, the integration team was always looking for best practices and ideas for improvements from the company they had acquired, ideas they could incorporate back into the standard CEMEX processes.

Sometimes, an innovation leader follows the innovation into the company by joining the implementation and support team. This can represent an important career opportunity for that person. It can work well if the person is comfortable being aligned with the specific innovation—that is, if she or he believes the ongoing development of that innovation is likely to be significant and challenging. For example, at one time banks, retailers, and travel companies didn't do customer relationship management as we know it today. Yet now, in some of these industries, it has become typical for companies to have sizable customer relationship departments staffed with specialists. These new business competency centers started with a relatively small innovation or pilot.

In 1994, Nick Gassman of British Airways was assigned temporarily from the IT function into the revenue management department, where pricing and yields were optimized.[17] Through personal interest, he became the first staff member to understand the strategic importance of the Internet, and the Web in particular, to the future of the travel industry. He wrote a white paper about it, which led to his being assigned to help marketing understand the Web. In late 1995, he co-delivered British Airways' first Web site. By the late 1990s, he had become an important player in devising new online business strategies for the company. Today he is the "usability" manager for the airline, responsible for making sure it's easy to buy and fly through online processes, which account for over 50 percent of all tickets sold. For someone like Gassman, introducing an innovation can become a new career passion, and their growing knowledge and experience can be invaluable to the firm.

If a company does not have an innovation team and is not experienced in bringing in innovation, outside consultants can play the role of the innovation leaders in helping with knowledge transfer and rollout. Consultants can assist with the specific innovation and, as mentors, help develop the skills required to bring in subsequent innovations.

Transferring Across the Business

One of the most difficult stages of innovation transfer is rolling out across business units after a successful initial deployment in one unit. The ideal situation is to create enough groundswell of demand from the initial success that the innovation takes on a life of its own and doesn't need to be pushed. To maximize credibility, transfer between business units should be championed by the unit that already adopted the innovation, although a central innovation leader or team can and should help coordinate activities. Demonstrations and open houses are useful for raising awareness, but the biggest driver is word of mouth about the success and benefits of the initial deployment. Innovation leaders or project staff from the first business unit should be available to help jump-start deployment in other units.

Gaps between rolling out the implementation among several units can provide time for reflection and learning, though they shouldn't be so long that the innovation loses momentum. At these review points, any extended or ancillary benefits explored in the evaluation phase can be considered. It's also possible that the initial implementation revealed new secondary options that had not been anticipated. When this happens, the business case for later implementations should be updated to reflect the value of these new options.

Ultimately, the innovation must offer significant enough benefits that it stands or falls on its own merits over time. If, despite best efforts, an innovation does not gain momentum after attempts to transfer, you might be wise to wait until some significant change occurs—for example, in the maturity of the innovation or in the processes it supports. In the meantime, there will be many other innovation candidates worthy of your attention.

Finishing the STREET Journey

And so, after transferring the innovation to those who will drive and derive its ultimate value, we arrive at the end of our journey through the STREET process. Along this journey, as an innovation leader, you've understood the scope of your company's business value and risk contexts in order to focus innovation activities on the most relevant opportunities and stay in line with the company's ability and desire to manage risk. You've broadened your tracking activities to include a range of sources and types of innovation, rather than just those that are thrust on you by external market hype. You've prioritized your options using ranking techniques that turn implicit assumptions into explicit discussion points, and presented the results with graphical models that lead to rational and defensible choices. You've determined which innovations are worth adopting early, despite the risk, because they hit at the heart of your business value context, and which should wait until they are more mature. In short, you've been selectively aggressive in choosing innovation candidates that will bring value to your organization, and you've avoided the hype cycle traps pressuring you to adopt too early or too late.

For promising candidates, you've evaluated a range of factors to better understand the benefits, costs, and risks associated with adopting the innovation, particularly if the candidate is still moving through the early stages of its hype cycle when there is little existing knowledge to draw on regarding any of these factors. You've looked beyond the immediate benefits to drive opportunity and solve problems, and you've also considered less tangible value propositions, such as making someone look good or feel good. You've examined in detail the challenges that can derail an innovation's success, including performance, integration, penetration, and payback issues, and you've taken specific measures to minimize the risks—for example, using prototypes and pilots as part of a staged evaluation with regular decision points. You've considered where the innovation is on the hype cycle, and how fast it's moving, to see how you can take advantage of competitive, public relations, supplier, and hiring opportunities as the cycle peaks and troughs.

You've developed strong networks with individuals and other teams within your organization that will be affected by the innovation, and you've helped them appreciate both the value and the challenges. You've presented the business value through vivid use cases and scenarios. You've used your knowledge of internal and external hype cycles to plan how to manage your company's varying and conflicting feelings toward the innovation.

In some cases, you've decided the innovation isn't quite ready to let loose on your organization—the value doesn't justify the current level of cost, or there is too high a risk that it won't deliver the expected value. In other cases, you've decided to continue, or worked with others to make that decision. Because you've found a champion with the authority and personality to drive the innovation into operational success, and because you've worked so hard to anticipate and mitigate sources of organizational and individual resistance, the innovation moves smoothly into operational use.

Or perhaps, like most innovation programs, you encounter a few more unexpected issues and pockets of resistance to change. We don't want to trivialize the work to be done in "operationalizing" the innovation, and there are many excellent guides to help traverse these challenging waters, from disciplines including change management and IT project management.

When these processes are executed well, the innovation starts to become a mainstream feature of the way your business operates. It is assimilated and spread across the organization by managers and users who now understand its value and actively want to exploit it fully. What was once a push action by a combination of external market forces and internal thought leader advocacy becomes a pull as the organization embraces the positive change that the innovation brings. The internal hype cycle for the innovation accelerates up the Slope of Enlightenment to the Plateau of Productivity.

In short, you have avoided the hype cycle traps of adopting too early or too late, of giving up too soon or hanging on too long. Instead, you've mastered the hype cycle's opportunities, followed the STREET process, and chosen the right innovation at the right time.

Eleven

Future Cycles

Fashions fade, style is eternal.

—Yves Saint-Laurent

A s an innovation moves out of the STREET process and into the Plateau of Productivity within the organization, any innovation leader has a choice to make. For this particular innovation, you've reached the natural ending of the innovation leader's task. Whether you are a full-time corporate innovation leader or a line manager dealing with a local innovation, it's time to look at what's next.

If you are a line manager, you will almost certainly need to stay involved with the innovation in some capacity. You'll need to oversee its ongoing usage, refinement, and evolution as one part of your role, even as you start to consider the bigger picture of the changes the innovation brings. What are the new opportunities, what are the new types of challenge arising, and how might variations on this innovation, or totally new ones, help things along? You may have many innovation balls in play at the same time, at different stages and demanding varying levels of your attention as they progress.

Sometimes innovations will be so substantial that they lead to the creation of new business processes, organization units, and job roles. In this case the innovation leader has to choose whether to change course and move into one of these new roles or stay with the area they came from.

Look again at figure 1-7 in chapter 1—where Alex Drobik wrote on his hype cycle chart the words "2006–2008: e-business ends." What he predicted, and what happened, is that e-business simply became "business as usual"—the new normal. To reach that stage, companies created departments, leaders, and teams skilled in designing services, Web interfaces, client-facing and internal processes, and the technological infrastructure to conduct business over the Internet. Like Nick Gassman at British Airways, many innovation leaders at that time decided to move permanently into a role in the newly formed e-business groups, which have since morphed into essential fixtures of current operational processes.

For innovation leaders who are part of a centralized group or function, the usual path is to let the innovation go on its way and switch their personal energies back to the pipeline of newer innovation candidates that are at earlier stages in the hype cycle. This person is a specialist serial incubator of innovations, someone who is impatient to move on to the next great innovation opportunity for their organization. In fact, it's important that they don't get tempted to dwell too long on innovations that are already launched and well on their way, even if there is a little more corporate kudos to soak up from the success. By hanging around too long, they may interfere with the transfer of ownership and independence of the mainstream managers who will make the innovation a routine part of daily business life. Also, for every day they spend on innovations that are already working, those new fledgling opportunities earlier in the cycle may be at risk of underdevelopment.

Your Future as an Innovation Leader

As we look at options for the future direction of an innovation leader, we want to mention one final topic: how the hype cycle can help you as an individual think about your professional career.

You can use the hype cycle to help navigate your professional life. After all, over the decades, your career will span many situations and projects where you will be called on to lead an innovation adoption or play a part in key decisions along the way. Simply whether you choose to show interest or stand on the sidelines can make all the difference to the outcome.

It has been noted many times in the last thirty years that the idea of a "job for life" died with the baby boomer generation. Anyone born from about 1965 onward can expect to work for a number of companies and have several career changes in their working life.

If you look at any professional area—marketing, law, finance, design—you will see waves of large-scale innovations ripple across that discipline over the years. Think about the "transparency" wave post Sarbanes-Oxley or the "new media" wave in marketing. Think about the "Six Sigma" wave in manufacturing or the "glass and steel" wave in architecture. Each one of these innovation waves followed a hype cycle. Each required individual professionals to explore the ideas involved, grow with them, learn by the scars of experience in multiple projects, and eventually perhaps become an accredited master as the innovation was codified. So today you can be a Cisco certified network professional or a Six Sigma "master black belt" where local area networking and quality improvement once were simple crafts.

It becomes possible to see your own career as a series of rides on overlapping hype cycles—rides on these vast waves of change that pass through your field of work. According to your personal capabilities and preferences, you may prefer to get on such cycles late when everything is well understood, risk is low, and jobs are plentiful but perhaps also commoditized, predictable, and modestly rewarded. Perhaps that's where your skills in fixing problems and attention to detail allow you to contribute best and feel most comfortable. Or maybe your willingness to challenge the status quo and take risks guides you to try new things early, perhaps contributing to their evolution, learning from the earliest examples, and getting highly paid, but with some risk that the new concept will fizzle out in the trough and you'll be left with some low-value experience on your résumé.

When a career opportunity, a development project, a training course, or a new role comes along, use the hype cycle in your thinking about what to do. Whole careers can be built or destroyed by choosing which hype cycles to ride, when and how. For that reason, before we finish, it's worth considering how the nature of innovation adoption and the hype cycle itself are going to evolve in the future.

The Future of the Hype Cycle

The first thing to say is that the importance of innovation is not likely to decline. Our nations rely on innovation to improve productivity and fuel economic growth. But to be competitive, nations and organizations don't necessarily have to excel at originating innovation—they have to be able to *apply* innovation successfully. Take a look at this excerpt from the U.S.

National Intelligence Council's look ahead for the period leading up to 2020: "The greatest benefits of globalization will accrue to countries and groups that can access and adopt new technologies. Indeed, a nation's level of technological achievement generally will be defined in terms of its investment in integrating and applying the new, globally available technologies—whether the technologies are acquired through a country's own basic research or from technology leaders."[1]

As emerging economies such as those of India and China become major powers and many more nations join the race for their share of the leading edge of the knowledge economy, the pace of competition is heating up. For example, a decade ago companies such as Microsoft and Google would typically keep their R&D at headquarters—somewhere on the U.S. West Coast. Today those same companies place R&D centers wherever they find pools of talent—the United Kingdom, India, or China, for example. The sources of innovation are expanding.

In response to this trend, companies that once originated their own innovations are now much more prone to outsource them. Using *open innovation*, a term coined by Henry Chesbrough, companies such as Eli Lilly and Procter & Gamble have been systematizing this approach in recent years.[2] The cost of entry to tap into external innovators has been driven down sharply by online innovation networks of various forms, such as those offered by InnoCentive, NineSigma, and yet2.com. Open innovation is passing though its own hype cycle, but we think it is highly significant because it is rapidly changing the corporate attitude toward innovation adoption.

Because of developments like this, in the future managers will be more inclined to look outward from their organizations to solve problems or take opportunities by applying innovations. The assumption that what's needed next will naturally and usually come from within your own R&D resources is breaking down. Take the example of IBM. The R&D function of this information technology powerhouse is renowned for the number of patents it generates—in 2007 it claimed more U.S. patents than any other company in the world for the fifteenth year in a row, a record of which it is proud.[3] Yet from 2000 to 2007, it acquired over fifty small and midsize companies, already several times the number it bought in the previous decade. Many of these were acquired not just for their customer bases but for their innovations. IBM is following a trend pattern we see elsewhere, including some of the newest companies around. For example, Google, though it is renowned for its own inventiveness, acquired sixteen companies in 2007 alone. By acquiring and incorporating a steady flow of hot new sites and ideas, the company continues to benefit from the same forces of rapid, viral, Web-based innovation that spawned it in the first place.

At the other end of the spectrum from buying entire companies, technology is making innovation adoption easier and more granular through services delivered over the Web. Developments like software-as-a-service are gathering pace quickly. For example, Salesforce.com's AppExchange and SAP Business ByDesign make it particularly easy for small and mid-size enterprises to experiment with software applications that previously required a major investment. By accessing new ideas and business methods encapsulated in business software and delivered over the Web, companies try out new approaches more rapidly and scale up and down as needed. This reduces the contracting overhead and decision inertia required to evaluate and adopt an external innovation. As this technology progresses, it will be possible for companies to mix and match different elements from different sources, using "mash-ups" of software to be able to create a wider range of "cocktail-mixed" innovations that might be better suited to their particular needs.

A little farther into the future, we can foresee the same effects progressing from the intangible realm of bits and software into the concrete world of physical innovation, through the development of low-cost 3-D printers. These printers, sometimes called "fabbers," resemble inkjet printers, but instead of putting ink on paper, the jet deposits resin, plastic, or another material, layer by layer, to build up a physical 3-D object from a 3-D data model. They originated in rapid prototyping for industrial design, and, in recent years, the quality (color, detail, strength) of the models has increased, and printer and supply costs have decreased to a level that will trigger broad appeal within five to ten years. This will make it possible to exchange designs for models, toys, spare parts, artificial medical or dental parts, and many other types of objects and replicate them at will using local machines. Instead of buying a physical item, companies can buy the design, or one of many variations or design mash-ups, adapt it to their specific needs, and print it themselves. The same explosion of choice and speed of process change that software has enjoyed will apply in adopting physical innovations. This new means of innovation exchange between firms is likely to accelerate the "buy, don't build" attitude toward innovation in a realm that has to date been held back by the constraints of centralized, large-scale manufacturing and delivery over physical distance.

These improvements to the efficiency of adoptive innovation are likely to increase the overall speed of the hype cycle. We expect hype cycles in some markets to be shorter, on average, than they were in previous decades. The network also brings with it faster information-sharing and learning-sharing cycles. Later in the evolution of an innovation this may mean companies work through the Trough of Disillusionment a little more quickly than they were able to in the past. Over time perhaps a repeated pattern of shorter troughs will allow companies to become a little more bullish about adopting innovations.

At the same time, the initial excitement about newly discovered innovations is likely to be amplified by network conversation. We expect hype peaks to be higher and sharper than they have been in the past as global news media and the blogosphere suddenly swarm to new innovations for short periods before equally quickly moving on to the next.

However, the ability of the Web to deliver news and ideas rapidly across organizational and geographic boundaries is often counterbalanced by its tendency to divide a community into specialized subcommunities. Different Web communities may be at different points in their exposure to the innovation, so the news still takes time to spread. One community after another hears about an innovation, evaluates it and compares results, and then comes to its own conclusions, creating its own peaks and troughs along the way. Late-adopting communities can pull in experience from a community that is farther along, leading to a dampening effect on the hype cycle, though not a total elimination of the effect.

Certainly, a highly hyped, mass-market phenomenon—such as the launch of the iPhone in 2007—can follow an accelerated path, with all the innovation's benefits and foibles laid open to the world as soon as they're discovered. But that occurs only when there is already broad awareness and understanding of the type of innovation it represents—mobile phones in general in the case of the iPhone. In most cases, the amount by which the hype cycle can be shortened will be limited by the progress of its fragmented sub–hype cycles among different groups of adopters.

The geographic origin of innovations to be adopted is also likely to be changing. It has been well observed by C. K. Prahalad in his work on the "bottom of the pyramid" that the world's poorest need to be brought into the commercial network by trade, not continually excluded from it by poverty and lack of access.[4] Network technologies are gradually penetrating poorer nations, making many smaller businesses in fairly remote regions directly accessible to large ones halfway around the globe from them, and vice versa. Some of the myriad businesses that are formed by the application of microcredit and other mechanisms will tackle old problems in new ways. Prahalad has also pointed out that innovation under conditions of constraint can yield new and interesting solutions—where perhaps trying to solve the same problem better in a rich and satiated market has been making little progress.[5] For example, irregular electrical supply forces you to think differently about how to power a laptop. Unmade roads make you think differently about how to build a cheap but robust automobile suspension.

These trends combined will lead to many more innovations, many more hype cycles, and a need for adoptive innovators to pay very close attention to what's going on. The sharpening of these cycles will tend to make timing issues more acute, windows of opportunity shorter, and the consequences of missing an opportunity potentially more hard hitting.

But the same forces that cause this may also yield partial solutions. Keeping track of hype cycles is also set to become easier and perhaps less labor intensive in the future. Software to keep track of proxy indicators of hype, such as the number of Web sites mentioning a particular term or the number of people searching for it, is becoming cheap and easy to access. Indeed, sometimes it's even free of charge—take a look at Google Trends as an interesting example.[6] To do a better job of hype assessment, it would be useful to be able to look at what people are saying about an emerging innovation and categorize their musings into various levels of positive and negative support for it. These "sentiment analysis" software tools are improving, though they remain a specialist niche for now. Applied to mass Web discourse, they could help us in the future to plot and keep track of hype cycles more accurately and more cost-effectively.

Approaches and tools from the field of management science will further support innovation adopters. Improved understanding of how personalities interact in team environments will help innovation leaders draw on the skills and characteristics they need to support progress at the various stages of the hype cycle. Social network analysis tools, which troll electronic interactions such as e-mails and blogs, will show more clearly who are the visionaries, who are the influencers, who are the builders, and who are the people who bring ideas and projects to closure.

The field of behavioral economics, which examines how people make decisions—and, in particular, which factors lead to consistent and predictable biases in decision making—clearly offers key insights for the hype cycle. Indeed, many of the examples of decision heuristics in chapter 2 were drawn from research in this field. Behavioral economics has only recently entered the radar screen of a few organizations, primarily as a way to understand customer motivations and preferences. We believe it also has a strong future in the executive ranks as an invaluable source of intelligence about how and why we make the decisions that we do.

The management science of innovation adoption will continue to improve, along with the growing focus on bringing in innovation from outside your organization. We hope the hype cycle and STREET will be useful tools for you as you navigate this trend through your career, and we encourage you to track advances and improvements in the methods around these tools.

Having said that, our final advice is to remember to keep the topic of innovation itself in perspective. We started writing this book in 2007, at the peak of an economic cycle and after four years of boom-level worldwide economic growth—a time when innovation was quite naturally high in the minds of business leaders and a topic of many business magazine and journal articles. While we believe it's important to make the most of the spur to innovation that comes with a strong economy, we'll also be watching to see how long this focus lasts. In a different economic setting, will executives defend their core long-term innovation activities? Or will they starve them of funds and energy—forgetting for a while that, as the saying goes, "you can't cost-cut your way to success"?

So it may just be that this whole innovation topic, and the hype cycle along with it, is just another fad. Is it peaking? In the trough? Or will it pull through to the Plateau of Productivity? More than anything, we hope we've equipped you to decide for yourself.

Notes

Preface

1. Joseph Weizenbaum, *Computer Power and Human Reason: From Judgment to Calculation* (San Francisco: W. H. Freeman, 1976).

2. See Carlota Perez, *Technological Revolutions and Financial Capital* (Cheltenham, UK: Edward Elgar Publishing, 2003), for recent work incorporating Nikolai Kondratiev's long wave theories; and Joseph A. Schumpeter, *Business Cycles: A Theoretical, Historical, and Statistical Analysis of the Capitalist Process* (New York: McGraw-Hill, 1939).

3. Everett M. Rogers, *Diffusion of Innovations*, 5th ed. (New York: Free Press, 2003).

4. Geoffrey A. Moore, *Crossing the Chasm: Marketing and Selling High-Tech Products to Mainstream Customers* (New York: HarperInformation, 1991).

5. "Paul Saffo and the 30 Year Rule," *Design World* 24, 1992.

6. Paul Saffo, "'Revolution' the Hype Word of Computer Industry Advances," *Infoworld*, February 4, 1991, 60.

7. Howard Fosdick, "The Sociology of Technology Adaptation," *Unisphere*, February 1993.

Chapter One

1. Roger Partington, interview with author, September 7, 2007.

2. Steve Masters, "CV: Mike Winch of Supermarket Chain Safeway," *Computing*, August 5, 1997.

3. "Why Supermarkets Are Planning the Loyalty Card," *Times* (London), August 11, 1995.

4. Alexandra Jardine, "Analysis—Why Loyalty's Not as Simple as ABC . . . ," *Marketing*, May 18, 2000.

5. Karen Fletcher, "Is Safeway Wrong to Drop Its Card?" *Marketing Direct*, June 1, 2000; and "How Rewarding Is the Loyalty Card?" *Grocer*, August 12, 2000.

6. Jardine, "Analysis—Why Loyalty's Not as Simple as ABC . . . ."

7. "The Amazing Electric Telegraph," History House, http://www.historyhouse.com/in_history/telegraph_1/, citing Jill Lepore, *A is for American: Letters and Other Characters in the Newly United States*" (New York: Alfred A. Knopf, 2002).

8. Tom Standage, *The Victorian Internet: The Remarkable Story of the Telegraph and the Nineteenth Century's On-line Pioneers* (New York: Walker Publishing, 1998).

9. Peter Schwartz and Peter Leyden, "The Long Boom: A History of the Future, 1980–2020," *Wired*, July 1997.

10. Personal communication with author, June 2007.

11. Alexander Drobik, "The End of E-Business," Gartner Research Note, November 9, 1999.

12. Information about Tesco came primarily from Clive Humby, Terry Hunt, and Tim Phillips, *Scoring Points: How Tesco Continues to Win Customer Loyalty*, 2nd ed. (London: Kogan Page, 2007).

13. Ibid., *Scoring Points*, 89.

14. Ibid., 90.

15. Tesco, "Retailing Services," http://www.tescocorporate.com/publiclibs/tesco/retailing services.pdf.

16. *Guardian*, "Sir Terry Leahy at the Guardian's Summit," *Public* magazine, http://www .guardian.co.uk/public/story/0,,1406231,00.html.

17. Humby, Hunt, and Phillips, *Scoring Points*, 271–272.

18. Ibid., 79.

19. Ibid., 91.

20. BBC News, "Morrisons Seals Safeway Takeover," Business, March 8, 2004, http://news .bbc.co.uk/1/hi/business/3542291.stm.

21. The observation first made by Intel cofounder Gordon E. Moore in 1965 and still true today—that the number of transistors that can be placed on an integrated circuit is increasing exponentially, doubling approximately every two years.

22. This term originates in computer software development culture. A beta version is the first version released outside the team that develops it, so it can be tested in the real world. Beta software usually includes all the main design features but also carries known flaws, bugs, and weaknesses.

Chapter Two

1. Researchers have found that this progression holds true across different technologies and metrics. In *Innovation: The Attacker's Advantage* (New York, Summit Books, 1986), Richard Foster tracks the development of artificial hearts as measured by patient survival time, and in *The Innovator's Dilemma: When New Technologies Cause Great Firms to Fail* (Boston: Harvard Business School Press, 1997), Clayton Christensen tracks the densities of computer disk drives.

2. The idea that the hype cycle consisted of two underlying curves was pointed out by Gartner analyst Hubert Delany in 1997, in the context of describing why Web technologies were moving so rapidly through the hype cycle. It was probably no coincidence that he was also creating equations to draw the hype cycle at the time. Mathematicians seem to spot rapidly that the hype cycle is best described by two equations rather than a single one.

3. The term *irrational exuberance* was coined by Alan Greenspan, then chairman of the Federal Reserve Board, in a speech he made to the American Enterprise Institute in 1996. It became a research topic in its own right—for example, it is the title of a book by Yale economics professor Robert Shiller.

4. Abraham H. Maslow, *Motivation and Personality*, 2nd. ed. (New York: Harper & Row, 1970), chap. 4.

5. John H. Lienhard, "The Survival of Invention," *Engines of Our Ingenuity*, no. 2080, http://www.uh.edu/engines/epi2080.htm. Copyright 1988–2006 by John H. Lienhard (Dr.); University of Houston. Used with permission.

6. Followers of the Chinese philosopher Mo Tzu collected their writings in a book called the *Mo Ching*.

7. Lienhard, "The Survival of Invention."

8. Memetics was first suggested in the late 1970s by ethologist Richard Dawkins, but its own peak of hype came in the early 2000s with the publication of *The Meme Machine* by psychologist Susan Blackmore. The subject of memetics has recently been in its own Trough of Disillusionment but shows signs of moving to the Slope of Enlightenment.

9. The prevalence of "management by airline magazine" has led to an academic article on the topic: Neil C. Ramiller, "Airline Magazine Syndrome: Reading a Myth of Mismanagement," *Information Technology & People* 14, no. 3 (2001): 287–303.

10. Charles MacKay, *Extraordinary Popular Delusions and the Madness of Crowds* (New York: Three Rivers Press, 1980). Originally published in 1841 under the title *Memoirs of Extraordinary Popular Delusions.*

11. Daniel Kahneman, Paul Slovic, and Amos Tversky, *Judgment Under Uncertainty* (Cambridge: Cambridge University Press, 1980).

12. Scott Plous, *The Psychology of Judgment and Decision Making* (New York: McGraw-Hill, 1993), 239.

13. Francis Bacon, *Novum Organum*, 1620.

14. Palm, http://www.palm.com/us/company/corporate/timeline.html.

15. Everett M. Rogers, *Diffusion of Innovations*, 5th ed. (New York: Free Press, 2003).

16. Robert G. Fichman and Chris F. Kemerer, "The Illusory Diffusion of Innovation: An Examination of Assimilation Gaps," *Information Systems Research* 10, no. 3 (1999): 255–275.

17. W. Bruce Chew, Dorothy Leonard-Barton, and Roger E. Bohn, "Beating Murphy's Law," *Sloan Management Review* 32, no. 3, Spring 1991.

Chapter Three

1. R. P. Feynman, *Appendix F, Personal Observations on Reliability of Shuttle*, in Steven J. Dick and Steve Garber, *Report of the Presidential Commission on the Space Shuttle Challenger Accident* (commonly referred to as the Rogers Commission Report), June 6, 1986.

2. TELUS Communications Company, "Q. What Is the Size and Growth Rate of the Canadian Wireless Phone Industry?" Press Room, FAQs, http://www.telusmobility.com/about/press_room/faqs.shtml#5.

3. Conversation with author, April 2, 2007.

4. Everett M. Rogers, *Diffusion of Innovations*, 5th ed. (New York: Free Press, 2003), 281. Rogers describes five categories of adopter on the basis of innovativeness: innovators (2.5% of adopters), early adopters (13.5%), early majority (34%), late majority (34%), and laggards (16%).

5. The categorization of companies into types A, B, and C on the basis of their aggressiveness in adopting technology innovation was developed by Gartner analysts David Cearley and Bill Kirwin, and the concept of enterprise personality was developed further by Bill Kirwin, Diane Morello, Phil Redman, and Joseph Feiman.

6. Seth Godin, *The Dip: A Little Book That Teaches You When to Quit (and When to Stick)* (New York: Penguin Group, 2007), 24.

7. Since we've now spoiled the experiment for you, you'll have to try it on family and friends to see for yourself. Go to http://viscog.beckman.uiuc.edu/media/HypeCycle.html to see the video or to view the Ig Nobel Prize–winning paper "Gorillas in Our Midst," which describes the results.

8. Karen Gomm, "Sainsbury's will miss date for chip-and-Pin roll-out," *Computer-Weekly.com*, September 6, 2004.

9. Dan Simons, interview with author, August 9, 2007.

10. Susannah Patton, "The Truth About CRM," *CIO*, June 6, 2001, http://www.cio.com.au/index.php/id;601839273.

11. John S. Hammond, Ralph L. Keeney, and Howard Raiffa, "The Hidden Traps in Decision Making," *Harvard Business Review*, January 2006.

12. Eric Abrahamson and Gregory Fairchild, "Management Fashion: Lifecycles, Triggers, and Collective Learning Processes," *Administrative Science Quarterly* 44 (1999): 708–740.

13. Paula Phillips Carson, Patricia A. Lanier, Kerry David Carson, and Brandi N. Guidry, "Clearing a Path Through the Management Fashion Jungle: Some Preliminary Trailblazing," *Academy of Management Journal* 43, no. 6 (2000): 1143–1158.

14. Scott Plous, *The Psychology of Judgment and Decision Making* (New York: McGraw-Hill, 1993), 180.

Chapter Four

1. Norwich Union, "'Pay As You Drive' Insurance," http://www.norwichunion.com/pay-as-you-drive/.

2. Progressive, "Use Less, Pay Less: A Simple Concept That Reduces the Cost of Car Insurance Now Available to Michigan and Oregon Drivers," http://newsroom.progressive.com/2007/January/Tripsense-mich-ore.aspx.

3. Designer and researcher Bill Buxton calls this phenomenon the "Long Nose of Innovation," a play on the "Long Tail" effect of low-frequency, but collectively high-volume, transactions that occur outside of blockbuster products. Bill Buxton, "The Long Nose of Innovation," *BusinessWeek*, January 2, 2008.

4. From a supplier perspective, the Trough of Disillusionment coincides with the "chasm" in Geoffrey A. Moore's classic book on technology marketing, *Crossing the Chasm: Marketing and Selling High-Tech Products to Mainstream Customers* (New York: HarperInformation, 1991). During this stage, suppliers want to increase product adoption from a few early adopters to a majority of mainstream adopters but have difficulty in making the transition.

5. Everett M. Rogers, *Diffusion of Innovations*, 5th ed. (New York: Free Press, 2003).

6. "Wired for Take-off All the Way to Salt Lake," *Newsweek*, April 29, 2002.

Chapter Five

1. The idea that our modern world might benefit from examining the way the Amish evaluate technology is argued powerfully and engagingly in Howard Rheingold, "Look Who's Talking," *Wired*, January 1999.

2. Ibid.

3. Joe Mackall, *Plain Secrets: An Outsider Among the Amish* (Boston: Beacon Press, 2007), 164.

4. Ibid., 156.

5. C. M. Fiol and E. J. O'Connor, "Waking Up! Mindfulness in the Face of Bandwagons," *Academy of Management Review* 28, no. 1 (2003): 59.

6. E. B. Swanson calls this "contextually differentiated reasoning." E. B. Swanson and N. Ramiller, "Innovating Mindfully with Information Technology," *MIS Quarterly* 28, no. 4 (2004), 559.

7. The STREET process started out life as the four-stage STEP technology evaluation process (specification, tracking, evaluation, production), first published as a Gartner research note by analyst Martin Muoto in July 1994. It evolved into the current six-stage version in 2003. Along with minor changes in terminology, we added the rank stage to stress the importance of prioritizing multiple candidates to avoid hype cycle traps, and the evangelize stage on the basis of feedback from leaders of emerging technology groups regarding the large amount of time they spend marketing their ideas to executives and business leaders within their organizations.

8. Fidelity: http://fcat.fidelity.com/.

9. Paul Jones, communication with author, March 3, 2008.

10. HM Treasury, "Budget 2007 Summary," http://budget2007.treasury.gov.uk/page_09.htm.

11. A 2001–2002 survey of forty-five Gartner clients showed that nearly 60% of type A organizations had a full-time emerging technology group. Less than 30% of type B and C organizations had a full-time group, relying instead on task forces and other part-time contributors.

12. Ben Elgin, "Managing Google's Idea Factory," *BusinessWeek*, October 3, 2005.

Chapter Six

1. "One-on-one with Bill Gates," transcript of interview between Peter Jennings and Bill Gates, ABC News, February 16, 2005, http://abcnews.go.com/WNT/Story?id=506354&page=3.

2. TEA, "TEA/ERA Theme Park Attendance Report 2006," http://www.themeit.com/attendance_report2006.pdf.

3. The Walt Disney Company, "Company Overview," October 2007, http://corporate.disney.go.com/corporate/overview.html.

4. Ibid.

5. Disney World and Orlando Unofficial Guide, "Pal Mickey," http://wdisneyw.co.uk/palmickey.html.

6. This idea is referred to as a *core ideology* in James C. Collins and Jerry I. Porras, "Building Your Company's Vision," *Harvard Business Review*, September 1996, 65–77.

7. The Neiman Marcus Group, Investor Relations, "Company Overview," http://phx.corporate-ir.net/phoenix.zhtml?c=118113&p=irol-irhome.

8. Ryanair, "Careers," http://www.ryanair.com/site/EN/about.php?page=Jobs&sec=working.

9. Lexus, About Lexus, "The Lexus Covenant," http://www.lexus.com/about/corporate/lexus_covenant.html.

10. Ibid.

11. Michael Treacy and Fred Wiersema, *The Discipline of Market Leaders: Choose Your Customers, Narrow Your Focus, Dominate Your Market* (Reading, MA: Addison-Wesley, 1995).

12. Ryanair, "About Us," http://www.ryanair.com/site/EN/about.php?page=About&sec=charter.

13. Singapore Airlines, "The Experience," http://www.singaporeair.com/saa/en_UK/content/exp/index.jsp.

14. C. K. Prahalad and Gary Hamel, "The Core Competence of the Corporation," *Harvard Business Review*, May–June 1990.

15. W. Chan Kim and Renée Mauborgne, "Creating New Market Space," *Harvard Business Review*, January–February 1999.

16. BP, "BP Annual Review 2007," http://www.bp.com/liveassets/bp_internet/globalbp/globalbp_uk_english/set_branch/STAGING/common_assets/downloads/pdf/ara_2007_annual_review.pdf.

17. BP, "BP to Shutdown Prudhoe Bay Oil Field," news release, August 7, 2006; and "BP Safety Focus Is Crucial: Turnaround Depends on Reducing Its Risks, Fixing U.S. Troubles," *Wall Street Journal*, January 2, 2008, http://online.wsj.com/article/SB119921101740160441.html.

18. Christian Annesley, "Tesco Says Heat-seeking Tool Is Beating Customer Queues," *ComputerworldUK*, October 2, 2007, http://www.computerworlduk.com/management/it-business/it-organisation/news/index.cfm?newsid=5439.

19. GE 2004 Annual Report, Letter to Stakeholders: "Increasing Organic Revenue Growth," http://www.ge.com/ar2004/letter4.jsp.

20. James C. Collins and Jerry I. Porras, "Building Your Company's Vision," *Harvard Business Review*, September 1996, 65–77.

21. Boeing, "Boeing Chooses Chicago as Center of New Corporate Architecture," news release, May 10, 2001, http://www.boeing.com/news/releases/2001/q2/news_release_010510a.html.

22. Del Quentin Wilber, "Tale of Marooned Passengers Galvanizes Airline Opponents," *Washington Post*, February 16, 2007, http://www.washingtonpost.com/wp-dyn/content/article/2007/02/15/AR2007021501853_pf.html.

23. "An Extraordinary Stumble at JetBlue," *BusinessWeek*, March 5, 2007, http://www.businessweek.com/magazine/content/07_10/b4024004.htm.

24. JetBlue Airways, "JetBlue's Customer Bill of Rights," http://www.jetblue.com/about/ourcompany/promise/index.html.

25. Securities and Exchange Commission, Sarbanes-Oxley Act of 2002, "Public Law 107-204—July 30, 2002," http://www.sec.gov/about/laws/soa2002.pdf.

26. Marks & Spencer, "Marks & Spencer launches 'Plan A'—£200m 'Eco-plan,'" news release, January 15, 2001, http://www.marksandspencer.com.

27. Stuart Rose, "Staying Green in a Tough Economic Climate," *HBR Green*, March 4, 2008, http://www.hbrgreen.org/2008/03/the_hard_economics_of_green.html.

28. Todd Brown, UPS, interview with author, November 7, 2007.

29. Peter Schwarz, *The Art of the Long View* (New York: Currency, 1991).

30. Thierry Post, Martijn J. van den Assem, Guido Baltussen, and Richard H. Thaler, "Deal or No Deal? Decision Making Under Risk in a Large-Payoff Game Show," *American Economic Review, March 2008*.

31. Everett M. Rogers, *Diffusion of Innovations*, 5th ed. (New York: Free Press, 2003).

32. Robert Kaplan and David Norton, *Strategy Maps: Converting Intangible Assets into Tangible Outcomes* (Boston: Harvard Business School Press, 2004).

33. C. K. Prahalad, *The Fortune at the Bottom of the Pyramid: Eradicating Poverty Through Profits* (Upper Saddle River, NJ: Wharton School Publishing, 2004).

34. "Succession Planning: And the Next CEO Is . . . ," http://www.directorship.com/and-the-next-ceo-is--- , October 1, 2007.

Chapter Seven

1. DISA information is from Fritz Schulz, interview with author, September 4, 2007.

2. Bill Gates, "A Robot in Every Home," *Scientific American*, January 2007.

3. Martin Kagan, interview with author, November 6, 2007.

4. Mitch Wagner, "Second Life Casino Owner Left Scrambling After Gambling Ban," *Information Week*, July 27, 2007.

5. Transcript of first-quarter 2003 Unilever PLC earnings conference call, May 2, 2003. FD (Fair Disclosure) Wire English © CCBN and FDCH e-Media. All rights reserved. Via Dow Jones Factiva.

6. Nick Donofrio, interview with Diane Morello of Gartner, September 12, 2007.

7. Erin Byrne, interview with author, February 8, 2008.

8. Frank Finocchio, interview with author, December 6, 2007.

9. Netflix, "$50,000 Progress Prize Is Awarded on First Anniversary of $1 Million Netflix Prize," news release, November 13, 2007.

10. Peggy Mihelich, "Million-Dollar Prize Offered for Soldier 'Power Pack,'" *CNN.com*, July 17, 2007, http://www.cnn.com/2007/TECH/07/16/wearable.power.prize/index.html.

11. Fred Balliet, interview with author, November 8, 2007.

12. Fritz Schulz, interview with author, September 4, 2007.

13. Balliet, interview.

14. Finocchio, interview.

Chapter Eight

1. Note that the hype cycle represents just a portion of the overall lifecycle. An innovation may develop in the labs for many years before something triggers it up to the peak. There is also a lengthy stage after the innovation hits the plateau, as penetration spreads through the majority of the adopting population. This full cycle is likely to be decades long.

2. Dan Gossett, Michelin, interview with author, February 13, 2008.

3. Fred Balliet, interview with author, November 8, 2007.

4. Martin Kagan, interview with author, November 6, 2007.

Chapter Nine

1. This quote is commonly attributed to Paul Saffo. Saffo himself points out that he was not the first to utter these words—they are a piece of folk wisdom that he heard from a rancher neighbor. However, Saffo was the first and most persistent in applying the quote to the technology arena and examining the implications for a technology's progress. See Paul Saffo, "Six Rule for Effective Forecasting," *Harvard Business Review*, July–August, 2007.

2. Jim Wasil, interview with author, February 28, 2008.

3. Richard Zultner, "TQM for Technical Teams," *Communications of the ACM* 36, no. 10 (October 1993): 80.

4. Thanks to Romilly Powell and Dave Aron of Gartner for the foundational work on the list of benefits.

5. Thanks to Romilly Powell and Dave Aron of Gartner for the foundational work on the list of risks.

6. Cyrus Farivar, "Maps More Real Than Virtual," *New York Times*, July 9, 2006, http://www.nytimes.com/2006/07/09/automobiles/09TECH.html?_r=1&oref=slog. From The New York Times on the Web, © The New York Times Company. Reprinted with permission.

7. UK Passport Service, Biometrics Enrolment Trial Report, Atos Origin, May 2005 http://www.ips.gov.uk/passport/welsh/downloads/UKPSBiometrics-Enrolment-Trial-Report-Management-Summary.pdf.

8. Ministry of the Interior and Kingdom Relations, "Evaluation Report, Biometrics Trial, 2b or Not 2b," 2005, http://www.europeanbiometrics.info/images/resources/88_630 _file.pdf.

9. Marissa Mayer, "Nine Lessons Learned About Creativity at Google," Entrepreneurial Thought Leaders Lecture, May 17, 2006, http://edcorner.stanford.edu/authorMaterialInfo .html?mid=1554.

10. "Why One Winery Switched to Artificial Cork," *Wines & Vines*, August 1993.

11. Douglas R. Hofstadter, *Godel, Escher, Bach: An Eternal Golden Braid* (New York: Basic Books, 1979).

12. Scott Plous, *The Psychology of Judgment and Decision Making* (New York: McGraw-Hill, 1993).

13. Ibid.

14. J. Edward Russo and Paul J. H. Schoemaker, *Decision Traps: Ten Barriers to Brilliant Decision-Making and How to Overcome Them* (New York: Doubleday/Currency, 1989), cited in Plous, *The Psychology of Judgment and Decision Making*, 239–240.

15. W. Edwards, "Conservatism in Human Information Processing," in *Formal Representation of Human Judgment*, ed. Benjamin Kleinmuntz (New York: Wiley, 1968), cited in Scott Plous, *The Psychology of Judgment and Decision Making*, 138.

16. Robert Fichman, Boston College, Carroll School of Management, personal communication with author, February 22, 2008.

17. Jim Wasil, interview with author, February 28, 2008.

Chapter Ten

1. Gary Hamel, *The Future of Management* (Boston: Harvard Business School Press, 2007), 54.

2. Diane Lindquist, "From Cement to Services: Cemex's Lorenzo Zambrano Revolutionized the Low-Tech Cement Business by Investing in Technology; Now Companies Want to Buy That Expertise," *Chief Executive*, November 2002.

3. Adrian J. Slywotzky and and David J. Morrison, *"How Digital Is Your Business?"* (New York: Crown Business, 2000).

4. Remarks by CEMEX CEO Lorenzo Zambrano at global analyst meeting, July 19, 2001, http://www.cemex.com/pdf/ir/LHZ_rem.pdf.

5. VISION Consulting, Client Stories, "CEMEX: Culture and Service Reinvention to Reposition a Commodity Business as a Service Business," http://www.vision.com/clients/client_stories/cemex.html.

6. "CEMEX: Transforming a Basic Industry Company," Stanford Graduate School of Business Case GS-33, December 7, 2005.

7. Remarks by CEMEX CEO Lorenzo Zambrano at global analyst meeting, July 19, 2001, http://www.cemex.com/pdf/ir/LHZ_rem.pdf.

8. Lindquist, "From Cement to Services."

9. Bill Breen, "Change Is Sweet," *Fast Company*, May 2001, http://www.fastcompany.com/magazine/47/changeweb.html.

10. Guy Kawasaki, *Selling the Dream: How to Promote Your Product, Company, or Ideas, and Make a Difference Using Everyday Evangelism* (New York: HarperBusiness, 1992).

11. Ibid.

12. Jim Wasil, interview with author, February 28, 2008.

13. Erin Byrne, interview with author, February 8, 2008.

14. MySpace page, *Business Management*, February 8, 2007, http://www.busmanagement.com/pastissue/article.asp?art=269715&issue=208.

15. Martin Kagan, interview with author, November 6, 2007.

16. Donald A. Marchand, Rebecca Chung and Katarina Paddack, "CEMEX: Global Growth Through Superior Information Capabilities," Case IMD134 (Lausanne, Switzerland: International Institute for Management Development, 2003).

17. Nick Gassman, personal communication with author, November 22, 2007.

Chapter Eleven

1. National Intelligence Council, *Mapping the Global Future: Report of the National Intelligence Council's 2020 Project*, December 2004, http://www.dni.gov/nic/NIC_globaltrend 2020.html.

2. Henry W. Chesbrough, *Open Innovation: The New Imperative for Creating and Profiting from Technology* (Boston: Harvard Business School Press, 2003).

3. "In 2007, IBM received 3,125 U.S. patents from the USPTO. This is the fifteenth consecutive year that IBM has received more US patents than any other company in the world." IBM, Intellectual Property and Licensing, http://www.ibm.com/ibm/licensing/.

4. C. K. Prahalad, *The Fortune at the Bottom of the Pyramid: Eradicating Poverty Through Profits* (Upper Saddle River, NJ: Wharton School Publishing, 2004).

5. C. K. Prahalad, "The Innovation Sandbox," *Strategy + Business*, Autumn 2006, http://www.strategy-business.com/press/article/06306?pg=0.

6. Google Trends, http://www.google.com/trends.

Index

About the Authors

JACKIE FENN is a Gartner Fellow at the IT industry research and advisory company Gartner, Inc., covering emerging technology trends and innovation management. She helps commercial and government organizations spot the trends and innovations that will make a difference to their business, and also guides them in setting up emerging technology groups and processes. Before joining Gartner, Jackie was a principal consultant at service provider Logica in the United Kingdom and the United States, working on knowledge-based systems, speech recognition, multimedia, and interactive television. She's been a part of the IT industry for over twenty-five years as a practitioner and analyst. She lives in Massachusetts.

MARK RASKINO is a Gartner Fellow at the IT industry research and advisory company Gartner, Inc. His research focus is emerging macrotrends in business information technology and business leader needs of IT. He is a frequent keynote speaker at events around the world. Mark has over twenty-five years' experience in the sector, and before joining Gartner eight years ago, he was an e-business leader at British Airways. He lives in London.